The "Bible" for All Games Players . . .

A card room without a Hoyle is like a hotel room without a Bible. And in this volume my friend, Richard Frey, has done a job that should make his book the "Bible" for all games players.

To learn a new game, to play old favorites better, to settle any question that comes up, this book is authoritative and makes the most complex games and rules easy to understand. Furthermore, it is up to the minute in the most popular games played today. Its rules for bridge bidding include the latest changes. It tells about the newest forms of Canasta. It gives some hot tips on bettering your play in many other games.

Turn to any game you know, or to any game you want to learn, and a few sentences will convince you that here is a reference book that is fun to read. A must for anyone who wants to play a game and play it correctly.

CHARLES H. GOREN

Fawcett Crest Books
by Richard L. Frey:

ACCORDING TO HOYLE

HOW TO WIN AT CONTRACT BRIDGE

ACCORDING TO HOYLE

Revised and Enlarged

OFFICIAL RULES OF MORE THAN 200 POPULAR
GAMES OF SKILL AND CHANCE
WITH EXPERT ADVICE ON WINNING PLAY

by Richard L. Frey

Author:

*How to Win at Contract Bridge
in 10 Easy Lessons*

Editor-in-Chief:

Official Encyclopedia of Bridge

A FAWCETT CREST BOOK

FAWCETT PUBLICATIONS, INC., GREENWICH, CONN.

CONTENTS

Accordion	192
Aces	64
Acey Deucey	235
All Fives	223
All Fours	66
All Threes	224
Auction Euchre	41
Auction 45's	51
Auction Partnership Pinochle	152
Auction Pinochle	144
Auction Pitch	68
Authors	186
Baccarat	214
Backgammon	226
Bank Craps	268
Baseball	29
Belotte	164
Bergen	224
Bet or Drop	19
Bézique	159
Big Forty	196
Bird Cage	270
Black Jack	205
Black Lady	57
Blackout	216
Blind and Straddle	19
Blind Opening	19
Blind Tiger	19
Block Game	226
Bolivia	106
Boodle	59
Booray or Bouré	176
Brazilian Canasta	107
Butcher Boy	30
Calculation	197
Canasta	97
Canfield	194
Card Games for Children	184
Casino	178
Categories or Guggenheim	255
Checkers	246
Check Pinochle	158
Chemin-de-fer	215
Chess	237
Chicago	59
Chile	106
Chilean Canasta	106
Chinese Bézique	162
Chuck-a-luck	270
Cinch	66
Cincinnati	28
Clab	164
Clabber	164
Clob	164
Clock	197
Cold Hands	30
Concentration	190
Contract Bridge	110
Contract Bridge Strategy	122
Contract Bridge Variations	133
Contract Rummy	86
Craps	266
Crazy Eights	64
Crazy Jacks	64
Crazy Sevens	64
Cribbage	72
Cribbage Solitaire (Domino)	200
Cribbage Solitaire (Square)	200
Criss-Cross	28
Cuban Canasta	108
Cutthroat Bridge	135
Cutthroat Contract	135
Cutthroat Euchre	40
Dealer's Choice	27
Devil and the Tailors, The	249
Dice Games	266
Dominoes	221
Domino Hearts	56
Double-Barrelled Shotgun	29
Double Hasenpfeffer	43
Double Klondike	193
Double-Pack Pinochle	155
Down-the-River	23
Draughts	246
Draw Casino	183
Draw Game, The	221
Draw Poker	15
Duplicate Bridge	131

Eight-card Stud 23
Eights 64
Euchre 37

Fan Tan 62
Faro 212
Firehouse Pinochle . . . 158
Five Hundred 44
Five Hundred for 5 or 6 . 48
Five-Hundred Rum . . 95
Five-Hundred Rum
  Variations 96
Five or Nine 63
Flip 28
Forty-five 51
Forty-fives, Auction . . 51
Forty Thieves 196
Four-deal Bridge
  (Chicago) 138
Four-five-six 271
Four-hand Cribbage . . 77
Four-hand Five Hundred . 48
Fox and Geese 249
Freezeout 30

Garbage 27
Gin Rummy 88
Gin Rummy for 3, 4, 5,
  and more 92
Giveaway Checkers . . 249
Go Fish 186
Golf 198
Goulash (Pinochle) . . 140
Goulashes (Bridge) . . 133

Hasenpfeffer 42
Hazard 270
Hearts 53
High-card Pool 35
High-Low-Jack 66
High-low Poker 26
High-low Seven-card
  Stud 27
High-low Stud 26
Honeymoon Bridge . . . 136
Hurricane 29

I Doubt It 188
Italian Canasta 107

Jackpots 15
Joker Canasta 109
Joker Hearts 55

Kalaber 164

Kalabriás 164
Kaluki 81
Klab 164
Klaberjass 164
Klob 164
Klondike 192
Klondike, Double . . . 193
Knock Rummy 94
Kriegspiel 244

Losing Game, The . . . 249
Lowball 26
Low Poker 26

Mah Jongg 257
  Modern Game . . . 263
Matador 224
Memory 190
Mexican Stud 28
Michigan 59
Mill, The 250
Muggins 223
Multiple Golf 198

Napoleon at St. Helena . 196
Newmarket 59

Oh Hell 216
Oh Pshaw 216
Oklahoma Gin 92
Old Maid 185
Old Sledge 66
Omnibus Hearts 57

Panguingue 82
Parliament 62
Partnership Auction
  Pinochle with a Widow 154
Partnership Casino . . 182
Partnership Hearts . . . 56
Partnership Pinochle . . 152
Pass-out 19
Password 254
Patience 191
Pedro 70
Pelmanism 190
Persian Rummy 96
Pig 185
Pinochle 140
Pitch 68
Play or Pay 63
Poker 9
Poker Dice 272
Poker Solitaire 199
Poker Squares 199
Progressive Jackpots . . 18

Railroad Euchre	40	Stealing Bundles	187
Rauber Skat	174	Stops	59
Red Dog	35	Straight Draw Poker	19
Roulette	252	Straight Hearts	53
Royal Casino	183	Stud Poker	21
Round-the-Corner Gin	92	Stuss	213
Rubicon Bézique	161	Swedish Rummy	64
Rummy	78		
Russian Bank (Crapette)	201	Thirty-one	77
		Three-card Monte	29
Samba	105	Three-card Poker	29
Saratoga	59	Three-hand Bridge	135
Setback	68	Three-hand Casino	182
Seven-card Stud	23	Three-hand Cribbage	76
Sevens	109	Three-hand Euchre	40
Seven-toed Pete	23	Three-hand Pinochle	143
Seven-Up	66	Tiddly-Wink	225
Shotgun	29	Trictrac	226
Six-card Stud	23	Twenty-one	205
Six-hand Partnership		Two-card Poker	29
Pinochle	155	Two-hand Bridge	136
Six-pack Bézique	162	Two-hand Canasta	105
Skat	167	Two-hand Euchre	40
Slapjack	184	Two-hand Five Hundred	47
Snake	236	Two-hand Hearts	56
Sniff	223	Two-hand Pinochle	140
Snip Snap Snorem	61	Two Pots to Win	29
Solitaire	191		
Spade Casino	183	Uruguay	106
Spider	195		
Spite & Malice	218	Whiskey Poker	20
Spit in the Ocean	27	Wipe-Off	158
Spoil Five	48	Word Squares	254

Poker

POKER has been called the national card game of the United States, but it is also an international game, popular almost anywhere cards are played. It has many forms and is played differently in different lands and communities, but the basic principle is everywhere the same: to build "structures" consisting of two or more cards of a kind . . . sequences of cards . . . hands composed all of the same suit.

There are no official laws of Poker in the same sense that there are official laws of Contract Bridge. Poker is a game for the rugged individualist, and every game reserves the right to make its own laws. But any game will profit by adopting one set of published laws and abiding by it, and the following laws are offered as worthy for adoption.

STANDARD POKER LAWS
Applying to all forms of the game

PLAYERS. Any number from two to fourteen, but the original players in a Draw Poker game may by agreement limit the eventual number of players to seven or eight; in a Stud Poker game, the original players may by agreement limit the number to nine.

CARDS. The pack of 52, with the cards in each suit ranking: A (high), K, Q, J, 10, 9, 8, 7, 6, 5, 4, 3, 2. There is no rank of suits.

Wild Cards. Any card or cards may be designated as *wild*. The holder of a wild card may designate any other card for which the wild card stands. It is quite usual to play with a 53-card pack, including the joker, the joker being wild.

The Bug. The joker in a 53-card pack is often designated as the *Bug.* The Bug is a wild card with limitations: It may be counted as an ace, and it may be counted as a card of any suit and rank necessary to make a *flush* or *straight* (which terms are defined in the next section).

9

OBJECTS OF THE GAME. Each player endeavors to hold a better *poker hand* than any other player in the game. A poker hand consists of exactly five cards.

Rank of Poker Hands. The following list states the combinations that make up valuable poker hands, and their rank.

Five of a kind ranks highest when there is any wild card in the game.

Straight flush ranks highest when there is no wild card. It consists of five cards in suit and sequence, with the ace ranking either high or low: ◇A-K-Q-J-10 (the highest possible hand, also called a *royal flush*), or ◇5-4-3-2-A, or any sequence in between, as ♠10-9-8-7-6.

Four of a kind is next highest. It consists of the four cards of any one rank together with any fifth card; for example ♡7-◇7-♣7-♠7-◇Q constitute four sevens.

A *full house* ranks next; it consists of any three of one kind and any pair of another kind, as ♠6-♡6-◇6-♠A-♠A. It is referred to by the three-of-a-kind it contains; the example shown would be "sixes full."

A *flush,* ranking next, consists of any five cards of the same suit, but not in sequence, as ◇J-◇9-◇8-◇6-◇3, referred to as a "jack-high flush."

A *straight* consists of any five cards of two or more suits in sequence of rank, with the ace ranking either high in the sequence A-K-Q-J-10 or low in the sequence 5-4-3-2-A. It ranks next under a flush.

Three of a kind are any three cards of the same rank plus two other cards which do not constitute a pair and do not include the fourth card of the same rank; ♠9-◇9-♡9-♣K-◇3 would be referred to as "three nines."

Two pairs, which rank next under three of a kind, constitute two cards of one rank, two cards of another rank, and any fifth card which is of neither of those ranks; it is referred to by the higher of the two pairs. Thus, ♠Q-♣Q-♠8-♣8-♠4 would be "queens up."

One pair—any two cards of the same rank, together with three other cards which do not combine with the other two to form any of the higher-ranking hands above: ♠K-♣K-♡7-♡6-♡4 are a pair of kings.

No pair—the lowest-ranking hand—losing to any hand containing a pair or any better combination, consists of any five cards not meeting the specifications above.

Object of Betting. The players in the game bet with one

another as to which has the best poker hand. Each deal is a separate game, in that its result does not affect any preceding or subsequent deal. All the bets are placed together and form a *pot*. A player who does not wish to bet that he has the best hand may *drop*, thus relinquishing any chance to win the pot.

The ultimate object in Poker is therefore to win the pot, whether by actually holding the best hand or by inducing other players to drop and leave the pot to be taken, uncontested, by a single player still willing to bet.

SEQUENCE OF PLAY. *Rotation*. The turn to deal, the cards as they are dealt, and the turn to bet all pass from player to player to the left. Once a player has dropped, the turn skips him and takes up with the next player to his left who has not dropped.

Chips. The unit of exchange is almost invariably the poker chip, which may represent money.

Procedure. First the cards are shuffled and dealt by the proper dealer; then there may be one or more *betting intervals* in which the players may bet on their hands (or, if unwilling to bet, may drop); and, at the end of the last betting interval, there is a *showdown* at which each player who has not previously dropped exhibits his cards face up. Whichever of these players has the highest-ranking poker hand wins the pot.

THE SHUFFLE, CUT AND DEAL. Any player may shuffle the pack of cards, have them cut by the player at his right, and deal them one at a time, face up, in rotation beginning with the player at his left, until a jack falls to any player; that player becomes the first dealer.

The Shuffle. Any player may shuffle, the dealer last. The cards must be shuffled at least three times.

The Cut. The player at dealer's right must cut the pack, leaving at least five cards in each packet. (Traditionally, the player at dealer's right could refuse to cut.)

Dealing. The cards are dealt one at a time in rotation to the left.

BETTING. In any form of Poker there are one or more *betting intervals*. In each betting interval, one player in the game has the privilege or duty of making the first bet. Each player in rotation after him may either

(a) *drop*, by discarding his hand; in this case, he no

longer participates in the pot, and cannot win the pot regardless of what may later occur;

(b) *call*, which means that he places in the pot enough chips to make his contribution to the pot *during that betting interval* as great as the contribution of any other player, but no greater;

(c) *raise*, which means that he places in the pot enough chips to call, plus one or more additional chips.

To illustrate this: There are seven players in the game, designated as A, B, C, D, E, F and G. A is the first bettor. A bets one chip. B calls by putting in one chip. C drops, discarding his hand. D raises, putting in three chips—one chip to call and two to raise. E calls, putting in three chips. F raises, putting in six chips—three to call and three to raise. G drops.

It is now the turn of A again. A calls, putting in five chips; this makes his total contribution to the pot six chips during this betting interval. B drops; he relinquishes his chance to win the pot, and the chip he previously put in the pot remains there. D calls, putting in three chips to bring his total contribution up to six. E raises five chips by putting in eight chips. F raises by putting in ten chips. A drops, thus losing the six chips he had already put in. D calls by putting in ten chips. E calls by putting in five chips, and now the betting interval is ended. D, E and F are still in the pot, and each during this betting interval has put sixteen chips into the pot.

A betting interval ends when every active player has had at least one turn to bet and when the bets have been *equalized*—that is, when every player has either contributed the same amount as every other player has contributed during the betting interval, or has dropped.

A player may drop or bet only in turn.

Checking. In many forms of Poker, a player in turn is permitted to make "a bet of nothing" by saying "Check," provided no previous player has made a bet during that betting interval. The effect of the check is that the player merely wishes to stay in the pot by making a bet so insignificant that it is not worth the trouble of putting that amount into the pot. If the first bettor checks, each active player thereafter may check until any player chooses to bet, after which a player may stay in the pot only by at least calling the previous bet.

THE SHOWDOWN. When the bets have been equalized in the last betting interval, every player who has not previously dropped must expose all his cards face up on the table. The highest-ranking poker hand wins the pot.

It is not necessary for a player to announce the value of his poker hand as he puts it down, nor is he bound by any such announcement if he makes it. "The cards speak for themselves." The player with the winning hand takes in the pot. (If a player begins to take in the pot even though he does not have the winning hand, a player with a better hand must protect himself by promptly objecting.)

If any wild cards are being used, the player holding them must indicate their rank or suit when he shows them. Thereafter, the cards speak for themselves. If he fails to designate a wild card as such, it is taken at its face value.

If at any stage of the game every player but one has dropped, the latter takes the pot without showing any of his cards.

Breaking Ties. When two players have hands of the same type, the higher-ranking hand is determined as follows:

If each has a straight or straight flush, the one including the highest card wins (6-5-4-3-2 beats 5-4-3-2-A).

If each has three of a kind, four of a kind, or (with wild cards) five of a kind, the one composed of the higher-ranking cards wins. When there are many wild cards, two players may have three or four of a kind in the same rank. The tie is then broken by the unmatched cards, as described in the two next paragraphs.

If each has two pairs the one with the highest pair wins; A-A-3-3-4 beats K-K-Q-Q-5. If each has the same higher pair, the hand with the higher of the two lower pairs wins; A-A-6-6-5 beats A-A-5-5-9. If each has the same two pairs, the one with the higher fifth card wins; A-A-6-6-7 beats A-A-6-6-5.

If each has one pair, the higher pair wins; K-K-5-3-2 beats J-J-A-K-Q. If the two pairs are the same, the winner is determined by comparison of the other three cards in the two hands, depending first on the highest card (J-J-A-3-2 beats J-J-K-Q-10); then on the next higher card (J-J-A-4-3 beats J-J-A-3-2); and finally on the third card (J-J-A-K-7 beats J-J-A-K-6).

If each has a flush, or if each has a hand of lower rank than one pair, the hand containing the highest card wins;

A-7-5-3-2 beats K-Q-J-7-4. The highest cards in the two hands being identical, the winner is determined by the rank of the next-highest card, and so on down to the lowest card in the two hands, if necessary.

When two players have hands which are in all respects identical, except for the suits of the cards, and when they are jointly highest in the showdown, they divide the pot as evenly as possible and determine ownership of an odd chip or chips by lot. In determining the rank of poker hands, the suits are meaningless.

IRREGULARITIES. *Incorrect Pack.* If proved before the pot has been taken in, that deal is void and each player withdraws from the pot as many chips as he has put in it, but results of previous deals are not affected.

Misdeal. In the event of a misdeal, the next dealer in turn deals, after a new shuffle and cut; any ante placed in the pot remains there, but the regular ante is made for the next pot also. It is a misdeal: if attention is called in time to an irregularity in the shuffle or cut or to a deal out of turn; or if the pack is discovered to be imperfect at any time before the pot has been taken in.

Incorrect Number of Cards. If in dealing the dealer gives a card to the wrong player, he may rectify the deal before proceeding, transferring such cards as are necessary.

Incorrect Number of Hands. If dealer omits a player, he must give his own hand to the omitted player nearest his left. If dealer deals too many hands, he must assign one hand to each player and any excess hand becomes dead.

Irregularity in Betting. In correction of a betting irregularity, no chips once placed in the pot may be removed.

If a player bets, calls or raises out of turn, the turn reverts to the proper player. When the offender's turn comes, he is deemed to have bet the number of chips he put in. If he put in too few chips to call, he may add enough chips to call. He may not raise, and if he put in more chips than he needed to call, those chips are forfeited to the pot.

If a player announces a bet, in or out of turn, and does not accompany the announcement with a contribution of chips to the pot, the announcement is void. If he puts into the pot more chips than he announced, the additional chips are forfeited to the pot unless the improper announcement was a slip of the tongue and is corrected before any other player calls attention to it.

Draw Poker

IN THE ORIGINAL Poker game, each player received five cards face down, did not show any of them until the showdown, and never had a chance to improve beyond the five cards originally dealt to him. This was "Straight" Poker.

Draw Poker was the first of a long line of innovations designed to create more betting action. Each player could discard any number of his original cards and receive new cards to replace them.

Continued attempts to liven up the game by encouraging betting led to eventual adoption of a rule that in certain circumstances (as after a passed-out deal, or after some player held a big hand) the next pot should be a "jack," meaning that the stakes would be jacked up by raising the limit and increasing the amount of the ante. This created bigger pots, and the rule was added that the betting could not even be begun on a hand weaker than a pair of jacks. The resultant game, Jackpots, became the principal form of Draw Poker played in the United States.

JACKPOTS

THE ANTE. Before each deal, each player in the game antes one [white] chip of lowest value.

PLAYERS. Seven make the best game, eight make a full table.

DEALING. Each player receives five cards, all face down.

OPENING THE POT. The first betting interval commences when the deal is completed. Eldest hand has the first turn. He may either:

(a) *Open* the pot by making a bet, if he has a pair of jacks or any higher-ranking poker hand; or

(b) *Check*, meaning that he does not make a bet at the time but reserves the right to call or raise a bet later. A player may check whether or not he has as good a hand as a pair of jacks.

If eldest hand checks, the next player in rotation may

15

either open or check; and so on. Once any player makes a bet, the pot is open and each player in turn thereafter must either drop, call or raise.

Deal Passed Out. If every player including the dealer checks on the first round, the deal is passed out. Each player antes another chip. The next player in turn deals. (If dealer is anteing for all players, only the next dealer in turn antes.)

THE DRAW. When the bets in the first betting interval have been equalized, dealer picks up the undealt portion of the pack. Each player who is still in the pot, in rotation beginning nearest the dealer's left, may discard one or more cards, face down, at the same time announcing the number of cards he has discarded. The dealer then takes an equivalent number of cards from the top of the pack and gives them to that player, to restore his hand to five cards.

Each player in his turn receives the full number of cards demanded before the next player discards and draws.

Dealer draws last, and must announce the number of cards he discards.

Standing Pat. A player who does not wish to draw to his original five cards must so signify by announcing the fact or by knocking on the table when his turn to draw comes. Such a player *stands pat.*

Splitting Openers. The player who opens the pot is permitted to discard one or more of the cards essential to the combination which permitted him to open, and need not announce that fact. He is permitted to place his discard face down in the pot, so that it may be referred to later as evidence that he held proper openers.

Shuffling the Discards. If dealer has given the next-to-last card of the pack, and if the demands of the players in the draw are still not satisfied, he must shuffle together the bottom card and all cards previously discarded, have them cut by the player who will next receive a card in the draw, and proceed with the draw with the new pack so created. The discard of the opener and the discard of the player next to receive cards are not included if they have been kept separate and can be identified.

Reviewing the Draws. At any time during the draw, until the first legal bet has been made thereafter, any player may demand that each other player state the number of cards he drew, and the other players must so state, truthfully.

FINAL BETTING AND SHOWDOWN. When the draw is completed, the player who opened the pot must either check or bet. If this player has dropped, the next player in the pot to his left has the first turn. Each other player in turn may then check, or, if any bet has been made, may either call, raise or drop until the bets are equalized.

When all players have checked, or when all bets are equalized, every player who has not previously dropped shows his full hand in the showdown and the highest-ranking poker hand wins the pot.

PROVING OPENERS. Before his hand is discarded for any reason, the opener must prove that he held sufficient strength to justify opening the pot. Inability to prove openers is subject to penalty—see "False Openers" below.

IRREGULARITIES IN DRAW POKER. The following sections apply only to Draw Poker. Remedies and penalties for irregularities which may occur not only in Draw Poker but also in other forms of Poker are covered in the general laws on pages 9-14.

Card Exposed in The Deal. If one card is exposed in dealing, the player to whom it is dealt must keep it and there is no misdeal. If more than one card is exposed in dealing, a misdeal may be called by any player receiving such an exposed card, provided that player has not intentionally seen the face of any other card dealt to him.

Foul Hand. If a player's hand is foul, he cannot win the pot. He is deemed to drop whenever the irregularity is discovered, and any chips he has placed in the pot are forfeited. If he has made the final bet and has not been called, the chips in the pot remain there for the next deal.

Incorrect Hand. If one player is dealt too many cards and announces the fact before he has looked at the face of any of them, the dealer must draw the excess from his hand and restore it to the top of the pack. If a player is dealt too many cards and has seen the face of any of them, his hand is foul.

If a player has too few cards and has not seen the face of any of them, the dealer must deal him enough cards from the top of the pack to give him the proper number.

If a player has too few cards and has seen the face of any of them, he may play on but may never have his hand filled out to the full five cards (if he discards two cards, he may not draw more than two cards, and so on). A hand with fewer than five cards may never constitute a straight, flush or straight flush.

Card Exposed in the Draw. If the first card drawn by a player is exposed in the draw, the player must accept that card. If any other card demanded by that player is exposed in the draw, such card must be placed among the discards. After all other players have drawn, such exposed card is replaced by the dealer from the top of the pack.

Incorrect Number of Cards Drawn. If a player does not receive the exact number of cards he asked for, he may cause the dealer to make correction provided he has not looked at the face of any of the cards drawn.

If the next player in turn has received one or more cards in the draw, a player who has received the wrong number may play on with a short hand if this causes him to have too few cards, and may leave the excess on the table, unseen, if the draw would have given him too many cards. If a player receives too many cards in the draw and looks at all of them, his hand is foul.

If a player permits another player to his left to draw out of turn, the former may not receive cards in the draw; but he may stand pat and play on if he has not already discarded, and he may play on with a short hand if he has already discarded.

False Openers. If the opener cannot prove on demand that he held openers, his hand is foul. If all other players have dropped, each other player may withdraw from the pot any chips, except his ante, that he has contributed. The antes and any chips contributed by the opener remain for the next deal.

The opener is deemed to lack openers if his hand contains more than five cards.

PROGRESSIVE JACKPOTS

This is the same game as Jackpots, except that when a hand is passed out and everyone antes again, at least a pair of queens is required for openers in the next deal; if this is passed out, at least a pair of kings is required in the next deal; if this is passed out, at least a pair of aces in the next deal. The sequence is seldom carried beyond a pair of aces.

STRAIGHT DRAW POKER

This game is sometimes referred to as "Pass-out" and sometimes as "Bet or Drop." It differs from Jackpots as follows:

No minimum holding is required to make the opening bet before the draw.

In each turn, a player must either bet—at least one white chip, usually called a "white check"—or drop. Once he has dropped he may no longer compete for the pot. If any bet has been made before him, he must at least call to stay in.

BLIND OPENING

This form of Draw Poker, in the United States also called "Blind Tiger" (and in former times called "Blind and Straddle"), has become the standard form of Poker in most countries. Except in big-city clubs, it is little played in the United States.

Betting. Before the deal, the dealer puts one chip in the pot. This is the *ante.* The player at his left (formerly called the *age*) must put in one chip to open the pot; this bet is the *blind.* The next player to the left must put in two chips, constituting a *blind raise* of one chip; this bet is sometimes called the *straddle.* All these bets are made before any cards are dealt.

When the cards have been dealt and the players have looked at their hands, the turn begins at the left of the last blind bettor. Each player in turn may stay in by calling or raising the highest previous bet; in some games the first voluntary bet must be a raise, so the first voluntary bettor would have to put in three chips, or in some games four chips (called a *double*). The limit before the draw is usually two chips. In some games the ante and blind are two chips each, the blind raise four chips, and the first voluntary bet six or eight chips; if it is six chips, the limit before the draw is two chips, and if it is eight the limit is four. The blind bettors (including the dealer) count their blind bets toward what they later need to call.

Once a voluntary bet is made, betting proceeds as in any

other form of Draw Poker. After the draw, there is a final betting interval in which the limit is usually four or five chips. In this betting interval there is usually a one-chip minimum bet, but in some games players are permitted to "check free" (stay in without betting) until a bet is made.

When no player before the age makes a voluntary bet in the first betting interval, the age may either call the blind bet, or raise, or propose to the blind raiser that they divide the dealer's ante. If the blind raiser refuses the proposal, the age may raise, call, or drop.

WHISKEY POKER

The deal is five face-down cards to each player, as in Draw Poker, plus one extra hand which receives its cards next before the dealer. The extra hand is the widow.

Eldest hand may take the widow, *knock*, or pass. If he passes, the next player in rotation has the same options, and so on as long as each successive player passes. If any takes the widow, he places his original hand face up on the table and the widow becomes his hand. If any *knocks*, the widow is immediately turned face up.

After the hand on the table is exposed, each player in turn has the option of taking one card from it in exchange for one card from his hand, or taking all five cards in exchange for his hand, or passing, or *knocking*. But a player may not pass in two successive turns, after the hand on the table is exposed.

Play continues for any number of rounds, until there is a knock. The knock (also called *close*) is a call for a showdown. Each hand thereafter, not including the knocker, has one more turn, following which all hands are exposed and the best hand wins.

Settlement may be in any one of three ways:

1. Each player antes one chip before the deal, and the high hand in the showdown takes the pot.

2. Each hand antes one chip before the deal; the low hand in the showdown must match this pot; and the high hand in the showdown takes it all.

3. There is no ante, and the low hand in the showdown pays an agreed amount (usually one chip for each player in the game) to the high hand.

Stud Poker

Any procedure not specifically described below is governed by the general laws beginning on page 9.

PLAYERS. Seven, eight or nine make the best game. Stud Poker is a better game for two, three or four players than is Draw Poker, for there is more action in betting.

DEALING. The dealer gives one card face down to each player in rotation; then one card face up to each player.

A player's face-down card is his *hole card* and is not shown until the showdown.

After these cards have been dealt, the pack is temporarily laid aside and the deal is interrupted for a betting interval. When the bets in this betting interval have been equalized, the dealer gives another face-up card, in rotation, to each player who has not dropped. The deal is again interrupted for a betting interval. After this betting interval, a third face-up card is given to each player who has not dropped, and after another betting interval each such player receives a fourth face-up card, completing his hand of five cards. Now there is a final betting interval, after which each player who is in the showdown turns up his hole card and the highest hand takes the pot.

BETTING. There is no ante in Stud Poker, except by agreement.

In the first betting interval, the player with the highest card showing must make a bet; if two or more players tie for highest-showing card, the player nearest the dealer's left (that is, the player who received his card first) bets first. In each subsequent betting interval, the highest poker combination showing designates the player with the first right to bet. After the first betting interval, it is not obligatory to bet. The first bettor may check, and any player thereafter may check if there has been no previous bet.

Dropping. A player who drops must turn his face-up cards down, and should not expose his hole card. (He is said to *fold.*)

DEALER'S OBLIGATIONS. The dealer is expected to designate the player who must bet first in each betting interval, as by pointing to the proper player and saying "First queen bets." The dealer is also expected to call attention to combinations of three showing cards which make it possible that the holder will eventually have a straight or a flush; thus, if all three of a player's showing cards are hearts, the dealer should announce "Possible flush."

BETTING LIMIT. It is customary in Stud Poker to have one limit during the first three betting intervals, and a higher limit for the final betting interval and also for any earlier betting interval in which any player has an "open pair."

IRREGULARITIES. Only irregularities peculiar to Stud Poker are dealt with here. Other irregularities and the remedies and penalties for them will be found on page 14.

Misdeal. No misdeal may be called after all hole cards and at least one face-up card have been dealt. When there is a misdeal, the same dealer deals again.

Card Improperly Exposed. If dealer deals any player's first card face up, he must deal that player's second card face down to serve as his hole card. If dealer deals both of a player's first two cards face up, that player may stay in and dealer must deal his third card face down. There is no penalty on the dealer if he improperly deals any one of the first three cards face up to a player; but if, having dealt the first three cards face up to a player, dealer also gives that player his fourth card face up, such player may withdraw from the pot all the chips he has placed in it and drop out; or that player may stay in and dealer must give him his fifth card face down.

If dealer has given a player all five of his cards face up, that player may either stay in or may drop out and withdraw from the pot all the chips he has placed therein, and dealer must replace them.

Card Faced in Pack or Prematurely Dealt. Any card dealt by the dealer before the close of a betting interval, or found faced in the pack, is dead and must be discarded. The deal is continued, each player receiving the card he would have received in regular rotation if no such card had been prematurely exposed or found faced; and when all cards in regular rotation have been dealt, players who failed to receive cards on that round are served in rotation.

A player who would have received an exposed card may demand a shuffle and cut of the remaining cards before a replacement card has been dealt to him.

Impossible Call. If a player calls a bet in the last betting interval, though it is impossible for any hole card to give him a hand that would beat the four cards of the hand showing against him, and if attention is called to this before the pot is gathered in, the player who so called may withdraw the number of chips with which he called the bet, unless at the time he called there was a player to his left who had not dropped.

SEVEN-CARD STUD
(Seven-Toed Pete, Down-the-River)

Each player receives three cards before the first betting interval—two cards face down, dealt one at a time, then one card dealt face up. There is then a betting interval. There are then three more rounds of cards dealt face up, one at a time, with a betting interval after each. Finally, one more card is dealt face down to each player who has not dropped, after which there is a final betting interval and a showdown in which each player turns up his three face-down cards and selects five cards as his poker hand.

If a card supposed to be dealt face down is instead dealt face up by dealer, and if due correction is not made through the sixth and seventh cards, the rules applying respectively to the fourth and fifth cards in five-card Stud Poker (page 22) are used; but if dealer gives a player his seventh card face up, having dealt the first six cards properly, that player has no recourse.

In other respects the rules of Stud Poker apply.

SIX-CARD STUD, EIGHT-CARD STUD

In Six-card Stud, the first card is dealt face down, the next four cards each face up, and the last card face down; there is a betting interval after each round of dealing from the second card on.

In Eight-card Stud Poker, the first two cards are dealt face down, the next four cards face up, and the last two cards face down, with a betting interval after each round of dealing from the third on.

In each case, a player chooses any five of his cards to be his poker hand in the showdown.

Variations of Poker

OPTIONAL LAWS

SPECIAL HANDS. Depending upon the locality in which the game is played, and the personal preferences of the players, certain special combinations of cards may be given values along with the standard poker hands enumerated on page 10. Some of these hands are:

Big Tiger, or *Big Cat.* King high, eight low, no pair. Ranks above a straight, below a flush.

Little Tiger, or *Little Cat.* Eight high, three low, no pair. Ranks above a straight, below a Big Tiger.

Big Dog. Ace high, nine low, no pair. Ranks above a straight, below a Little Tiger.

Little Dog. Seven high, deuce low, no pair. Ranks above a straight, below a Big Dog.

Skeet, or *Pelter.* Nine, five, deuce with one card between the nine and five in rank and one card between the five and deuce in rank, no pair. Ranks above a straight, below a flush. The skeet is seldom played when Tigers and Dogs are also played. When all five cards of a skeet are of the same suit, the hand is a Skeet Flush and ranks above a straight flush.

As between Tigers (Cats), Dogs and Skeets, ties are broken as in the case of any other poker hand containing no pair—by the highest card, then the next highest, and so on.

Skip Straight. This is also called a Dutch Straight, or Kilter. It consists of a progression of cards each separated by one step in rank from the adjacent one—for example, Q, 10, 8, 6, 4 or K, J, 9, 7, 5. It ranks above three of a kind but below a straight. As between two skip straights, the one containing the highest-ranking card wins.

Round-the-Corner Straight. A sequence of cards, treating the thirteen cards as an unending sequence, so that 3-2-A-K-Q is a "straight." Beats three of a kind, loses to a skip straight or straight. As between two round-the-corner straights, the one with the higher card at the top of the sequence wins: 5-4-3-2-A beats 4-3-2-A-K.

Blaze Any five face cards. Beats two pairs, loses to three of a kind; however, a blaze including three of a kind need not be called a blaze. As between two blazes, each composed of two pairs, ties are broken as between any two hands composed of two pairs.

Four flush. This is played principally in Stud Poker, whereas the other special hands are played principally in Draw Poker; however, in many Jackpot games, a player is permitted to open on a four flush even though that hand is given no special value in the showdown. In Stud Poker, a four flush (when played) beats a pair but loses to two pairs. A four flush is any hand containing four cards of one suit. As between two four-flush hands, one containing a pair beats one containing no pair; if neither contains a pair, ties are broken as between any two hands containing no pair.

POPULAR WILD CARDS. The following are most frequent choices of cards to be designated as wild:

Deuces;

One-eyed cards, or "cards with profiles" (♠J, ♡J and ♢K);

Low hole card in each hand (in Seven-card Stud);

Any card selected in the hand and all other cards of the same rank in the same hand;

Any card selected by the player, but only the one card.

DOUBLE-ACE FLUSHES. When it is not required (in accordance with the rules some players use) that a player designate a wild card as some card other than the ones he already holds, a flush may be headed by two or even three aces; thus, if deuces are wild, the holding ♢A ♣2 ♢7 ♢5 ♢4 would beat ♠A ♠K ♠9 ♠8 ♠5, because the holder of the former hand could cause the ♣2 to serve as an additional ♢A.

In games in which the low hand wins, and in which ace ranks as the low card, some permit a hand to be designated as "Double Ace Low," and yet be deemed not to contain a pair.

ROYALTIES. Royalties, or *premiums*, or *bonuses*, (in England, *penalties*), are sometimes paid by unanimous agreement of the players, made before the game begins. In such cases, any player holding four of a kind or a straight flush receives an extra payment from each other player, regardless of the result of the pot.

LOW POKER, or LOWBALL

Straight Draw Poker is played, as described on page 19. There is no minimum requirement for betting, and in each turn a player must either bet (or at least call the previous bet) or drop. Straights and flushes do not count.

In the showdown, the lowest hand wins the pot, with the ace the lowest card in the pack. Since straights do not count, the lowest possible hand is 5-4-3-2-A, which is called a *bicycle*. Aces are low in every case; a pair of aces ranks lower than a pair of deuces.

Low Poker is frequently played in connection with a Jackpots game. If a deal is passed out at Jackpots, the cards are not gathered up and reshuffled; instead, the betting takes up with eldest hand and the game becomes Lowball.

Variant. Occasionally Lowball is played with no difference from the standard rank of the hands, so that the lowest possible hand is 7-5-4-3-2 of two or more suits; straights and flushes count, and the ace ranks high. In the showdown the cards speak for themselves, and the combination 5-4-3-2-A is a straight; the holder is not permitted to call the ace the high card in his hand.

HIGH-LOW POKER

Any standard form of Poker may be played, but in the showdown the highest-ranking poker hand and the lowest-ranking poker hand divide the pot equally. (The lowest-ranking poker hand, of course, is 7-5-4-3-2 of two or more suits.) If there is a chip left over after the pot has been divided as evenly as possible, that chip goes to the high hand. If two or more players tie either way, they divide half the pot.

HIGH-LOW STUD. Regular five-card Stud Poker is played, but in the showdown the high and low hands divide the pot. Before taking his last card, any player has the option of turning up his hole card and taking his last card face down. If the dealer improperly exposes such a card, the player may not take it; and after all other players still in the pot have been served, the player receives the next card from the top of the pack. The penalty on the dealer is that, if he is still in the pot, his hand becomes foul.

HIGH-LOW SEVEN-CARD STUD. Seven-card Stud is played as described on page 23, but in the showdown each player may select any five of his cards to represent his high hand, and any five of his cards to represent his low hand. High and low split the pot, but the same player may win both ways.

DECLARATIONS. In many games, each player is required to declare, after the bets have been equalized in the last betting interval but before any face-down cards are exposed for the showdown, whether he is going for high, for low, or for both. He is bound by his announcement, and if he declares for high, he may not compete for low; if he declares for low, he may not compete for high; and if he declares for both, he must at least tie for winning hand both ways or he cannot win either way, and even if there is only one other player in the showdown, that player takes the entire pot.

Others play that each player in the showdown must decide in advance whether he will go for high, for low, or for both, but need not make his decision public. Without permitting other players to see him, he must take into his hand a white chip if he is going for low; a red chip if he is going for high; a blue chip if he is going for both.

DEALER'S CHOICE

In the usual informal Poker game, the dealer may choose which form or variation of Poker will be played. Sometimes he is not limited to forms of poker, but may select such games as Fan Tan, Red Dog, or any other game suitable to the number of players at the table. Sometimes each dealer in turn plays a series of games, and this is known as "Garbage."

There is one special rule applicable to Dealer's Choice: When the game selected is Jackpots, or any other game in which the hand can be passed out, when a hand is passed out everyone antes again but the same dealer redeals.

The following are popular "Dealer's Choice" games:

SPIT IN THE OCEAN. Each player gets four cards, dealt one at a time face down. The dealer then places one card face up in the center of the table. This card is wild, and every other card of the same rank is wild. The card thus shown in the center of the table is considered to be the fifth card of every player in the game.

In most games of Spit in the Ocean, every player antes before the deal. There are several methods of betting:

Variant 1. There is only one betting interval, which occurs after the deal is completed. When the bets are equalized, there is a showdown.

Variant 2. As in Stud Poker (except that the cards are dealt face down) there is a betting interval after each round of one card is dealt to each player who has not dropped, and a final betting interval after the card is faced in the center.

Variant 3. After the face-up card is dealt, there is a betting interval; then each player who has not dropped may discard one or more of his face-down cards and draw enough cards, also face down, to restore his hand to four cards. The rules of Draw Poker apply. There is then a final betting interval before the showdown.

MEXICAN STUD or FLIP. Stud Poker is played, except as follows: Each player receives his first two cards face down, and may turn up one of them, after which there is a betting interval; each round thereafter is dealt face down, but after the deal each player must turn one of his face-down cards up. Thus there is only one hole card in each hand at any one time.

Each player should select the card to turn up before any other player has turned up his card, so that all cards are turned up simultaneously; but if any player turns his card up before the other players have selected theirs, any other player may change his selection before turning up his card.

CINCINNATI. Among the many names for this game are Lame Brains, Rickey de Laet, and, in one variant, Criss-Cross.

Five cards are dealt face down to each player, one at a time, and five more face-down cards are dealt to the center of the table. One of the cards in the center is turned face up, and there is a betting interval; then another, and so on, with a betting interval after each card, until all five are exposed. In the showdown, each player selects five cards from among the five cards of his hand plus the five exposed cards on the table. No card is wild unless the dealer so designates before dealing.

CRISS-CROSS. The center cards are laid out in the form of a cross, and the center card is turned up last. Each player must select one or the other bar of the cross, giving him only eight cards to select from. Otherwise the game is the same as Cincinnati. The dealer may, if he wishes, designate the center card and all other cards of the same rank to be wild cards. This designation must be made before the deal begins

SHOTGUN. Draw Poker is played, except that after each player has received three cards the deal is interrupted for a betting interval; then each player who has not dropped receives another face-down card, and there is another betting interval; then each player who has not dropped receives a fifth face-down card and there is another betting interval. There is then a draw, followed by a final betting interval and showdown.

DOUBLE-BARRELLED SHOTGUN. Shotgun, as described in the preceding paragraph, is played as a high-low game; and there are four additional betting intervals, because after the draw each player turns up one card of his hand at a time, with a betting interval following each. High and low hands split the pot.

TWO POTS TO WIN. Any form of Poker may be played, but the pot accumulates until any player has won the pot a second time, whereupon he takes the pot.

TWO-CARD POKER, or HURRICANE. Each player receives only two cards, dealt one at a time, face down. There is a betting interval, and the high hand in the showdown wins the pot. Usually all players ante before the deal. Straights and flushes do not count in the showdown; a pair of aces is the highest possible hand.

THREE-CARD POKER, or THREE-CARD MONTE. One card is dealt face down for each player, with a betting interval; then one card face up to each player, with a betting interval; then another card face up to each player, which ends the deal. There is a final betting interval and a showdown. The highest possible hand is a straight flush (three cards in sequence in the same suit); then three of a kind, then a flush (all three cards of the same suit), then a straight (any three cards in sequence), then a pair, and then high card.

BASEBALL. Either five-card or seven-card Stud Poker is played, with the following special rules:
All nines are wild.
Any three in the hole is wild.
If a player is dealt a three face-up, he must either "buy

the pot," which means that he puts into the pot as many chips as are already there, in which case his exposed three and all other threes are wild; or he must drop out of the pot. If he does buy the pot, no other player need match that amount to stay in.

A player who is dealt a four face-up is immediately dealt another face-up card in addition to the four.

However many cards a player may have at the end, he must select five of them to be his hand in the showdown.

BUTCHER BOY. The cards are dealt in rotation face up. When a duplicate of any card previously dealt appears, it is transferred to the player who received the card of that rank previously. There is a betting interval, with this player betting first.

When bets are equalized, the deal resumes, the next card being dealt to the player who would have gotten the last card (or, if he has dropped, to the active player nearest his left).

This process continues until any player has four of a kind, at which point the game ends and that player takes the pot.

As many play, at this point the pot is divided between the high and low hands, the player with four of a kind being high even though another player has a straight flush in five cards. As among the other hands, each must select five cards if he has more than five. In a hand of fewer than five cards, a missing card ranks as the lowest card in the pack, so that 7-5-4-3 is lower than 7-5-4-3-2.

COLD HANDS. Each player puts up an agreed amount, after which the cards are dealt, face up, one at a time until each player has five. The highest poker hand showing takes the pot. Some play that one may discard from a cold hand and draw, as in Draw Poker.

FREEZEOUT. Any form of Poker may be played; usually, the game is either Straight Draw Poker or Stud Poker. Each player takes an original stake; it is not necessary for all players to start with the same amount. No player may add to his original stake nor drag down any part of it or of his winnings after play begins. When a player loses all he has, he drops out and play continues among the remaining players until one player has all the starting stakes.

Poker Probabilities

POSSIBLE POKER HANDS IN A 52-CARD PACK

Straight Flush (including 4 Royal Flushes)	40
Four of a Kind	624
Full House	3,744
Flush	5,108
Straight	10,200
Three of a Kind	54,912
Two Pairs	123,552
One Pair (84,480 of each, aces to deuces)	1,098,240

No pair:

Ace High	502,860	
King High	335,580	
Queen High	213,180	
Jack High	127,500	
Ten High	70,380	
Nine High	34,680	
Eight High	14,280	
Seven High	4,080	
		1,302,540

Total	2,598,960

POSSIBLE POKER HANDS IN A 53-CARD PACK
(with the joker included as a wild card)

Five of a Kind	13
Straight Flush	204
Four of a Kind	3,120
Full House	6,552
Flush	7,804
Straight	20,532
Three of a Kind	137,280
Two Pairs	123,552
One Pair	1,268,088
Less than one pair	1,302,540
Total	2,869,685

POSSIBLE POKER HANDS WITH DEUCES WILD
Number of Deuces

	None	One	Two	Three	Four	Total
Five of a Kind		48	288	288	48	672
Royal Flush	4	80	240	160	..	484
Straight Flush	32	576	2,232	1,232	..	4,072
Four of a Kind	528	8,448	19,008	2,832	..	30,816
Full House	3,168	9,504	...	...	..	12,672
Flush	3,132	7,264	2,808	...	..	13,204
Straight	9,180	37,232	19,824	...	..	66,236
Three of a Kind	42,240	253,440	59,376	...	..	355,056
Two Pairs	95,040	...	...	...	..	95,040
One Pair	760,320	461,728	...	...	..	1,222,048
No Pair	798,660	...	...	...	..	798,660
Total	1,712,304	778,320	103,776	4,512	48	2,598,960

In Draw Poker, if there is no legal minimum for making the opening bet, the minimum strength that justifies opening is as follows:

PLAYERS YET TO SPEAK	STRENGTH REQUIRED
7	Pair of Aces
6	Pair of Kings
5	Pair of Kings
4	Pair of Queens
3	Pair of tens
2	Pair of eights
1	Ace-King high

In a conservative game it may be assumed that every additional player who stays in believes he has a better hand than any of the players before him. On this is based the following table of the minimum strength required to stay in when the pot has already been opened and others are in it:

PLAYERS ALREADY IN POT	REQUIRED TO STAY IN
1	Kings
2	Two low pairs
3	Queens up
4	Kings up
5	Aces up
6	Three of a kind

Flushes and Straights. At the start of a Draw Poker hand, you can see only five cards. There are forty-seven cards you do not know. If you hold four cards of a suit, nine of the unknown forty-seven cards are of the same suit as your four, and if you draw one of them you will have a flush. Therefore if you stay and draw one card, you have nine chances in forty-seven to fill your flush. The odds are 38-to-9, or somewhat more than 4-to-1 against you.

If you have a bobtail straight, such as 8-7-6-5, the odds are 39-to-8, or almost 5-to-1 against filling it, for there are only eight cards that will help you (in this case, the four nines and the four fours).

Therefore you should draw to a flush only when the pot gives you about 4-to-1 odds; to a bobtail straight only when the pot gives you 5-to-1 odds.

DRAWING THREE CARDS TO A PAIR
Total Number of Cases: 16,215

RESULT	FAVORABLE CASES	ODDS AGAINST
Two pair	2,592	5.25 to 1
Triplets	1,854	7.74 to 1
Full House	165	97.3 to 1
Four of a Kind	45	359. to 1
Any improvement	4,656	2.48 to 1

DRAWING TO A PAIR AND ACE KICKER
Total Number of Cases: 1,081

RESULT	FAVORABLE CASES	ODDS AGAINST
Aces up	126	7.58 to 1
Another pair	20	17 to 1
Total two pair	186	4.81 to 1
Triplets	84	12 to 1
Full House	9	119 to 1
Four of a Kind	1	1080 to 1
Any improvement	280	2.86 to 1

DRAWING TWO CARDS TO TRIPLETS
Total Number of Cases: 1,081

RESULT	FAVORABLE CASES	ODDS AGAINST
Full House	66	15½ to 1
Four of a Kind	46	22½ to 1
Any improvement	112	8⅔ to 1

DRAWING ONE CARD TO TRIPLETS

RESULT	FAVORABLE CASES	ODDS AGAINST
Full House	3	14⅔ to 1
Four of a Kind	1	46 to 1
Any improvement	4	10¾ to 1

ODD DRAWS

DRAW	ODDS AGAINST	RESULTS
Four to an Ace	11 to 1	Two pairs or better
Three to A-K of same suit	12 to 1	Two pairs or better
Two to straight flush (e.g. ◇J 10 9)	11 to 1	Straight or better
except: K, Q, J or 4, 3, 2	13½ to 1	Straight or better
A, K, Q or 3, 2, A	20 to 1	Straight or better
Two to a flush	23 to 1	Flush
Two to open-end straight	22 to 1	Straight

SPECIAL CONSIDERATIONS. In many forms of Poker, or in standard forms played with different stakes and limits, there are special considerations.

The Bug. A straight is good enough to win in almost every case, and drawing to a three-card sequence plus the Bug, such as Bug-10-9-8, is twice as good as the draw to a usual bobtail straight. Such a hand is therefore worth a play in many cases where a bobtail straight such as J-10-9-8 would be dropped, and is even worth a raise when three other players are already in the pot. This is not true of draws to a flush.

High-Low Poker. A full house has a better chance to win high than a seven-high hand to win low. When many players are raising and re-raising, a good low hand should be viewed with caution and the holder should be content to call; a good high hand should be played as strongly as in a Jackpots or regular Draw Poker game.

High-Low Seven-Card Stud. At the start, you should play for low, not for high. The holding 7-5-4 is far better than an original holding of a pair of kings.

Deuces Wild. The average winning hand in a five- or six-hand game is three aces, including at least one deuce. A "natural" combination is not so good as a combination including one or more deuces, because the chances that other players will hold deuces is increased. When the pot has been opened, it is seldom wise to stay in without a deuce in the hand, unless holding three of a kind or better.

Red Dog (High-Card Pool)

ESSENTIALLY a gambling game, Red Dog is more often played by family groups for meaningless stakes than by serious gamblers.

PLAYERS. Any number up to ten may play.

CARDS. The 52-card pack. In each suit, the cards rank: A (high), K, Q, J, 10, 9, 8, 7, 6, 5, 4, 3, 2. There is no rank of suits.

PRELIMINARIES. Each player puts up some agreed number of chips, which may be as few as one per player in large games and as many as ten per player when only three or four are playing. These chips form a pool, which is the common property of all participants, in equal shares.

Anyone picks up a shuffled pack, has it cut by any other player, and deals one card face up to each player in rotation. The player receiving the highest card is the first dealer and thereafter the deal rotates to the left.

DEALING. After a shuffle and cut, the dealer distributes the cards, face down, one at a time to each player in rotation to his left, beginning with the player at his left, until each player has five cards. The dealer places the remaining cards face down before him to serve as the *stock*.

When there are nine or ten players in the game, only four cards are dealt to each player.

THE PLAY. *The object of play* of each player in turn is to beat whatever card is on top of the stock when his turn comes. To beat this card, he must have in his hand a card of higher rank in the same suit.

Betting. Each player in turn makes a bet against the pool, not against the other players. The eldest hand has first turn, which then passes in rotation from player to player to his left.

Each player must bet at least one chip; the maximum bet is the number of chips in the pool at the time (called "betting the pot").

Settlement of Bets. Dealer then turns face up the top card of the stock. If the player's hand contains any card to beat it, he shows that card and withdraws his bet; the dealer then removes from the pool and pays him an equivalent amount. The player's other cards are placed aside unseen.

If the player cannot beat the card shown, the chips he bet are added to the pool and he shows his entire hand, face up.

Renewal of Pool. If a player's winning bet leaves no chips in the pool, each player contributes the amount originally required to form a new pool, and play continues.

IRREGULARITIES. If a player is dealt too few cards, he may choose whether to play on with the cards dealt him or to withdraw.

If a player is dealt too many cards, the dealer must draw the excess from his hand, offered face down after being shuffled; and play continues.

If a player bets an amount greater than the number of chips in the pool, he is deemed to have bet the amount of the pool.

STRATEGY. If there are more cards that a player can beat than can beat him, he has a good bet; if the converse is true, he has a poor bet and should bet the minimum.

The simplest way to determine the chances of winning and losing is to consider every suit a sequence from 2, which is low, up to 14, representing the ace. Assuming that five cards have been dealt to each player, there are 47 unknown cards at the start. Subtract the highest card held in each suit from 14, counting a void suit as 1; the sum of the differences will be the number of cards which one's hand cannot beat. Since there are 47 unknown cards altogether, if there are 23 or fewer such cards outstanding, the player has a better-than-even chance to win; if there are 24 cards or more, he has a less-than-even chance.

Euchre

IN ONE PERIOD (1880-1905) this was the most popular "family" game in the United States. It is closely related to three other "national" games: Écarté in France, Napoleon in England, and Spoil Five in Ireland.

PLAYERS. Four players, in two partnerships. Euchre has been adapted to any number of players from two to seven. These variants are described after the four-hand game.

CARDS. The pack of 32. The rank of cards in each suit is, in general: A (high), K, Q, J, 10, 9, 8, 7. But in the trump suit, the jack (called *right bower*) is elevated to the highest trump, and the second-highest trump is the other jack of the same color as right bower (called *left bower*). *Example:* If hearts are trumps, the trumps rank: ♡J (high), ◇J, ♡A, K, Q, 10, 9, 8, 7. The trump suit always contains nine cards; the *next* suit (same color as the trump) contains seven; the *cross* suits (opposite color from the trump) each contain eight.

PRELIMINARIES. Draw cards for partners, seats, and first deal. The two lowest play against the two highest; lowest card has choice of seats and is the first dealer. In drawing, the ace is low, below the seven. Two or more players drawing equal cards must draw again. Partners sit opposite each other.

Dealer has the right to shuffle last. The pack is cut by the player at his right. The cut must leave at least four cards in each packet. It is usual to use two packs alternately, dealer's partner shuffling the still pack during the deal.

DEALING. Five cards are dealt to each player, in two rounds of 3-2 or 2-3, as dealer chooses. The cards are dealt in rotation to the left, beginning with eldest hand.

After dealing the last packet to himself, dealer places the rest of the pack face-down on the table, and turns the top card face up. This *turn-up* proposes the trump suit for the deal.

MAKING. Eldest hand may pass or may accept the turn-up
for trump. The latter choice is signified by saying "I order
it up" (since dealer alone has the right to take the turn-up
into his hand). If eldest hand passes, the next player has
the same option, and so on. If partner of the dealer wishes
to accept the turn-up suit, he says "I assist." Opponent at
right of dealer accepts in the same words as eldest hand,
by ordering it up.

Should any player, including dealer, accept the turn-up,
dealer at once discards one card from his hand. The discard is by custom placed crosswise under the undealt
cards. The turn-up belongs to dealer in place of his discard.
By custom the turn-up is not placed in dealer's hand, but
is left on the pack until duly played.

If all four hands pass, dealer puts the turn-up, still face
up, crosswise under the undealt cards, signifying that the
proposed trump has been *turned down*. Eldest hand then
has the right to name the trump suit, or to pass; in the
latter event, dealer's partner may *make it* or pass, and
so on. But no player may *make it* the suit of the rejected
turn-up.

Naming the other suit of same color as the rejected turn-
up is called *making it next;* naming a suit of opposite color
is *crossing it*.

If all four hands pass in the second round, the cards are
thrown in, and the next dealer deals.

PLAYING ALONE. The hand that makes the trump, whether
in the first or second round, has the right to declare "I
play alone." The partner of the *lone player* then lays his
cards face down on the table and does not participate in
the play, but duly shares the increased winnings if the
lone player succeeds.

THE PLAY. If the maker plays alone, the opening lead is
made by the opponent at his left; otherwise, the opening
lead is made by eldest hand regardless of the position of
the maker.

A lead calls upon each other hand to follow suit if able;
if unable to follow suit, the hand may play any card. A
trick is won by the highest trump, or by the highest card
of the suit led. The winner of a trick leads to the next.

The object of play is to win at least three tricks. If the
making side fails to win three it is *euchred*. The winning
of all five tricks by one side is called *march*.

SCORING. Maker of trump, if playing with partner, wins: for making 3 or 4 tricks, 1 point: for march, 2 points. Maker playing alone wins: for 3 or 4 tricks, 1 point; for march, 4 points. In any case, if making side is euchred, opponents win 2 points.

Four-hand Euchre is usually played for a game of 5 points, but this is sometimes increased by agreement to 7 or 10.

IRREGULARITIES. *Misdeal.* There may be a new deal by the same dealer if a card is exposed in dealing; a card is faced in the pack; or if the pack is found imperfect. When a pack is found imperfect, previous scores stand.

A deal by the wrong player may be stopped before a card is turned up; if the error is not noticed until later, the deal stands.

Error in Bidding. A player who *orders it up* when he is partner of dealer, or *assists* when he is an opponent of dealer, is deemed to have accepted the turn-up for trump. If a player names for trump the suit of the turn-up after it has been turned down, his declaration is void and his side may not make the trump.

Declaration Out of Turn. If a player makes a declaration (or turn down) other than a pass, out of turn, it is void and his side may not make the trump.

Lead Out of Turn. If a hand leads out of turn and all other hands play to the trick before the error is noticed, the trick stands. But if any hand has not played, the false lead must be taken back on demand of any player and becomes an exposed card. Any cards played to the incorrect lead may be retracted without penalty. An opponent of the incorrect leader may name the suit to be led at the first opportunity thereafter of the offender or his partner to lead; such call must be made by the hand that will play last to the trick.

Exposed Cards. A card is deemed exposed if it is led or played out of turn; dropped face up on the table except as a regular play in turn; played with another card intended to be played; or named by a player as being in his hand. An exposed card must be left face up on the table and must be played at the first legal opportunity.

Revoke. Failure to follow suit to a lead when able is a revoke. A revoke may be corrected before the trick is quitted, and if it is corrected any opponent who played after the revoke may retract his card and substitute another. If a player so mixes the tricks that a claim of revoke against his side cannot be proved, the claim must be considered proved.

Upon proof of established revoke, the non-revoking side has the option of scoring the hand as played or of taking the revoke penalty. The revoke penalty is 2 points, which may be either added to the score of the non-revoking side or subtracted from the score of its opponents. If the revoke was made by the opponents of a lone hand, the penalty is 4 points.

THREE-HAND (CUTTHROAT) EUCHRE

In a three-hand game only three hands are dealt. A separate score is kept for each player, but the maker of trump is always opposed by the other two playing in temporary partnership. There is no call of "alone," because the maker is necessarily a lone hand (and is so treated in applying the laws on irregularities). The scoring: Maker scores, for 3 or 4 tricks, 1 point; for march, 3 points. If maker is euchred, each opponent scores 2 points.

TWO-HAND EUCHRE

From the regular Euchre pack discard the sevens and eights, reducing it to 24 cards. Two hands are dealt. All rules, including scoring, are as at four-hand, except that there is no declaring "alone," since no partnership play is possible in any case.

RAILROAD EUCHRE

Railroad Euchre is any form of the game in which special features are adopted. Any or all of the following may be included:

Joker. The joker is added to the pack and always ranks as the best trump, above the right bower. One suit is agreed upon in advance to be the proposed trump in case the joker is turned up.

Playing Alone. A player announcing alone may discard one card from his hand and receive the best card from his partner's hand. (The selection is made by partner, without exposure of any cards.) This exchange is additional to dealer's right to take up the trump, so that dealer may make two discards. He takes partner's best before taking the turn-up, so that if the card from partner does not suit him he can discard it for the turn-up. If dealer's partner plays alone, dealer may give him the turn-up.

Opposing Alone. After a player announces a lone hand, either opponent may announce that he will oppose alone. This lone opponent is entitled to discard one card and receive partner's best card. Euchre of a lone hand by a lone opponent counts 4 points.

Laps. If a game is won by a total of more than 5 points, the excess over 5 is carried forward to the next game. The object of laps is to preserve the incentive for playing alone, whatever the score.

Slam. A game counts double if the losers did not score a point.

Jambone is a lone hand played with the cards exposed. Either opponent may direct the card to be played from the exposed hand at each turn, but opponents may not consult. The only object in calling jambone is to try for the increased score for march, which counts 8 points. Lone opposition is not allowed against jambone.

Jamboree is simply a bonus, 16 points, for holding the five highest trumps. It may be scored only by the maker of trump. Dealer gets credit for jamboree made with the help of the turn-up.

AUCTION EUCHRE

PLAYERS. Five, six or seven. The same rules can be adapted, if desired to any lower number of players.

CARDS. For *five-hand,* use the pack of 32 cards; *six-hand,* use 36 cards (adding the sixes); *seven-hand,* use full pack of 52. The joker may be added, if desired; it ranks as the highest trump, over the right bower.

PRELIMINARIES. All participants draw cards from a spread pack. Lowest card has first deal and choice of seats. Next-lowest sits at his left, and so on around the table.

DEALING. Cards are dealt in packets to the left, beginning with eldest hand. A widow is dealt after the first round of the deal. *Five-hand and six-hand:* Each player receives five cards, in rounds of 3-2 or 2-3, and the widow is two cards. *Seven-hand:* Each player receives seven cards, in rounds of 3-4 or 4-3, and the rest of the pack goes to the widow.

A method of scoring peculiarly suited to five-hand and seven-hand is *set-back*. All players commence with equal numbers of chips. When a player wins, he puts chips from his pile into the pool. When he is euchred, he draws chips from the pool. The first player to get rid of all his chips wins the game.

HASENPFEFFER

THIS IS A simplification of Euchre, said to have been invented by the Pennsylvania Dutch.

PLAYERS. Four, in partnership.

CARDS. The pack of 24, made by deleting all cards below the nine from the pack of 52, plus the joker, making 25 cards in all. The joker is the highest trump; the second is the jack of the trump suit (*right bower*); the third is the jack of the other suit of same color as the trump (*left bower*). The other trumps are: A (fourth-best), K, Q, 10, 9. In plain suits the rank is; A (high), K, Q, J, 10, 9.

PRELIMINARIES. Cards are drawn; lowest card has choice of seats and deals first. In cutting, all suits rank ace high. If equal cards are drawn for low, the tying players must draw again.

Dealer shuffles last, and the pack is cut by the player at his right. The cut must leave at least four cards in each packet.

DEALING. Cards are dealt to the left, commencing with eldest hand. Each player receives six cards, dealt three at a time. The last card is placed face down on the table to form the widow.

BIDDING. Each player in turn, commencing with eldest hand, has one chance to bid or pass. A bid specifies the number of tricks the player (with help of partner) will contract to win if allowed to name the trump suit. The high bidder names the trump, takes the widow card into his hand, then discards any one card. If all four players pass without a bid, the holder of the joker must acknowledge it and must then bid three. (Should the joker be the widow, and all four pass, the deal is abandoned.)

THE PLAY. The high bidder makes the opening lead. A lead calls upon each other hand to follow suit if able, if unable to follow suit, the hand may play any card. A trick is won by the highest trump, or by the highest card of the suit led. The winner of a trick leads to the next.

SCORING. If the contracting side makes at least its contract, it scores one point for each trick taken. If it fails, the amount of the bid is deducted from its score (the side is said to be *set back*). In either case, the opposing side scores one point for each trick it wins. Game is 10 points. If both sides reach 10 in the same deal, the contracting side counts first and so wins.

IRREGULARITIES. Use the laws of Euchre.

STRATEGY. As there are eight trumps, a holding of three in one hand should be counted worth one probable long-card trick. Each high trump (sufficiently guarded) is an additional trick, and each side ace should be counted a trick. The bidder is also entitled to include in his bid the expectation that partner can win one trick, The normal minimum for a bid of three is thus any three trumps and a side ace. It pays to be forward, rather than conservative, in bidding.

See also Euchre, *strategy*.

DOUBLE HASENPFEFFER

This variant is played with the Pinochle pack of 48 cards, without the joker. Three, four or six may play. With an even number partnerships are usually arranged, partners sitting alternately. The whole pack is dealt, with no widow. The lowest bid permitted is for half of the tricks, and the dealer must bid this number if all others pass. The high bidder may elect to play *alone,* in which case he may discard two cards and ask for the best two his partner can give him. If a lone player fails to make his contract, he is set back by as many points as there are cards per hand; if he makes contract, he scores twice this amount. If dealer fails to make a forced bid, he is set back only half. Scoring in all other cases is as in Hasenpfeffer. Game is 62 points.

Five Hundred

THE RULES of Five Hundred were originally copyrighted in 1904 by the United States Playing Card Company. At that time the game most widely played in the United States was Euchre. Five Hundred largely supplanted Euchre and for some years was the major social card game.

PLAYERS. Two to six may play. The rules below are given for three-hand, but the four-hand partnership game (page 48) is equally good.

CARDS. (For three-hand.) The pack of 32, with the joker added. The cards in the trump suit rank: joker (high), J (*right bower*), J (of the other suit of same color as the trump, *left bower*), A, K, Q, 10, 9, 8, 7. The cards in each plain suit rank: A (high), K, Q, J, 10, 9, 8, 7.

The suits rank: hearts (high), diamonds, clubs, spades. For bidding purposes, *no trump* ranks above hearts.

PRELIMINARIES. Draw for first deal. Lowest card deals; in drawing, the ace ranks below the two and the joker is the lowest card.

Dealer has the right to shuffle last, and the pack is cut by the player at his right. The cut must leave at least four cards in each packet.

The turn to deal passes to the left.

DEALING. Cards are dealt to the left, beginning with eldest hand. Each player receives ten cards, in rounds of 3-4-3. After the first round, three cards are dealt face down in the center to form a widow.

BIDDING. Commencing with eldest hand, each player in turn may make one bid or pass. Each bid names a number of tricks, from six to ten, together with the intended trump suit or no trump. Each bid must be for a greater number of tricks than the previous bid, or for the same number in a higher-ranking declaration. The highest bid becomes the contract, and the two other players combine in temporary partnership against the bidder.

If all hands pass without a bid, the next dealer deals. (In some circles, if a deal is passed out, the hand is played at no trump, each player for himself. Eldest hand leads. Each trick won counts 10 points.)

44

THE PLAY. Highest bidder takes up the widow, then discards any three cards, face down. He makes the opening lead, and may lead any card. A lead calls upon each other hand to follow suit, if able; if unable to follow suit, the hand may play any card. A trick is won by the highest trump, or by the highest card of the suit led. The winner of a trick leads to the next.

At no trump, the joker is a trump suit in itself. The joker may not be played unless one is void of the suit led, but when played, it wins the trick. When the joker is led, the leader must specify the suit for which it calls.

The object of play is to make or defeat the contract. Although the opponents combine against the bidder, they must keep their tricks separate for scoring purposes. The bidder makes nothing extra for extra tricks over his contract, unless he wins all ten tricks and his bid was for less than 250.

SCORING. The value of every possible bid is shown in the scoring table.

TRICKS	6	7	8	9	10
♠	40	140	240	340	440
♣	60	160	260	360	460
♦	80	180	280	380	480
♡	100	200	300	400	500
No trump	120	220	320	420	520

If the bidder makes his contract, he scores the value of his bid. If he took all ten tricks, and his bid was for less than 250, he scores 250 instead of the value of his bid. If the bidder is *set back*—fails to make contract—the value of his bid is subtracted from his running total. Thus it is possible for a player to have a minus score.

Each opponent of the bidder, whether the contract is made or set, scores 10 for each trick taken by himself.

Game is 500. If two or more players *go out* in the same deal, bidder wins; as between opponents alone, the first to win a trick that makes his total 500 wins. An opponent may *count out* by winning a trick that gives him 500, and the hand is then abandoned unless the bidder would also go out if he made contract.

NULLO. An additional declaration allowed in some circles is *nullo*, an offer to win no tricks at no trump. The value of nullo is 250, so that for bidding purposes it ranks higher than eight spades and lower than eight clubs. If nullo takes the contract, the bidder loses if he wins a single trick, and each opponent scores 10 for each trick taken by the bidder.

IRREGULARITIES. *Misdeal.* There must be a new deal by the same dealer if too many or too few cards are given to any hand; if a card is found faced in the pack or is exposed in the dealing; if the pack is found to be imperfect.

Bid Out of Turn. In a partnership game, if a player bids out of turn the bid is void and his side may make no further bid on that deal. In a game where each plays for himself, there is no penalty for a bid out of turn; the bid is void.

Wrong Number of Cards. If two hands (not including the widow) are found to hold an incorrect number of cards, there must be a new deal by the same dealer. If one hand and the widow are incorrect, the incorrect hand loses the right to bid, and any other player draws a sufficient number of cards from the excess and gives them to the deficient hand.

If, during the play, the bidder and widow alone are incorrect, the bidder loses at once, but the hand is played out to determine how many tricks the opponents can win. In this event some tricks at the end may be short. If the opponents are found to have an incorrect number of cards, the bidder and widow being correct, bidder at once wins the value of his game, and may continue play in the effort to win all the tricks.

Exposed Cards. A card illegally exposed by a player who has a partner (including opponents of the bidder at three-hand) must be left face up on the table. Any adversary may call for the play of the exposed card in regular turn, and the card must be played if it can be without revoking.

Play Out of Turn. If a player leads out of turn, and all others play to the trick before the error is noticed, it stands without penalty. If noticed earlier, the error must be corrected; the lead becomes an exposed card; the other cards on the trick are retracted; the correct leader may lead. If the correct leader is partner of the offender, the adversary at his right may call upon him to lead or not to lead a trump, or may forbid the suit of the exposed card to be led.

If a player plays when it is the turn of the hand at his right to *play* (but not to *lead*), the premature card stands as played without penalty; it may not be retracted.

Revoke. If a hand fails to follow suit when able, the offender may correct it before the trick is quitted and before he plays to the next trick. If it is not corrected, play ends immediately the revoke is noticed. If the revoke was by the bidder, he loses the value of his bid and the opponents score for whatever tricks they have taken up to that time. If the revoke was made by an opponent of the bidder, the bidder scores his bid and the opponents score nothing.

Looking at Quitted Tricks, or bidder looking back at his discard. The opponent at the offender's right may call a suit the next time the offender leads.

STRATEGY. As there are ten trumps, an average share is between three and four. The minimum trump length for a bid is four, but with only four they should include two of the three highest trumps or be heavily compensated with side strength. Most contracts go to hands with five or more trumps.

CHANCE OF FINDING AT LEAST ONE TRUMP IN WIDOW

When you hold 4 trumps	1091/1771	5:3 for
When you hold 5 trumps	955/1771	5:4 for

CHANCES OF FINDING ONE IMPROVING CARD IN WIDOW

"Places open"

1	231/1771	7:1 against
2	441/1771	3:1 against
3	631/1771	9:5 against
4	802/1771	6:5 against
5	955/1771	5:4 for

An approximate method of hand valuation is to count as a trick each trump in excess of 3, each top trump as good as the ace, and each side ace or guarded king.

Since each hand has only one turn to bid, it is important to bid the full value.

Play. With five or more trumps, the bidder should lead trumps at once in order to draw two for one. Even four trumps should be opened if the other suits are stopped.

The opponents should try to get the bidder in the *middle* by letting the lead come from his right rather than his left.

TWO-HAND FIVE HUNDRED

The deal is the same as for three players, a dead hand being placed at dealer's left. The winning bidder takes the widow and discards three cards; then the two hands are played out. Since the ten cards of the dead hand are not in play, bidding can and must be somewhat speculative.

FOUR-HAND FIVE HUNDRED

The four-hand game is played in two partnerships, the partners sitting alternately. The pack is of 42 cards (A to 5 in each suit, plus ♡4 and ◇4); the joker is usually not used, but it may be if desired. Each player is dealt ten cards, and the additional two or three cards go to the widow. Rules are the same as at three-hand, but the play is always two against two. A single score is kept for each side.

FIVE HUNDRED FOR FIVE OR SIX

The full pack of 52 (to which the joker may be added) is used in five-hand. Each player is dealt ten cards and the remainder goes to the widow. During the bidding, each is for himself but the high bidder then chooses partner(s) according to either of these alternative plans:

(a) A bid of six or seven entitles him to one partner; a bid of more entitles him to two; he names the players to be his partners, regardless of their position at the table;

(b) The bidder names a specific card, and the holder thereof becomes his partner, but must say nothing to reveal his identity until the card is duly played.

For six-hand play, in two partnerships of three each, the recommendation by the proprietors of the game is to use "the 62-card pack, the regular pack of 52 plus four 11's, four 12's, and two 13's." These added cards rank in order above the ten and below the jack or queen. Each player is dealt ten cards, and the remaining two (or three, with joker) go to the widow.

SPOIL FIVE

PLAYERS. From two to ten may play, but the best game is for five or six. Each plays for himself.

CARDS. The pack of 52. The ♡ A is always the third-best trump, consequently there are 13 trumps when hearts are trumps, but 14 when any other suit is trump. The rank of spot cards is different in the red and black suits; the mnemonical phrase goes "Highest in red; lowest in black."

The rank of cards in the trump suit is as follows:

Hearts: ♡ 5 (high), J, A, K, Q, 10, 9, 8, 7, 6, 4, 3, 2.

Diamonds: ◇ 5 (high), ◇ J, ♡ A, ◇ A, K, Q, 10, 9, 8, 7, 6, 4, 3, 2.

Clubs or *Spades:* 5 (high), J, ♡ A, A, K, Q, 2, 3, 4, 6, 7, 8, 9, 10.

The rank of cards in the plain suits is as follows:

Hearts or Diamonds: K (high), Q, J, 10, 9, 8, 7, 6, 5, 4, 3, 2, (◇ A).

Clubs or Spades: K (high), Q, J, A, 2, 3, 4, 5, 6, 7, 8, 9, 10.

PRELIMINARIES. Players may take seats at random. Any player distributes cards around the table, one at a time, face up, and the first jack marks the first dealer.

Dealer has the right to shuffle last, and the pack is cut by the player at his right. The cut must leave at least five cards in each packet.

Prior to the first deal, each player antes one chip into the pool. So long as this pool is not won, each successive dealer antes one additional chip. When the pool is taken, all hands ante one chip each to form a new pool.

DEALING. Cards are dealt to the left, beginning with eldest hand. Each player receives five cards dealt in rounds of 3-2 or 2-3. The deal completed, the next card is turned up for trump.

ROBBING. If the turn-up is an ace, dealer is entitled to take it in exchange for any card he chooses to discard. He must make his discard before the opening lead; having done so, he need not pick up the ace to establish his ownership.

If any player holds the ace of trumps, he is entitled to take any other turn-up in exchange for any discard. At his first turn to play, and before playing, he must pass his discard face down to dealer, who gives him the turn-up in exchange. (Or dealer, holding the ace, puts his discard under the stock and takes the turn-up.) The turn-up card so received need not be played to the current trick.

THE PLAY. Eldest hand makes the opening lead. A lead calls upon each other hand either to follow suit or trump; that is, he may trump even when able to follow suit. If unable to follow suit, the hand may play any card. A trick is won by the highest trump, or by the highest card of the suit led. The winner of a trick leads to the next.

Reneging is a privilege enjoyed by the three highest

trumps. The lead of an inferior trump does not compel the holder to play the trump 5, J, or ♡ A; if he has no smaller trump, he may discard. But the lead of a superior trump always calls for the play of an inferior; if the trump 5 is led, no player may renege, even with a singleton trump J or ♡ A.

Each player is for himself, and his primary object is to win at least three tricks. The second object is to win all five tricks. If unable to win three tricks, the player tries to prevent any other player from doing so. Consequently the game actually becomes a temporary partnership of the have-nots against the haves. When no hand wins three tricks, the game is spoiled.

When a player has won three tricks, he must immediately abandon his cards, or announce that he will *jink* it. In the latter event, play continues and he must win all five tricks, else the game is spoiled.

SETTLEMENT. A player who wins three tricks takes the pool; if he wins five tricks, he wins the pool plus an additional chip from each other player. If the game is spoiled, the pool is left intact to be won in a subsequent deal.

IRREGULARITIES. If a hand is found to have the wrong number of cards, during the play, it must be returned to the stock face-down and the owner drops out of the current deal. He may not take the pool in that deal, but no change is made in the ownership of tricks already played.

If a player robs when he does not hold the trump ace, leads or plays out of turn, reneges to the lead of a superior trump, fails to follow suit or trump when able, or exposes a card after any player has won two tricks, he forfeits the right to win the current pool on that or any subsequent deal. His rights are restored after the current pool is won. In any event, he must ante to the pool whenever he is dealer.

STRATEGY. Three out of five hands are spoiled, on the average, in a five-hand game. Of the cases where one player wins three tricks, four out of five result from abnormal length or strength.

Most of the strategy of play is concerned with spoiling. The renege privilege should be used to save a singleton high trump for later use against any dangerous opponent. When one opponent seems likely to win the first three tricks, and almost sure to win three tricks sooner or later, it is often good strategy to conceal possession of a winning trump (as by reneging) in the hope that the opponent will decide to jink it, whereupon the trump will spoil the pool.

FORTY-FIVE

Forty-Five is Spoil Five without the spoil. It is played two-hand, or by partnerships of two against two or three against three, seated alternately. The side that wins three tricks scores 5 points, or 10 for taking all five tricks. The side that first reaches a total of 45 wins the game.

AUCTION 45'S

Four play, two against two as partners; or six, in two partnerships of three. Partners are seated alternately.

In drawing for partnerships, the cards rank from ace high to deuce low; but in the play the rank of the cards is as in Spoil Five. Each player is dealt five cards, three at a time, then two; or two at a time, then three.

BIDDING. Eldest hand has first turn to bid, and thereafter the turn passes to the left. Each bid names a number of points, in multiples of 5, without specifying a suit; the highest bid is 30. Each player except the dealer must go higher than the preceding bid; the dealer, when his turn comes, may say "I hold," which means he will take the contract at the highest preceding bid, without going over. If the dealer holds, each player who has not previously passed may bid again, again provided he goes over the preceding bid. When the dealer does not hold, the highest bidder's side must play at the contract named. When the dealer holds and is not overcalled, dealer's side must play at the contract named.

DISCARDING AND DRAWING. The high bidder (or dealer, if he was allowed to hold) names a trump. Then each player in turn discards face down as many as he pleases of his original cards and dealer restores his hand to five cards from the top of the stock. (In six-hand play, some allow the dealer then to rob the pack as in Cinch, to replace his own discards.)

THE PLAY. The first lead is made by the hand to the left of the player who named the trump, and play proceeds as in Spoil Five, including the requirement of following suit or trumping, and the privilege of reneging when holding one of the three highest trumps. All players of a partnership combine to fulfil their joint contract or to defeat the adverse contract.

SCORING. Each trick counts 5, and the highest trump in play counts an additional 5 (making 10 in all for the trick it wins). If the contracting side fulfils its contract, it scores all the points it makes; if it falls short of its contract, the amount of the contract is deducted from its score. The opposing side in either case scores all the points it makes.

If a side bids 30 and wins all five tricks, it scores 60.

Game is won by the first side to reach 120 points. A side having 100 points or more may not bid less than 20.

IRREGULARITIES. *New Deal.* There must be a new deal by the same dealer if a card is exposed in dealing, or any player receives the wrong number of cards, or the dealer fails to adhere to the plan of dealing that he has commenced (as regards the number of cards to be dealt in each round).

Incorrect Hand. If, after the first bid but before the draw, any hand is found incorrect, a short hand is supplied with additional cards from the top of the stock, and excess cards are drawn from a hand and discarded by the right-hand opponent.

If, after the draw but before the opening lead, any hand is found incorrect, it must be rectified in the same way. If in giving cards to replace discards the dealer exposes a card, the player to whom it would have gone may refuse it, and then take a replacement after all other hands have drawn.

If, after the opening lead, any hand is found incorrect, or if a player exposes one of the three highest trumps, the offender must discard his entire hand and stay out of the play for the remainder of that deal; and his side may not score in that deal. If the offender's side named the trump, it loses its contract.

If any lower card is exposed illegally, after the opening lead, it must be placed face up on the table and played by the holder at his first legal opportunity.

Hearts

HEARTS is a comparatively recent game, but has largely displaced all the older "nullo" games in which the usual object is to lose tricks instead of winning them. It is a round game (every man for himself) and may be played in one form or another by two to eight players. "Straight" Hearts, Heartsette, Black Lady, and Domino are suitable for three to six players. Two may play Domino or the variant described as Two-hand Hearts. Particularly interesting with four players is Omnibus Hearts, which has become the most popular form of the game.

"STRAIGHT" HEARTS

PLAYERS. Any number from three to six may play, each for himself.

CARDS. The pack of 52. With other than four players, strip out some small cards to equalize the hands. Three players: discard ♣2. Five players: discard ♣2 and ◇2. Six players: discard ♣2, ♣3, ◇2, ♠2. (*Variant.* In Heartsette, the full pack is used whatever the number of players. The cards are dealt out evenly as far as they will go. Odd cards form a widow, which is added to the first trick and goes to the winner thereof.)

The cards in each suit rank: A high, K, Q, J, 10, 9, 8, 7, 6, 5, 4, 3, 2. There is no relative ranking of suits and never a trump. (Hearts are often called "trumps" but do not actually have the trump privilege.)

PRELIMINARIES. Cards may be drawn for choice of seats and first deal. Low card deals. The deal rotates to the left. Dealer has the right to shuffle last, and the pack is cut by the player at his right. The cut must leave at least four cards in each packet.

DEALING. The entire pack is dealt out one card at a time, beginning with the eldest hand.

THE PLAY. Eldest hand makes the opening lead. A lead calls upon each other hand to follow suit if able; if unable to follow suit, a hand may play any card. A trick is won by the highest card of the suit led. The winner of a trick leads to the next.

The sole object of play is to avoid taking hearts in tricks. Each heart counts 1 against the player taking it. (*Variant.* In Spot Hearts, ♡A counts 14; ♡K, 13; ♡Q, 12; ♡J, 11; and all other cards their index value.)

SCORING. Settlement is by any of three methods:

Cumulative Scoring. The number of hearts taken by each player is recorded in a running total column. When play ends, the average of all scores is computed and each player is debited or credited his amount over or under the average.

For example, suppose the final scores are

A	B	C	D
51	132	38	91

The total of the scores is 312 and division by 4 gives the average of 78. The net differences from average are:

A	B	C	D
—27	+54	—40	+13

Players B and D pay, A and C collect, their differences from average.

Sweepstake. After the play of a deal, each player puts in the pot one chip for every heart he took. If one player alone was *clear*—took no hearts—he wins the pot. If two players were clear, they divide the pot; if there is an odd chip, it goes into the next pot. If every player is *painted*—takes one or more hearts—or if one player takes all thirteen hearts the pot is a *jack* and is added to the next pot.

Howell Settlement. Each player puts in the pot, for each heart taken, as many chips as there are players in the game other than himself. Each player then takes out of the pot one chip for every heart, out of thirteen, that he did *not* take. In other words, he receives from the pot as many chips as the difference between thirteen and the number of hearts he took.

For example, in a four-hand game:

	A	B	C	D
Hearts taken	6	4	2	1
Put in pot	18	12	6	3
Receive	7	9	11	12
Net	—11	—3	+5	+9

IRREGULARITIES. *Misdeal.* If dealer exposes a card in dealing, or gives one player too many cards, another player too few, the next player in turn deals.

Revoke. Failure to follow suit when able to do so constitutes a revoke. A revoke may be corrected before the trick is turned and quitted; if not discovered until later, the revoke is established, play is immediately abandoned, and the revoking hand is charged with all 13 points for the deal. If revoke is established against more than one player, each is charged 13 points. But the revoke penalty may not be enforced after the next ensuing cut after the deal in which the revoke occurred.

Incorrect Hand. A player discovered to have too few cards must take the last trick (if more than one card short he must take in every trick to which he cannot play.)

STRATEGY. A holding is dangerous not through the presence of high cards, but through the absence of low cards. The suit A-10-7-4-2 is usually impregnable; the suit Q-10-9-7 is dangerous.

A suit is distributed 4-3-3-3 only 10% of the time. In the other 90% of cases, some hand will be able to discard on the third round or earlier. With a holding that can be forced to win one or two of the first three rounds of the suit, play the high cards first, saving the low card.

♠ Q 6 2   ♡ A 10 9 7 6   ◇ Q 10 9   ♣ 5 4

With the opening lead, this hand should start the diamonds at once, in order to get rid of the high cards while there is the maximum of chance that no hand can discard on the suit.

Sweepstake scoring creates peculiar necessities. Taking one heart is as fatal as taking ten. A player has to take desperate chances to stay clear. Once he is painted, the player cares not how many more hearts fall to him; his sole concern is to try to paint every other player as well and so create a jack.

JOKER HEARTS

In three-hand play, the joker may be added to the pack. Each hand receives 17 cards.

In four-hand play, the joker may be added and the ♡2 discarded.

In any case, the joker is a heart, ranking between ♡J and ♡10. It wins any trick to which it is played, unless any of the four higher hearts is also played to the trick (whether in following suit or discarding), in which case that trick is won by the highest heart it contains.

DOMINO HEARTS

Only six cards are dealt to each player. The stock (rest of the pack) is placed face down on the table. Play is as usual, but a hand unable to follow suit must draw cards from the top of the stock until he can. When the stock is exhausted, the cards are played out with discarding permitted when a hand cannot follow suit. Each player drops out as his cards are exhausted, and if he wins a trick with his last card, the active player at his left makes the next lead. The only counting cards are the hearts, which cost one each. The player with the least minus score, when another reaches minus 31, wins.

TWO-HAND HEARTS

The pack of 52 is used. Thirteen cards are dealt to each player. The stock (rest of the pack) is placed face down on the table. The first lead is made by nondealer. The rules of play are as in Hearts, but after each trick the winner draws the top card of the stock and his opponent draws the next. Thus the hands are kept at thirteen cards until the stock is exhausted, whereupon the last thirteen are played out. Only the hearts count, one each, and the player with the lesser number wins by the difference.

PARTNERSHIP HEARTS

Four play in two partnerships, seated across the table. Each wins tricks individually (a take-all, for example, must be won by a single player) and scores on each deal are kept individually. But partners endeavor to assist each other in the pass and in the play. Pass is always between partners. A pass in a suit including a deuce, unless nullified by a cross-pass in the same suit, is usually an urgent request for partner to win an early trick and lead the deuce so passer can unload the ♠Q. (See Black Lady.)

Most games bar an opening heart lead; some play that

hearts may not be led until a player has been painted or the leader has no other suit. Some play that ♣2 must be led to the first trick. All play a compulsory drop of the Black Lady when void of suit led or when the ace or king has appeared on a spade lead.

BLACK LADY

All rules of Hearts apply, with the following additions:

Counting Cards. Each heart counts 1 against the player taking it in a trick, and the ♠Q (called *Black Lady, Black Maria, Calamity Jane*) counts 13. Many play that the ♠Q must be discarded the first time the holder is unable to follow suit to the card led; failure to do so is a revoke.

The Pass. Before the opening lead, each player selects any three cards of his original hand and passes them to his right-hand neighbor. Each player must pass before looking at the cards received from his left.

With five or more players, only two cards are passed.

(*Variant.* Some pass the cards to the left; some alternate passes on succeeding hands, clockwise, left, across, right.)

Scoring. Any of the three methods of settlement may be used, but cumulative scoring is largely preferred. If one player takes all thirteen hearts and the ♠Q, no score is recorded for the deal. (*Variant.* Many play the *take-all*, or *slam*: a player who takes all the fourteen counting cards wins 26, that is 26 is subtracted from his cumulative total.)

Strategy. See the section on the strategy of Omnibus Hearts (page 58).

OMNIBUS HEARTS

So called because it includes all the optional features introduced into Black Lady in various localities. Omnibus Hearts is considered by many to offer the greatest opportunity for skill among all the Hearts variants.

The game is best for four players, each for himself.

To the rules of "Straight" Hearts, add the following:

Counting Cards. Each heart counts 1 minus, the ♠Q counts 13 minus, and the ◇10 counts 10 plus. (*Variant.* Some use the ◇J, some the ◇8, instead of the ◇10, as the plus card.)

The Pass. Before the opening lead, each player passes three cards of his original hand to his left-hand neighbor.

The player must pass before looking at the cards received from his right.

Scoring. Cumulative scoring is used. A game lasts until any player reaches an agreed limit, as —100.

Each player is debited or credited for the counting cards he wins in tricks. But if one player takes all fifteen counting cards he scores +26, the others scoring nothing. (Called *take-all* or *slam.*)

Strategy. There are four possible campaigns of play. The cards to pass must usually be selected with one campaign in mind, but keeping open the possibility of a switch of plan according to the cards received.

Take-none is the mere effort to avoid being painted. It is "straight" Hearts. This plan is the necessary policy when the hand does not contain the right cards for a positive campaign.

Save-the-ten is open only to the hand dealt the ◇10 or to the hand that receives it in the pass. The ◇10 is won by the hand holding it only in one of two ways: (a) ◇10 becomes the master card through the early play of all higher cards; (b) ◇10 wins an early lead, despite outstanding higher cards, through fortuitous circumstance.

Catch-the-ten is the effort to snare ◇10 by winning the last several tricks, after ♠Q is gone, or, rarely, to drop ◇10 with top diamonds. Catch-the-ten is the natural policy of any hand with a modicum of high cards.

Take-all is naturally reserved for a hand of great strength, but this can be and usually is massed in two or three suits. The pass must rid the hand of these fatal weaknesses: ◇10, except in a near-solid suit; low hearts, except in a solid heart suit.

The take-all hand must usually make a few low leads in order to solidify its long suits before the opponents discover the take-all intention and play to prevent it.

The "normal" opening lead is a spade. It is the indicated lead for a hand not having a dangerous holding and intent on either take-none or catch-the-ten, and these two campaigns monopolize 80% of the game. Failure to open spades may indicate: (a) possession of ♠Q or higher spades without sufficient guards; (b) desire to rid the hand of a short, high holding in clubs or diamonds; (c) effort to establish the suit opened, for save-the-ten or take-all.

Stops or Michigan

THERE IS A LARGE FAMILY of games called "Stops." In most of these games, the object is to get rid of all one's cards by playing them in order; when a player cannot legally play he is "stopped" and loses his turn, which delays his going out. The Stops family is very old and many games of the family are obsolescent. The most popular current games are Michigan, Fan Tan, and Eights, which with their surviving variants are described on the following pages.

MICHIGAN

Michigan is also called Stops, Boodle, Newmarket, Saratoga, Chicago.

PLAYERS. Three to eight. Five or more make the best game.

CARDS. The pack of 52. The cards in each suit rank: A (high), K, Q, J, 10, 9, 8, 7, 6, 5, 4, 3, 2. Chips are used, as described below.

PRELIMINARIES. Players may take seats at random. Any player may deal first. The game should break up only at a time when all participants have dealt an equal number of times.

BOODLE CARDS. A layout is placed on the table, composed of four cards taken from another pack: ♡A, ♣K, ◊Q, ♠J. (Or any four cards, A-K-Q-J, of different suits.) Prior to the deal, the dealer antes two chips on each boodle card; each other player puts one chip on each.

DEALING. Cards are dealt one at a time to the left, beginning with an extra hand or *widow* placed between dealer and eldest hand. The whole pack is distributed, even though some hands contain one more card than others.

THE WIDOW. The dead hand or widow is the property of the dealer. He may exchange it for his original hand, if he wishes, or he may auction it to the highest bidder. If he does not take it himself, he must sell it. If all including the dealer refuse the widow, no player may look at it. In any other case, the player who takes the widow discards his original hand, which thereafter may not be looked at by any player.

THE PLAY. Disposition of the widow being decided, eldest hand leads any card, which may be of any suit but must be the lowest he holds in that suit. The hand (eldest or any other) holding the next-higher card in the same suit plays it, regardless of the position of the owner at the table. And so following: the sequence is built up in the suit until stopped by play of the ace or because a card of the sequence is in the dead hand. The hand that plays last before a stop may start a new sequence, provided that he can *change suit* from the previous sequence. If unable to change suit, the player must pass and the turn passes to his left. Every new sequence must be started with the lowest card of the suit in the hand of the player.

Each player plays his cards in a pile before himself. It is not permitted to spread a pile to inspect played cards. The rank of each card is stated verbally as it is played, and also the suit when a new sequence is started.

When a player plays a card that duplicates a boodle card, he takes all the chips on that card. If a boodle card is not cleared in one deal, the chips remain on it until duly won.

Play ends when any player gets rid of his last card.

SETTLEMENT. The player who *goes out* collects one chip for each card remaining in every other hand.

IRREGULARITIES. Should a player start a suit with a card not the lowest he holds in the suit, he must pay one chip to each other player and he may not collect for any boodle cards he plays subsequent to his error.

Should a player cause a stop by failing to play a card when able, play continues as usual, even though the card withheld may later enable the offender to get a stop. But the offender may not collect for any boodle cards he plays subsequent to the error; if at the end of the hand the chips are still on the boodle card of the suit of the card erroneously withheld, the offender must pay an equal amount to the player (if any) who held the duplicate; if the offender is first to get rid of his cards, he does not collect, but play continues to determine the winner.

STRATEGY. Buying the widow is always an advantage in giving the player complete knowledge of the stops in the dead hand. The price that is worth paying of course depends on several factors—the amounts on the boodle cards, the possible number of boodle cards in the widow as inferred from the number of bidders, the merits of the original hand. A hand with more than its average share of high cards (face cards and aces) should be retained even if it lacks any boodle card.

In the early play, the natural course is to start the longest suit in the hand. But with a money card in a shorter suit, one should usually prefer to lead this suit at every opportunity.

SNIP SNAP SNOREM

PLAYERS. Four to eight.

CARDS. The pack of 52.

DEALING. The cards are dealt out one at a time as far as they will go. It does not matter if not all hands are equal.

THE PLAY. All players are provided with equal numbers of chips. (An optional rule is that each hand with the lesser number of cards, when hands are not even, must ante one chip into the pool.)

Eldest hand leads any card. Each hand in turn must then either play a card of the same rank or pass. Whenever two consecutive hands play (not pass), the first of the two is *snipped* if he was the leader, or *snapped* if he played the second card of the rank, or *snored* if he played the third card. For snip the player pays 1 chip to the pool; for snap, 2 chips; for snorem, 3 chips. *Example:* West leads ◊5; North plays ♠5, and West must pay a chip; East passes; South plays ♡5; West plays ♣5, and South must pay three chips; North escapes snap through East's pass.

The hand that plays the fourth card of a rank makes a new lead; he may lead any card. The play ends when any player gets rid of his last card. Each other hand pays one chip to the pool for each remaining card, and the winner takes the pool.

VARIANTS. It is usual to call attention to the forfeit imposed on the previous player by saying "snip," "snap," or "snorem." In a juvenile variant, Earl of Coventry, the leader is supposed to improvise a line of verse, and each other card of the rank is supposed to be accompanied by a rhyming line. No payment is made for snip, etc., the sole object being to get rid of all cards. Similar in object is the German *Schnipp-Schnapp-Schnurr-Burr-Basilorum,* probably the parent game; but here each lead is built up in suit and sequence by *four* additional cards, and "play in turn" is meaningless as in Michigan. In an English variant, Jig, play is likewise in upward sequence but only three cards are added to the lead. Neither of these obsolete sequence games can be played under the surviving rules, which do not state whether the sequence in a suit goes "around-the-corner" nor what happens when there are not enough cards left unplayed in a suit to make a complete sequence of four or five.

FAN TAN

The game widely known as Fan Tan should better be called Sevens or Parliament. The true Fan Tan is a Chinese betting game played with beans, not cards.

PLAYERS. Three to eight.

CARDS. The pack of 52. The cards in each suit rank: K (high), Q, J, 10, 9, 8, 7, 6, 5, 4, 3, 2, A.

THE POOL. Equal numbers of chips are distributed to all players, and before the deal each player antes one chip into the pool.

DEALING. Cards are dealt one at a time to the left, beginning with eldest hand. The whole pack is dealt out; it does not matter if some hands have one more card than others. (An option rule is that each hand with fewer cards must ante an extra chip.)

THE PLAY. The turn to play rotates to the left, beginning with eldest hand. The characteristic feature of the game is that a player unable to play in turn must pay a chip to the pool.

All sevens are *set* cards, corresponding to foundations in Solitaire. A seven is always playable, and until the first seven is laid on the table no other card can be played. Once a seven is down, the six and eight of the same suit are playable, and thereafter cards in suit and sequence with them. The four sevens, as played, are laid in a row in the center of the table; the four sixes are laid in a row on one side, and the four eights in a row on the other. Thereafter, the suits may be built in sequence, on the eights up to the king, and on the sixes down to the ace. Only one card may be played in any turn.

Play ends when any player gets rid of his last card. Each other player puts one chip in the pool for each card remaining in his hand, and the winner then takes the entire pool.

IRREGULARITIES. If a player passes when able to play, he must pay a penalty of three chips to the pool (additional to the chip already paid for the pass). If he passed when able to play a seven, he must in addition pay five chips each to the holders of the six and eight of the same suit.

STRATEGY. The player can rarely do better than play from his longest suit, whenever any choice offers. Exception arises only when it can be inferred that withholding the natural play will postpone the time when another hand goes out.

FIVE OR NINE

Eldest hand, or the first after him able to play at all, has choice of playing a five or a nine as the first *set*. The first card played fixes the rank of the four set cards for that deal. In all other respects the game is identical with Fan Tan.

PLAY OR PAY

Eldest hand may lead any card. The player at his left must play the next-higher card of the same suit, or pass. And so following: All thirteen cards of the suit must be played before a new suit is begun. The sequence in the suit is continuous, that is Q, K, A, 2 etc., and must be built *up* only, not down. The player of the thirteenth card of the suit leads any card for a new sequence. In all other respects the game is identical with Fan Tan. (Play or Pay is actually the older game. In the original Fan Tan, elaborated from it, the first lead fixed the rank of the four *set* cards, which were then built both up and down in *continuous sequence*. The further elaboration Parliament, now called Fan Tan, eliminated eldest hand's free choice of the set and limited the building to the king on one side and the ace on the other.)

EIGHTS, OR CRAZY EIGHTS

Eights, played by two, is the best game of the Stops family so far as concerns the opportunity for skill. It is also called Swedish Rummy, but is neither Rummy nor Swedish. "Crazy Jacks," "Crazy" Sevens, Aces, etc., are the same game except that another card is the wild card.

PLAYERS. Two, three, or four playing in two partnerships.

CARDS. The pack of 52. Usually two packs are used alternately.

DEALING. Cards are dealt one at a time to the left. With two players, give each seven cards; with three or more, give each hand five cards. The remainder of the pack after the deal is placed face down to form the *stock*. The top card is turned over and placed beside it as the *starter*. This begins the *talon*, or pile of played cards.

THE PLAY. Eldest hand plays first. He must lay on the starter a card of either the same suit or the same rank. The play continues in turn in the same way: each card played (other than an eight) must match the top of the talon pile in suit or rank.

A hand unable to play must draw cards from the top of the stock until able. A player may draw from the stock even if able to play. After the stock is exhausted, a hand unable to play passes, and the turn passes to the left.

All eights are *wild*. An eight may be played at any time, even though the hand could legally play another card. The player of an eight designates a suit, any suit, and the next hand must then play any card of that suit or play another eight. (An eight may never be designated as calling for a rank.)

Play ends when any player gets rid of his last card, if the game is cutthroat. In four-hand partnership play, play ends when both hands of a partnership have gone out.

A hand must play in turn if able, whether before or after drawing from the stock. If the stock is exhausted and no hand can play, the game ends in a *block*.

SCORING. The player or side that goes out collects for all cards remaining in hands of the opponents: 50 for each eight, 10 for each face card, 1 for each ace, index value for all other cards.

If play ends in a block, the player or side with lowest total count collects the difference of counts from the opponents. If two players tie (in three-hand play) they split the winnings.

Score may be kept on paper. A running total is then kept for each player or side, and the first to reach 100 or more wins a game. The winner scores 100 for the game, plus the difference of final totals.

IRREGULARITIES. *Misdeal.* There must be a new deal by the same dealer if a card is exposed in dealing; if the wrong number of cards is given to any hand; or if the pack is found imperfect.

Wrong Number of Cards. If, after the first lead but before the first draw from the stock, it is found that any hand was dealt the wrong number of cards, the hand must be rectified and play continues. A short hand draws extra cards from the stock. A hand with too many cards is spread face down, and any other player draws the extra cards, which are buried in the middle of the stock.

False Block. When play ends in a block, all hands should be faced for inspection. If it is then found that any player passed when able to play, play must be continued upon demand of any other player. A hand that so causes a false block and consequent exposure of cards by a false pass is barred from winning, but must play on to determine the winner among the other players.

STRATEGY. The principal point to remember is to save eights for emergencies; when no other hand is near to going out, it is worthwhile digging into the stock to avoid giving up an eight. Keeping track of the cards played, at least to the extent of counting the number in each suit, is of course vital. Many opportunities arise to "corner" the remainder of a suit, as by wilfully taking the whole stock when it is low. A "corner," especially when fortified by one or two eights, may enable a hand with twenty or thirty cards to go out before a hand that holds only a few.

All Fours

THIS OLD ENGLISH GAME, based on scoring for "high, low, jack, and the game," spawned a large family of American games—Seven-Up (because 7 points win), Old Sledge, High-Low-Jack, Pitch, Setback, Cinch, Pedro, and others. For at least a hundred years, from the late 1700's to the Civil War era and the rise of Poker, it was the favorite of the American gamester. The basic game is described first, then the more popular developments.

SEVEN-UP (the basic game)

PLAYERS. Two or three may play, each for himself, or four in partnerships of two each.

CARDS. The pack of 52. The cards in each suit rank: A (high), K, Q, J, 10, 9, 8, 7, 6, 5, 4, 3, 2.

DEALING. The turn to deal moves in rotation to the left. Each player receives six cards, dealt in rounds of three at a time, beginning with eldest hand. The deal completed, the next card is turned for trump. If the turn-up is a jack, dealer immediately scores 1 point. When more than two play, only eldest hand and dealer may look at their hands until the turn-up is accepted or rejected.

BEGGING. Eldest hand commences by *standing* or *begging*. If he stands, thereby accepting the turn-up for trump, all players pick up their hands and play begins. If he begs, dealer then has the option of insisting on the turned trump or agreeing to choose a new trump.

If dealer wishes to play the turn-up suit as trump, he says "Take it" and eldest hand scores 1 point for *gift*. If dealer chooses to have another trump, he is said to *refuse gift*. Dealer is compelled to refuse gift if eldest hand is only 1 point short of game.

RUNNING THE CARDS. When gift is refused, dealer *runs the cards*, that is, he deals another round of three cards to each player and turns a new trump (the first having been discarded face down). If the second turn-up is of a different

66

suit from the first, it fixes the trump suit and play begins; should it be a jack, dealer scores 1 point. But if the second turn-up is in the same suit, it must be discarded, another round of three cards must be dealt, and a third card turned up. And so following—the cards are run until a new suit is turned up. If the pack is exhausted without the turn of a new suit, the deal is abandoned, and the same dealer deals again. (Dealer never scores for the turn of a jack in the suit of the first rejected turn-up.)

THE PLAY. If the pack has been run, each player discards enough cards to reduce his hand to six. Eldest hand makes the opening lead. A lead calls upon each other hand to follow suit or to trump; if able to follow, the hand has the option of doing so or of trumping. If unable to follow suit, a hand may play any card, trump or nontrump. A trick is won by the highest trump, if any; otherwise by the highest card of the suit led. The winner of a trick leads to the next.

The object in play is to score any or all of the four points from which the game derives its name, as below.

THE FOUR POINTS. All games of the All Fours family agree on the following constants in scoring. Each is worth 1 point.

High is the highest trump in play; it is scored by the holder.

Low is the lowest trump in play. In the basic All Fours, here described, low is scored by the player to whom it was dealt. In some descendant games, low is scored by the player who takes it in a trick.

Jack is the jack of trumps; it is scored by the player who takes it in a trick.

Game is a plurality of points for cards won in play, reckoned:

each ace	4
each king	3
each queen	2
each jack	1
each ten	10

In three-hand play, if dealer ties for high total with one opponent, the latter wins; if the two nondealers tie for high total, game is not scored.

The points are always scored in the given order: high, low, jack, game. (The jack will not always be in play. If there is only one trump in play, it is both high and low.)

SCORING. Each player or side is credited with the points it wins in play, scored in the given order. The first to reach a total of 7 wins the game.

IRREGULARITIES. *Revoke* is failure to follow suit or trump, when able to follow suit. A revoke may be corrected before the trick is turned and quitted or the next lead is made, otherwise it stands as established. Penalty for established revoke: Revoker may not win the game in that deal, and may count only to 6; if jack was not in play, 1 point is deducted from revoker's score; if jack was in play, 2 points are deducted.

Exposed Card. An illegally exposed card must be left on the table and played as soon as such play is legal. There is no penalty for exposure when two play.

AUCTION PITCH, OR SETBACK

A 19th Century development, Auction Pitch (usually called Pitch, or Setback) became the most popular member of the All Fours family. It yielded first place to Cinch for ten years or so, and then returned to favor.

PLAYERS. From two to seven may play, but the game is best for four, each for himself.

CARDS. The pack of 52 is used, the cards of each suit ranking: A(high), K, Q, J, 10, 9, 8, 7, 6, 5, 4, 3, 2.

PRELIMINARIES. Players may take seats at random. Cards are drawn for first deal; highest card deals. Dealer has the right to shuffle last, and the pack must be cut by the player at his right, the cut leaving at least four cards in each packet.

DEALING. Each player in rotation receives six cards, dealt in rounds of three at a time, beginning with eldest hand.

BIDDING. Each player in rotation, beginning with eldest hand, has one turn to bid. The lowest bid is one, the highest four. Each bid must be higher than the preceding bid. The high bidder names the trump.

THE PLAY. The high bidder leads first; this is called *pitching,* and the suit of the card pitched becomes trump. (Since a bid of four cannot be overcalled, no one bothers

to bid it; he merely pitches a trump when his turn comes.)
If able to follow suit to the card led, each player in turn
must either follow suit or trump. If unable to follow suit,
he may play any card. A trick is won by the highest trump,
if any; otherwise by the highest card of the suit led. The
winner of a trick leads to the next.

SCORING. One point each is scored for winning in play:
high, highest trump card in play; *low,* lowest trump card in
play; *jack,* jack of trumps; *game,* plurality of points when
each ace is counted 4, king, 3; queen, 2; jack, 1; ten, 10.

High and low are always counted; jack may not be in
play, and game is not scored if two players tie for it.

If the pitcher scores at least as many points as he bid,
he adds to his score all the points he makes. If he falls
short of his bid, the amount of the bid is subtracted from
his previous score (which may put him in the hole). In
either case, any opponent of the pitcher always scores as
many points as he makes.

Game. An individual score is kept for each player (or
chips are used). The first player to reach a score of 7 wins
the game. If two or more players could reach 7 on the
same deal, the pitcher's points are counted first and as
among other players the points are scored in order high,
low, jack, game. Some play a game of 10 points.

Smudge. If a player bids four and makes it, he wins the
game immediately, unless he was in the hole at the time, in
which case his score becomes 4. (Some play that any
player wins the game in the one deal when he makes all
four points, regardless of the bid.)

SETTLEMENT. The winner collects from each other player:
one chip for game; plus one chip for each time the loser
was set back; plus one chip from any player who was in
the hole when the game ended.

VARIATIONS. *Bunch.* In two-hand play the dealer may
offer "bunch"—meaning that his opponent must choose
whether to let dealer play at a contract of two, or have a
new deal by the same dealer.

Bidding Over. At one time, eldest hand (or, in some
games, dealer) had the right to assume the contract at
the highest previous bid, without "bidding over."

Joker. The 53-card pack, including the joker, may be
used. The joker is a trump but ranks below the lowest

trump in play and does not count as *low*. If the joker is pitched, spades become trump. There are 5 points in play, 1 point being scored by the player who wins the joker in a trick. In counting out, this point ranks between low and game. Usually 10 points are game.

IRREGULARITIES. *Misdeal.* It is a misdeal if an ace, jack or deuce is exposed in dealing. Since the deal is an advantage, a misdeal loses the deal.

Revoke (failure to follow suit or trump, when able to follow suit). A play once made cannot be withdrawn, so a revoke stands and play continues to the end. If the pitcher revokes, he cannot score and is set back the amount of his bid, while each other player scores what he makes. If any player except the pitcher revokes, all players except the revoker score what they make (including the pitcher, even if he does not make his bid). The revoking player cannot score, and has the amount of the bid deducted from his score.

Error in Bidding. An insufficient bid, or a bid out of turn, is void and the offender must pass in his turn to bid.

Error in Pitching. Once the pitcher plays a card, the trump cannot be changed.

If a player pitches before the auction closes, he is assumed to have bid four and play proceeds; except that any player in turn before him who has not had a turn to bid may himself bid four and pitch, whereupon the card illegally pitched, and any card played to it, must be withdrawn.

If the wrong player pitches after the auction is closed, the pitcher may require that card and any card played to it to be withdrawn; and, when first it is the offender's turn to play, the pitcher may require him to play his highest or lowest card of the suit led or to trump or not to trump; except that if the pitcher has played to the incorrect lead, it cannot be withdrawn and the pitcher must immediately name the trump, which he must then lead the first time he wins a trick.

PEDRO

The name Pedro is applied to a number of elaborations of Auction Pitch, all based on the addition of the five of trumps (*pedro*) as a counting card. The ten of trumps, won in a trick, is *game* and counts 1.

Pedro Sancho. Four to seven players. Each receives six cards. Eldest hand bids first. There is one round of bidding. Dealer has the privilege of taking the contract at the highest previous bid. The contracting player pitches the trump. All points scored are for trump cards won in tricks, counted in order:

High, highest trump in play		1
Low, lowest trump in play		1
Jack, the jack		1
Game, the ten	of trumps	1
Pedro, the five		5
Sancho, the nine		9

The maximum of points per deal is thus 18. Game is usually set at 100.

Dom Pedro, or *Snoozer,* is the same as Pedro Sancho with the addition of two more counting cards: the three of trumps, worth 3, and the joker (called *snoozer*) worth 15, bringing the total per deal up to 36 maximum. The trump three counts after the ten (game), and snoozer counts after the nine (sancho). Snoozer is always a trump, ranking below the two.

Cinch. For a brief period (1890's) this was the most popular game of the All Fours family, and many still consider it the best. It is a four-hand partnership game. In addition to the five of trumps (*right pedro*) there is a *left pedro*, the five of the suit of the same color as the trump, also counting 5 and ranking between the trump five and four.

Each player is dealt nine cards. A bid names any number of points up to 14 (the maximum). After the bidding, each player discards as many cards as he wishes (he may not discard a trump) and is dealt replacements to bring his hand up to six cards. The dealer may *rob the pack* (look at all unused cards and select those he wishes). The high bidder then pitches and play proceeds.

If the contracting side wins as many points as it bid, the side with the higher score wins the difference in scores. If the contract is not made, the opponents score the points they won plus the amount of the contract. Game is won by the first side to reach 51.

Cribbage

CRIBBAGE is believed to have been invented by Sir John Suckling (1609-1642). Probably it is an elaboration of an older game, Noddy. The original game was played with hands of five cards; the modern game gives each player six. That is virtually the only change from Suckling's directions.

PLAYERS. Two. There are variants for three and four players, described later.

CARDS. The pack of 52. The cards in each suit rank: K (high), Q, J, 10, 9, 8, 7, 6, 5, 4, 3, 2, A. The *counting values* are: K, Q, J, 10, each 10 (wherefore these are called *tenth cards*); ace, 1; each other card, its index value.

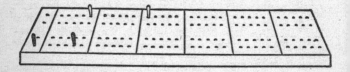

CRIBBAGE BOARD. Indispensable to scoring is the device known as the *cribbage board*. This is a rectangular panel, long and narrow, in which are four rows of 30 holes each. (See illustration.) At one end, or in the center, are two or four additional holes, called *game holes*. The board is placed between the two players, and each keeps his own score on the two rows of holes nearest himself. Each is supplied with two *pegs*. Before the first hand, the pegs are placed in the game holes. On making his first score, the player advances one peg an appropriate number of holes (one per point) away from the *game end* of the board. The second score is recorded by placing the second peg an appropriate distance ahead of the first. For each subsequent score, the rear peg is jumped ahead of the other, the distance between the two pegs always showing the amount of this last score.

The traditional mode of scoring is down (away from the

game end) the outer row, and up the inner row. "Once around" is a game of 61 points. "Twice around" is a game of 121 points.

PRELIMINARIES. Cards are drawn; the lower deals first. If cards of equal rank are drawn, both players draw again. Dealer has the right to shuffle last. Nondealer cuts, and must leave at least four cards in each packet.

DEALING. Each player receives six cards, dealt one at a time face down, beginning with nondealer. The turn to deal alternates. The dealer has an advantage.

LAYING AWAY. After seeing his hand, each player *lays away* two cards face down. The four cards laid away, placed in one pile, form the *crib*. The crib counts for the dealer. Nondealer therefore tries to lay away *balking cards*—cards that are least likely to create a score in the crib.

THE STARTER. After both hands have laid away, nondealer lifts off a packet from the top of the *stock* (the rest of the pack). Again, each packet must contain at least four cards. Dealer turns up the top card of the lower packet, which is then placed on top of the stock when the packets are reunited. The card thus turned up is called *1 the starter*. If it is a jack, dealer immeditely pegs 2, called *2 for his heels*.

THE PLAY. Nondealer begins the play by laying a card from his hand face up on the table, announcing its counting value. Dealer then shows a card, announcing the total count of the two cards. Play continues in the same way, by alternate exposures of cards, each player announcing the new total count. The total may be carried only to 31, no further. If a player adds a card that brings the total exactly to 31, he pegs 2. If a player is unable to play another card without exceeding 31, he must say "Go," and his opponent pegs 1, but before so doing, opponent must lay down any additional cards he can without exceeding 31. If such additional cards bring the total to exactly 31, he pegs 2 instead of 1.

Whenever a *go* occurs, the opponent of the player who played the last card must lead for a new count starting at zero. Playing the last card of all counts as a *go*. (Since nondealer makes the opening lead, dealer is bound to peg at least 1 in play.)

Besides pegging for 31 and go, the player may also peg for certain combinations made in play, as follows:

Fifteen. Making the count total 15 pegs 2.

Pair. Playing a card of same rank as that previously played pegs 2. Playing a third card of same rank makes *pair royal* and pegs 6. Playing the fourth card of the same rank makes *double pair royal* and pegs 12.

The tenth cards pair strictly by rank, a king with a king, a queen with a queen, and so on. (King and jack do not make a pair, although each has the counting value 10.)

Run. Playing a card which, with the two or more played immediately previously, makes a sequence of three or more cards, pegs 1 for each card in the *run*. Runs depend on rank alone; the suits do not matter. Nor does the score for run depend upon playing the cards in strict sequence, so long as the three or more last cards played can be arranged in a run. *Example:* 7, 6, 8 played in that order score 3 for run; 5, 2, 4, 3 played in that order score 4 for run.

Any of the foregoing combinations count, whether the cards are played alternately or one player plays several times in succession in consequence of a go. But a combination does not score if it is interrupted by a go.

SHOWING. After the play, the hands are *shown* (counted). Nondealer shows first, then dealer's hand, then crib. The starter is deemed to belong to each hand, so that each hand includes five cards. Combinations of scoring value are as follows:

Fifteen. Each combination of two or more cards that total fifteen scores 2.

Pair. Each pair of cards of the same rank scores 2.

Run. Each combination of three or more cards in sequence scores 1 for each card in the run.

Flush. Four cards of the same suit in hand score 4; four cards in hand or crib of same suit as the starter score 5. (No count for four-flush in crib.)

His Nobs. Jack of same suit as the starter, in hand or crib, scores 1.

It is important to note that every separate grouping of cards that makes a fifteen, pair, or run counts separately. Three of a kind, *pair royal*, count 6 because three sets of pairs can be made; similarly, four of a kind, *double pair royal*, contain six pairs and count 12.

The highest possible hand is J, 5, 5, 5, with starter the 5 of same suit as the jack. There are four fifteens by combining the jack with a five, four more by combinations of three fives (a total of 16 for fifteens); the double pair royal adds 12 for a total of 28; and *his nobs* adds 1 for maximum score of 29. (The score of 2 for *his heels* does not count in the total of the hand, since it is pegged before play.)

A *double run* is a run with one card duplicated, as 4-3-3-2. Exclusive of fifteens, a double run of three cards counts 8; of four cards, 10. A *triple run* is a run of three with one card triplicated, as K-K-K-Q-J. Exclusive of fifteens, it counts 15. A *quadruple run* is a run of three with two different cards duplicated, as the example 8-8-7-6-6 previously given. Exclusive of fifteens, it counts 16.

No hand can be constructed that counts 19, 25, 26, or 27. A time-honored way of showing a hand with not a single counting combination is to say "I have nineteen."

The customary order in showing is to count fifteens first, then runs, then pairs, but there is no compulsion of law. *Example:* A hand (with starter) of 9-6-5-4-4 will usually be counted "Fifteen 2, fifteen 4, fifteen 6 and double run makes 14," or simply "Fifteen 6 and 8 is 14."

MUGGINS. The hands and crib are counted aloud, and if a player claims a greater total than is due him, his opponent may require correction. In some localities, if a player claims less than is due, his opponent may say "Muggins" and himself score the points overlooked.

SCORING. The usual *game* is 121, but it may be set at 61 by agreement. Since the player wins who first returns to the game hole by going "twice around," the scores must be pegged strictly in order: his heels, pegging in play, nondealer's hand, dealer's hand, crib. Thus, if nondealer goes out on showing his hand, he wins, even though dealer might have gone out with a greater total if allowed to count his hand and crib.

When the game of 121 is played for a stake, a player wins a single game if the loser makes 61 points or more. If the loser fails to reach 61, he is *lurched,* and the other wins a double game.

IRREGULARITIES. *Misdeal.* There must be a new deal by the same dealer if a card is found faced in the pack, if a card is exposed in dealing, or if the pack be found imperfect.

Wrong Number of Cards. If one hand (not crib) is found to have the wrong number of cards after laying away for the crib, the other hand and crib being correct, the opponent may either demand a new deal or may peg 2 and rectify the hand. If the crib is incorrect, both hands being correct, nondealer pegs 2 and the crib is corrected.

ERROR IN PEGGING. If a player places a peg short of the amount to which he is entitled, he may not correct his error after he has played the next card or after the cut for the next deal. If he pegs more than his announced score, the error must be corrected on demand at any time before the cut for the next deal and his opponent pegs 2.

STRATEGY. The best balking cards are kings and aces, because they have the least chance of producing sequences. Tenth cards are generally good, provided that the two cards laid away are not too *near* (likely to make a sequence). When nothing better offers, give two *wide* cards—at least three apart in rank.

Proverbially the safest lead is a 4. The next card cannot make a 15. Lower cards are also safe from this point of view, but are better treasured for go and 31. The most dangerous leads are 7 and 8, but may be made to trap the opponent when they are backed with other close cards. Generally speaking, play *on* (toward a sequence) when you have close cards and *off* when you do not. However, the state of the score is a consideration. If far behind, play on when there is any chance of building a score for yourself; if well ahead, balk your opponent by playing off unless you will surely peg as much as he by playing on.

THREE-HAND CRIBBAGE

Each player receives five cards, and one card is dealt to start the crib. Each hand lays away one card to the crib, which belongs to the dealer. The cut for starter is made by eldest hand, who then makes the opening lead. The turn to play is to the left. When one player says "Go," the hand at his left must play if able, and if he does play, the third hand must also play if able. The point for go is scored by the last to play. Eldest hand shows first, then the player at his left, then dealer's hand, then crib. The turn to deal passes to the left.

FOUR-HAND CRIBBAGE

Cards are drawn; the two lowest play as partners against the two highest. Lowest card has choice of seats and deals first. Partners sit alternately. Five cards are dealt to each player. Each hand lays away one card to the crib, which belongs to dealer. Eldest hand cuts for the starter, and makes the opening lead. After a call of "Go," each succeeding player in turn has opportunity to play and thus to score for the go. The scores made by both partners of a side, in play and in showing, are pooled. Nondealing side shows first, then dealer's side, finally crib. Game is 121.

STRATEGY: With only five cards dealt to the original hand, the individual scores made in *showing* will usually be smaller and an increased part of the total score is pegged in the play. Discarding balking cards to an opponent's crib is a lesser part of the strategy and an ace may be more profitably retained for use in the play. In the late play, judgment of what partner may hold will exercise greater importance in deciding whether to play *on* or *off* to a run.

THIRTY-ONE

An uncomplicated game, especially good for a large number of players of almost any age group. CARDS: Pack of 52, ranking ace (high) to 2 (low). Cards count: Ace, 11; face cards, 10; other cards their index value. ANTE: Before the deal, each player antes an agreed number of chips to the winner's pool. DEAL: Three cards to each player, one at a time, face down, beginning with player at dealer's left; then three cards (the widow) face up in the center. THE PLAY: Each in turn, beginning with player at dealer's left, exchanges one card from his hand for one card in the widow. A player may not pass but may knock at any stage of the game if he thinks he holds the best hand. *Object of the game:* To hold three cards of the same suit totaling 31 (ace and two 10-cards). Next in value are three of a kind (aces, kings, etc.) or, failing three of a kind, the highest total of cards in the same suit. Exchanges with the widow continue until one player shows 31 and takes pool, or until a player knocks, whereupon each other player has one additional turn, in which he may stand pat or exchange a further card with the widow. Cards are then exposed and best hand wins.

Rummy

THE most popular family of card games in the United States is also the youngest: Rummy, which dates from the early 1900's. The first game of the family, called Conquian (Spanish *con quien*, with whom) entered Texas from Mexico; this name was soon corrupted to Coon-Can, and the English gave the game its lasting name by calling it Rum (queer) Poker. Elaborations on the original theme have been innumerable, but three main branches developed: The early Conquian (in which the object is merely to go out) became Panguingue in the Southwest and Basic Rummy elsewhere; Knock Rummy, in which one ends the play at will, became Gin Rummy; and 500 Rum, in which melded sets have a scoring value, flowered as the tremendous Canasta of the 1950's. The identity of the essential Rummy principle with that of the ancient Chinese domino game Mah Jongg has not failed to impress students of the game.

BASIC RUMMY

PLAYERS. From two to six may play.

CARDS. The pack of 52. The cards in each suit rank: K (high), Q, J, 10, 9, 8, 7, 6, 5, 4, 3, 2, A.

DEALING. Cards are dealt one at a time, to the left, beginning with eldest hand. Each hand comprises: with two players, ten cards; with three or four, seven cards; with five or six, six cards. The rest of the pack is placed face down to form the *stock*. The top card is turned up and set beside the stock to commence the *discard pile*.

In two-hand, the winner of each hand deals next. With more players, the deal rotates in turn to the left.

OBJECT OF PLAY. In all games of this family, the immediate object of play is to form the hand into *sets*. A set may be of either of two types: a *group* of three or four cards of the same rank, or a *sequence* of three or more cards of the same suit.

78

THE PLAY. Each player in turn must *draw* one card, either the top card of the discard pile or the top of the stock. He may then *meld* or *lay down* (place on the table) any *set* he holds. If he has more than one set, he may meld all in the same turn. He need not meld when able, but may keep the set in his hand. To complete his turn, the player must *discard* one card, face up on the discard pile.

Any player in turn may *lay off* (add one or more matching cards) on any melded set, his own or another player's. He may meld and lay off in the same turn.

The first player to get rid of all his cards, by melding, wins the deal, and play ends. When the draw enables him to meld all his remaining cards, he need not discard. But he may *go out* by melding all but one card, which he discards.

SCORING. Each other player pays to the winner the count of all cards left in his hand, reckoning each face card as 10, each ace as 1, and each other card its index value.

IRREGULARITIES. *Play Out of Turn.* If a player is not stopped before he has completed his turn by discarding, it stands as a play in turn and intervening players lose their turns. If the player out of turn has taken the top card of the stock, it is too late for rectification after he has added that card to his hand.

Illegal Draw. If, by playing out of turn or by drawing more than one card from the top of stock, a player sees a card to which he is not entitled, that card is placed face up on top of the stock. The next player in turn may either take the card or have it put in the center of the stock, face down, and proceed to play as if no irregularity had occurred.

Incorrect Hand. A player with too many cards discards without drawing; a player with too few cards draws without discarding, until his hand is restored to the correct number. If, after a player goes out, another player has too many cards he simply pays the value of all cards in his hand; if he has too few cards, he is charged 10 points for each missing card.

Cards Laid Down Illegally. If a player lays down cards that are not in fact a matched set, they must be restored to his hand if discovered at any time before the cards have been mixed. An opponent's card laid off on such a set remains on the table, but no card may then be added unless three or more cards, which themselves form a matched set, have been laid off. If a player announces that he is out when he is not able to get rid of all his cards, he must lay down and lay off all he can. In either case play proceeds as if no irregularity had occurred.

STRATEGY. Keen observation of the discards helps both toward improving one's own hand and blocking the opponent's. A knowledge of what cards are dead (buried in the discard pile) often shows that a combination of cards is not worth holding because it cannot be improved. Noticing what an opponent picks up will give a clue to what he has in his hand. Attention to what cards have *not* been discarded may be an even better guide to an opponent's hand.

Building Sets. The more chances there are to improve a combination of cards, the better it is. The combination ♡Q ◇QJ has four chances—♠Q-♣Q-◇K-◇10 and so is better than ♣KQ ◇Q, which only three cards can improve. It must be remembered that a dead card must not be counted as a chance; if an eight has been discarded previously, ♠8 ♣8 7 is no better than ◇6 ♡6 4, assuming that both black sixes and ♡5 are still available.

As between combinations offering the same number of chances, the lower is usually better to hold.

Discarding. In general, the highest unmatched cards in the hand should be discarded first; kings first of all, since they will fit into sequences only at one end.

Picking Up. It seldom pays to pick up the last discard unless it forms a set. For example, to pick up a discarded ♡8 when holding ♡7 and ♣8, in order to have a four-chance combination, is generally losing tactics. The opponent will be warned not to discard anything that might match ♡8.

RUMMY VARIATIONS

Among the variations from the foregoing rules, found in various localities, are the following:

Sequences. The ace ranks either below the two or above the king, so that ◇ A 2 3 and ◇ A K Q are both correct sequences. Or, as some play, the sequence in the suit is circular, so that ◇K A 2 may be melded " 'round the corner."

Final Discard. The player who goes out must complete his turn with a final discard. Consequently, when reduced to two cards or one the player cannot make a new meld but must depend upon laying off on previous melds.

Rummy. The winner collects double if he melds his whole hand at one time, having no previous meld. This is called *going rummy.*

"Rummy." If a player discards a card that he could have laid off on an existing meld, any other player may call "Rummy!", pick up and meld the card, and then make a discard.

Block. If none has gone out by the time the stock is exhausted, play ends, and the hand with the lowest count wins.

Borrowing. A player may borrow a card from any of his previous melds to complete a new meld, provided that he leaves a correct meld of at least three cards.

KALUKI

This is the same as Basic Rummy, except as follows:

Two full packs are shuffled together, with four jokers, making 108 cards. Ace ranks either high or low, so that A-K-Q and 3-2-A are valid sequences but 2-A-K is not. Each player is dealt fifteen cards.

A player's first meld must comprise cards totaling 51 or more. Aces count 15, face cards 10, other cards their index value. Jokers are wild, and when melded count the same as the cards they are designated to represent. A joker in the hand counts 25.

A player may not draw the discard or lay off until after he has made his initial meld, except that he may take the discard if he makes a correct meld in that turn. A melded joker may be captured ("traded") by any player in exchange for the natural card it represents.

The player who goes out scores all the points remaining in the other hands.

Panguingue

PANGUINGUE has achieved notable popularity in the Southwest United States and on the Pacific Coast; in this region there are many public gaming houses devoted to "Pan."

PLAYERS. Any number up to fifteen may play. The usual game is six or seven.

CARDS. Eight packs of 40 cards each, shuffled together, totaling 320 cards. The 40-card pack is made by stripping out the eights, nines and tens from the pack of 52. While the general practice is to use eight such packs, as few as five are used in some localities.

The cards in each suit rank: K (high) Q. J, 7, 6, 5, 4, 3, 2, A. Note that the jack and seven are in sequence. (In home play, it is easier to strip the pack of face cards instead of eights, nines and tens; the cards then rank in natural order.)

PRELIMINARIES. Cards are drawn; lowest card is eldest hand for the first deal and second-lowest is the first dealer. The rotation in Panguingue is to the *right*, not to the left as in most games. Eldest hand chooses his seat, and dealer sits on his *left*. Other players may take seats at random.

At the beginning, and occasionally thereafter, all eight packs are shuffled together, by various players, in batches of manageable size. At other times, the cards that were in play during the previous hand are shuffled with a batch from the stock and then placed at the bottom thereof, so that new cards come into play from the top of the stock.

DEALING. Each player receives ten cards, dealt to the *right* in rounds of five at a time. The rest of the pack is placed face down to form the *stock*. In practice, the stock is cut in two; the upper part or *head* is placed in the center of the table, while the *foot* is set aside, to be brought into play only if the head is exhausted.

The top card of the stock is turned face up and placed beside it, to commence the *discard pile*.

The deal does not rotate: the winner of one hand becomes eldest hand in the next, and the player at his left deals.

DROPPING. After looking at his hand, each player in turn beginning with eldest hand declares whether he will stay in the deal or drop out. If he drops, he pays a forfeit of two chips. All such chips are stacked on the foot of the stock, for which reason a player who drops is said to *go on top*. These chips go to the winner of the deal. The hands discarded by players who drop are placed crosswise under the foot of the stock; they do not belong to the stock and may not be drawn if both head and foot of the stock are exhausted.

THE PLAY. Each player in turn draws one card. He may either turn up the top of the stock, and use it in a meld or discard it; or he may take the top of the discard pile, but he may take the latter only if he can meld it at once. After drawing, the player may *meld* or *lay off* as many cards as he wishes. Having done so, he discards one card from his hand. His discard goes face up on the discard pile, and his turn ends when he discards. (In many public gaming clubs, the house rule is that *no* discards *may be* drawn: the top of the stock must be drawn at every turn.)

MELDS. The object of play is to meld eleven cards, and the first player to do so wins the deal. As in Rummy, the valid sets that may be melded are *groups* and *sequences*. ("Pan" players have their own colloquialisms. A meld is usually called a *spread;* a sequence is a *stringer* or a *rope*.)

Sequence comprises any three cards of the same suit, in sequence, as ♣J 7 6.

Group comprises three cards of the same rank. If the rank is ace or king (which cards are called *non-comoquers*), any three cards are valid regardless of suits. *Example:* ♠K ♣K ◇K is a valid meld. All other ranks are governed by the rule that the three cards must be (a) of different suits, or (b) all of the same suit. *Example:* ♣8 ♡8 ♠8 and ◇Q ◇Q ◇Q are valid melds, but not ♣5 ♣5 ♡5.

CONDITIONS. On melding one of several types of sets, a player immediately collects chips from every other player. These privileged melds are called *conditions*.

All threes, fives, and sevens are called *valle cards* (cards of value). All other ranks are *non-valle* cards. The distinction enters into the list of conditions, which is as follows:

1. Any *group* of valle cards, of different suits. (1 chip.)
2. Any *group* of valle cards, in the same suit. (4 chips in spades, 2 chips in any other suit.)
3. Any *group* of non-valle cards, in the same suit. (2 chips in spades, 1 chip in any other suit.)
4. Any *sequence* A, 2, 3. (2 chips in spades, 1 chip in any other suit.)
5. Any *sequence* K, Q, J. (2 chips in spades, 1 chip in any other suit.)

LAYING OFF. Having melded any set, a player may later *lay off* on it any additional cards that are in keeping with it. (Note that a player may lay off only on his own melds.) A *group* in different suits may be increased by cards of the same rank in *any* suit, a *group* in the same suit may be increased by cards of the same rank and suit; a sequence may be increased by additional cards in sequence of the same suit.

For each card laid off on a *condition*, the player collects again the value of the condition, except in the case of type 2 above (a group of three valle cards in the same suit), where an added card collects only 2 in spades, 1 in any other suit.

When three or more cards have been laid off on a meld, it may be split into separate melds provided that each part is valid in itself. *Example*: If a player melds ♣Q J 7, and later adds ♣K 6 5, he may break it into ♣K Q J and ♣7 6 5.

If splitting a meld forms a condition that did not previously exist, the owner duly collects for it. In the above example, the player would collect for ♣K Q J, which is a condition of type 5.

BORROWING. A player may *borrow* one or more cards from his own increased meld, to fill a new meld, provided that he leaves a valid meld. *Example*: If a player melds ♣K Q J, later lays off ♣7, he may then borrow ♣K to fill a new meld with two other kings. He could borrow ♣7 instead of ♣K, but could not borrow ♣Q or J as he would thereby break the sequence.

FORCING. If the top of the discard pile can be laid off on a meld of the in-turn player, he can be forced to draw it and meld it upon demand of any other player. The object of such a demand is to compel the player to discard, possibly to his disadvantage.

GOING OUT. The first player to meld eleven cards wins the deal. Since the hand contains only ten cards, a player with ten cards melded continues to draw and discard, though with no card in his hand, until he draws a card he can lay off. In this situation the player at his left is not permitted to discard a card that the first could lay off, unless he has no safe card to discard. If this rule is violated, and the first player goes out thereby, the offender must pay the losses of all players for that deal.

SETTLEMENT. The winner collects, from every player who did not drop, 1 chip for winning plus the total value of all conditions melded by the winner. (Thus he collects for his conditions twice over.) Some clubs have the rule that a player who has made no meld at all must pay the winner 2 chips.

IRREGULARITIES. *Wrong Number of Cards.* If a player finds that he has more or less than ten cards, before he has made his first draw, he may discard all his cards and demand a new hand from the top of stock. If, after his first draw, a player's hand is found incorrect, he must discard his hand and retire from that deal, must return all collections he has made for conditions, but must continue to make due payments to others for conditions and winning.

Foul Meld. If a player lays down any spread not conforming to the rules, he must make it valid on demand. If he cannot do so, he must return any collections made in consequence of the improper spread and legally proceed with his turn. If he has already discarded, he must return all collections he has made on that hand, discard his hand, and retire from the play until the next deal, but must continue to make due payments to others for conditions and winning. However, if he has made the meld valid before attention is called to it, there is no penalty.

Contract Rummy

VARIANTS of Contract Rummy are played under many different names, as Liverpool Rum, Joker Rummy, Progressive Rum, King Rummy. The first was probably the game developed by Ruth Armson, called Zioncheck. The basic idea of all is that a game comprises a fixed number of deals, and that in each deal the *rum hand* must be of pre-fixed character. This prescription is called the *basic contract* for the deal. It is impossible to cover all local variants, but the following is typical.

CARDS. With three or four players, use two packs of 52 shuffled together, plus one joker, 105 cards. With five to eight players use three packs of 52 plus two jokers, 158 cards. The ace ranks either high or low. An ace may be *laid off* on one end of a sequence even though it includes an ace on the other end; but sequences do not go "around the corner." All aces and wild cards count 15 each.

DEALING. A game comprises seven deals. The deal rotates to the left. In each of the first four deals, each player receives ten cards; in each of the last three deals, each player receives twelve cards.

THE PLAY. Drawing and discarding are as in Rummy, with this additional feature: If the player in turn refuses the discard, any other may claim it. If two or more claim it, it goes to the hand nearest the left of the in-turn player. On receiving the discard, the claimant must also draw the top card of the stock, and he makes no discard at that time. Play then reverts to the in-turn player, who draws the top of the stock (he may not draw the next card of the discard pile, having refused the first).

The first meld by a player must be the basic contract, as defined below. Thereafter he may *lay off* cards on any melds on the table, but he may not meld any additional sets. Play ends when one player gets rid of all his cards by melding and laying off.

BASIC CONTRACT. Each set of the basic contract must comprise exactly three cards (except in the 7th deal). Having a set of four or more, the player may meld only three; the additional cards may be laid off at a later turn. The basic contracts are:

1st deal: Two groups.
2nd deal: One group and one sequence.
3rd deal: Two sequences.
4th deal: Three groups.
5th deal: Two groups and one sequence.
6th deal: One group and two sequences.
7th deal: Three sequences, but with no unmatched cards; a complete hand. The first meld of this deal terminates the play.

Any three cards of the same rank form a valid *group* regardless of suits. When the basic contract calls for two or more sequences, they must be in different suits, or, if in the same suit, must be disconnected.

WILD CARDS. Jokers are *wild,* together with any others (usually deuces) designated by agreement. A wild card may be used to complete any set. A wild card in a sequence may be moved to either end by a player who wishes to lay off the natural card on the meld (but no sequence may be built beyond fourteen cards). When a joker is melded in a sequence, it may be claimed in exchange for the natural card by the holder thereof, provided that he has previously melded his basic contract. If two or more players are unable to claim a joker, it goes to the player whose turn to play comes first.

SCORING. When play of a deal ends, each player is charged with the count of all cards remaining in his hand, as in Rummy. Winner of the game is the player having the lowest total after the 7th deal.

Gin Rummy

THIS variant is essentially two-hand Knock Rummy (described later) with a limitation on knocking designed to give more defense to a player who is dealt a poor hand. Its invention is credited to E. T. Baker, a member of the Knickerbocker Whist Club of New York, in 1909. He called it Gin for the alcoholic drink, by analogy with the name of the parent game, which was then called Rum.

PLAYERS. Two. But there are methods by which three or more may play (page 92).

CARDS. The pack of 52. The cards in each suit rank: K (high), Q, J, 10, 9, 8, 7, 6, 5, 4, 3, 2, A.

PRELIMINARIES. Cards are drawn; higher card has choice of seat and deal. The player winning the right may either deal first himself or require opponent to do so. Thereafter the winner of each hand deals the next. Dealer has the right to shuffle last. Nondealer cuts the pack.

DEALING. Each hand receives ten cards, dealt one at a time beginning with nondealer. The rest of the pack is placed face down to form the *stock*. The top card of the stock is turned up and placed beside the stock, to form the first card up.

THE PLAY. Nondealer may take the first upcard or refuse it; if he refuses, dealer has the same option. If dealer also refuses, nondealer draws the top card of the stock. Thereafter, each in turn draws a card, either the upcard or the top of the stock, and then discards one (the new upcard) card face up on the previous discards. A player may not draw the upcard and discard it in the same turn.

The object of play is to form the hand into *matched sets*: three or four cards of the same rank, or sequences, three or more cards in sequence in the same suit. Cards that do not form part of a set are called *unmatched cards*.

After drawing, a player may *knock* if his unmatched cards (after he discards) will count 10 or less. In this reckoning, each face card counts 10, each ace 1, each other card its index value. On knocking, the player lays down ten cards, arranged in sets and with the unmatched cards segregated, then discards the eleventh card. If all ten of his cards are matched, his count is 0 and he is said to *go gin*.

If neither player has knocked by the time the fiftieth card has been drawn (and a following discard made), the cards are abandoned and there is no score for the deal.

LAYING OFF. Opponent of the knocker may *lay off* any of his unmatched cards that fit upon the knocker's matched sets, thereby reducing his own count of unmatched cards.

SCORING. If the knocker has the lower count in unmatched cards, he wins the difference of the counts. Should the opponent have an equal or lesser count, he is said to *undercut* the knocker. The opponent then scores the difference (if any) in the counts, plus a bonus of 25 points (in some games, 10 or 20 points). The knocker cannot be undercut if he has gone gin. A player who goes gin scores the opponent's count of unmatched cards, if any, plus a bonus of 25 (in some games, 20).

GAMES. The first player to accumulate 100 points wins the game. 100-point *game bonus* is added to his score. Each player then adds to his score 25 points (in some games 20) for each hand he has won; this is called a *box*, or *line, bonus*. The winner wins the difference in total scores. If the loser did not score a point, this difference is doubled; such a game is called a *shutout*, or *schneider*, and the loser is said to be *skunked*.

IRREGULARITIES. *New Deal*. A deal out of turn may be stopped at any time before the upcard is dealt; thereafter it stands as a correct deal.

There must be a new deal by the same dealer if it is found, before the completion of the deal, that the pack is imperfect or that a card is faced in the pack; or if a card is exposed in dealing, or if a player has looked at the face of a card.

Irregular Hands. If either player's hand is discovered to have an incorrect number of cards before that player has made his first draw, there must be a new deal.

After the first draw, if it is discovered that both players have incorrect hands, there must be a new deal. If one player's hand is incorrect and the other player's hand is correct, the player with the correct hand may decide either to have a new deal or to continue play. If play continues, the player with the incorrect hand must correct his hand by drawing without discarding, or by discarding without drawing, and may not knock until his next turn to play.

After a knock, a player with too few cards is charged 10 points for each card missing, and may not claim the undercut bonus; if the knocker's opponent has more than ten cards, the hand may not be corrected, the offender may not claim an undercut bonus, and can lose or tie but not win the hand.

If the player who knocks has an incorrect number of cards, the penalty for an illegal knock applies.

Imperfect Pack. When two packs are being used, a card from the other pack found in the stock is eliminated and play continues. If it is discovered, after the knock, that the pack is incomplete, the deal stands. Discovery that the pack is imperfect in any way has no bearing on any score that has been entered on the score sheet. (See also *New Deal,* above.)

Premature Play. If nondealer draws from the stock before dealer has refused the upcard, the draw stands without penalty as his first play (but dealer may still take the upcard). If a player draws from the stock before his opponent has discarded, the draw stands as his proper play.

Illegally Seeing a Card. If a player drawing in turn sees any card to which he is not entitled, every such card must be placed face up next to the discard pile. The offender may not knock until his next turn to play, unless he is gin. The nonoffender has the sole right to take any of the exposed cards until first thereafter he draws from the stock; then the offender has the same right until first thereafter he draws from the stock; when each player has drawn from the stock, the exposed cards are placed in the discard pile.

If a player drawing out of turn sees a card to which he is not entitled, the rule given in the preceding paragraph applies, except that the offender may never take such cards, but may draw only his opponent's discard or the top card of the stock in each turn.

Exposed Card. A card found exposed in the stock, or in the other pack or away from the table, is shuffled into the stock and play continues. Accidental exposure of a card in a player's hand is not subject to penalty.

Illegal Knock. If a player knocks with a count higher than 10, but his opponent has not exposed any cards before the error is discovered, the offender must leave his hand face up on the table until his opponent has completed his next play. However, if the knocker's hand is illegal only with respect to the count of his unmatched cards, his opponent may accept the illegal knock as legal.

If the knocker has more than 10 points, and the error is discovered after the opponent has exposed any of his own cards but before he has laid off any cards, the opponent may choose which of the following penalties to apply: To make the knocker play the rest of the hand with all his cards exposed; or to permit the offender to pick up his hand, in which event the offender may not score for any undercut or gin bonus in that hand.

If the knocker has an incorrect number of cards, his opponent may demand a new deal; or may require the offender to play with his hand exposed and to correct his hand on his next play or plays, either by drawing without discarding or by discarding without drawing.

If a player, after knocking, inadvertently discards a card that makes his knock illegal, he may replace that discard with a discard that makes his knock legal.

Looking Back at Discards. Players may agree in advance that looking back at discards will be permitted. In the absence of such agreement, a player who looks back at a covered discard loses his right to his next draw.

STRATEGY. Most important is the effort to keep two or three very low cards—aces, twos and threes—at all times, even when they are not matched and offer no prospect of forming sets. If the opponent wins, having the low cards reduces the loss. Most Gin hands are won on holdings of six or seven matched cards (two sets) plus other cards counting to 10 or less.

The initial effort to get some low cards into the hand means that the early discards are usually face cards and tens, even more than in other Rummy games. For the first two or three turns it will often pay to hold high pairs and two-card sequences, hoping the opponent's discards will fill them. After the fourth turn it is unsafe to hold them.

In the first four or five turns one should knock as soon as he can get his count down to 10. (Very occasionally he may

be wary of knocking with 9 or 10 on the fifth turn, for example if his opponent has picked up one or two discards, or
has discarded a low card, especially an ace or deuce.)

In later play—after the eighth turn— a count of about 5
justifies a knock. Waiting for gin, although able to knock,
is seldom justified unless the opponent can be assumed to
have a weak hand.

HOLLYWOOD SCORING

Hollywood Scoring is a method of scoring Gin Rummy as
though three games were being played simultaneously. The
scoresheet contains three double-columns for Games 1, 2,
and 3. The first score made by a player is entered in Game
1; his second score is entered in Game 1 and again in Game
2; his third score and subsequent scores are entered under
all three games. When any one game terminates, Game 4
may be opened up, and so on continuously, or the two remaining games may be finished without further extension.
If a player is shut out in Game 1, his first score is entered
in Game 2 alone, and his second in Games 2 and 3. Game
and box bonuses are awarded to each column independently of the other games in progress.

ROUND-THE-CORNER GIN

Ace may rank high or low in a sequence and sequences
may go around the corner (A-2-3, A-K-Q, K-A-2, etc).
As an unmatched card, an ace counts 15 points.

Game ends when one player reaches 125 points.

OKLAHOMA GIN

In Oklahoma Gin the rank of the upcard fixes the maximum number of points with which a player may knock in
that deal. Thus, if the upcard is a five, the knocker must
have 5 points or less. Any face card counts 10. Some play
that an ace calls for a gin hand, not merely a count of 1. A
usual added rule is that when the upcard is a spade all
scores accruing from that deal are doubled.

GIN RUMMY FOR 3, 4, 5, AND MORE

THREE-HAND PLAY. In the most popular method, only two
play at a time. Each player cuts; lowest stays out the first

hand, next-lowest deals. After the end of each hand the loser goes out and the idle player takes his place. Each player has his own scoring column for the hands he wins. The game ends when any player reaches 100, and after game and box bonuses have been added, each player settles separately with each other player (a player who is shut out pays the extra points only to the winner). An idle player may not advise either other player.

A second method is to play *chouette* (see page 230). One player is in the box. He plays a regular two-hand game against one of his opponents (the captain), but if he loses he pays both opponents and if he wins he collects from both. The opponents may consult but the captain has the final decision. When the captain loses a hand, the other opponent becomes captain. When a game ends, the captain becomes the man in the box.

A third method is for all three to play. Each receives ten cards. If the player at dealer's left refuses the first upcard, either other player, in turn, may take it. A player in turn may take either opponent's previous discard (unless one has already been taken). When a player knocks, the other players may lay off only on the knocker's original matched sets (if the knocker has ♡9 8 7 and one opponent lays off ♡6, the other may not add ♡5). An individual score is kept for each player. Game is 200, and each player settles separately with each other player. There is no undercut bonus; if the knocker is undercut, 20 points are deducted from his score, but an undercutter scores only if his score is lower than the knocker's.

PARTNERSHIP PLAY. Four or more players, in even numbers, may play in partnerships. Each member of a side plays a two-hand game against a member of the opposing side. When all hands are finished, the scores are combined and only one side scores; for example, if one member of side A wins by 12 points and the other member loses by 10 points, side A wins the hand by 2 points. When a player knocks, play in other games may be suspended until the result is known. At the end of each game, each player changes opponents. Game is 125 when there are four players, 150 when there are six or eight players, 175 when there are ten players, 200 when there are twelve players, etc. Drawn hands are not replayed. A player whose hand is ended may advise a teammate, if he has not seen any opposing hand.

KNOCK RUMMY

PLAYERS. From two to five.

CARDS. The pack of 52, the cards ranking as in Gin Rummy.

DEALING. When two play, each receives ten cards; three or more, seven cards.

THE PLAY. Drawing, discarding and rules as to sets are as in Gin Rummy. All sets are kept in the hand until a player is ready to knock, that is, lay down his whole hand and thereby end the play. A player may knock in his turn, after drawing, regardless of how far the play has progressed or even whether it has begun, and he duly discards one card.

SCORING. When any player knocks, each player counts the *deadwood* in his hand—the cards not matched with others in sets. Face cards count 10 each, all other cards their index value. The hand with the lowest total in deadwood collects from each other hand according to the difference of the counts. If the knocker is lowest, there is no further payment. But if another hand is lower than the knocker, this player wins from all and collects an extra penalty of 10 from the knocker. (Some play that the knocker in this case pays double.) If a player ties the knocker for low count, this player collects the winnings, while the knocker neither pays nor collects. If two or more players other than the knocker tie for low score, they divide the winnings.

If a player *goes rum* by knocking with a hand completely formed in sets, he collects an extra 25 from each player besides the count of his hand. A *rum hand* cannot be tied; if another besides the knocker has a complete hand, he pays the knocker 25.

STRATEGY. In two-hand play, many players knock on first turn if they are slightly below "average" (which is 65). That is, they knock with a deadwood count of 60 or less in their original ten cards. On the second turn, a count of 40 or under is a good knock. Thereafter, the minimum should be decreased by about 10 points per turn.

In three-hand play (when average for the seven cards is 45) it is wise to knock on the first turn with 35; in four- or five-hand play, with 30. Deduct 10 for each turn.

500 Rum

THIS is also called Pinochle Rummy, and its family includes the popular games of Canasta, Samba, Persian Rummy, Michigan Rum and Oklahoma.

PLAYERS. From two to eight may play. Best for three, four, or five. Four may play in two partnerships.

CARDS. The pack of 52. With five or more players, it is advisable to use two full packs, shuffled together. The cards in each suit rank: K (high) Q, J, 10, 9, 8, 7, 6, 5, 4, 3, 2, A. The counting value of cards is as follows: K, Q, J, each 10; cards from 10 to 2, index value; ace, 15 if left in hand or melded in a group of aces, but 1 if melded in A-2-3.

DEALING. Cards are dealt one at a time to the left, beginning with eldest hand. When two play, each receives thirteen cards. With any greater number of players, each receives seven cards. The rest of the pack is placed face down to form the *stock*. The top card is turned up and set beside it to start the *discard pile*.

OBJECT OF PLAY. To form sequences and three or more of a kind, especially those that have high scoring value (see *Scoring*, below).

THE PLAY. Each hand in turn draws either the top card of the stock or a card from the discard pile. *All* cards in the discard pile are available, and it is therefore spread so that all indexes are visible. But there are two restrictions upon drawing from the discard: (a) a discard may be drawn only if it is immediately melded; (b) any and all cards *above* the card drawn and melded must be taken also. (Such additional cards should be left on the table until the player's next turn, so that all others have fair opportunity to inspect and memorize them.)

After drawing from stock or discard, the player may meld as many cards as he can and wishes, and he ends his turn by discarding one card face up on the discard pile.

A player may add cards to any meld on the table—the fourth card of a group of three, or additional cards to a se-

95

quence. All such added cards are retained by the owner in front of himself, not placed with the original meld when the meld belongs to another player. Consequently, when a card fits with either of two melds (a group and a sequence), the owner must specify to which he chooses to attach it. A sequence increased by one player may be further increased by another, to the limits of the suit.

Play of a deal ends when one player gets rids of all cards in his hand by melding, or when the stock is exhausted. After the last discard play may continue so long as each hand in turn can draw from the discard and meld; but as soon as any hand passes, the play ends.

SCORING. At the end of play, each player adds the value of all cards he has melded, and from the total subtracts the count of cards left in his hand. *All* cards left in the hand are counted, regardless of whether they include possible melds. If the count of cards left exceeds the count of melds, the player scores minus for the deal.

A running total score is kept for each player, and when one reaches plus 500 or more, the game ends. Each player settles with each other according to the difference of their final totals. (There is no bonus for winning a game.)

IRREGULARITIES. See RUMMY, *Irregularities*, page 78.

PERSIAN RUMMY

PERSIAN RUMMY is an elaboration of partnership 500 Rum. The pack is increased to 56 cards by the addition of four jokers. Jokers count 20 each, and may be melded only in *groups* of jokers. If all four cards of a rank are melded at once, the meld counts double. *Example*: A meld of four aces counts 120, but if three are melded first and the fourth added later, the total is only 60. An ace counts 15 at all times and ranks above the king. Thus ♡A K Q is a sequence, but ♡A 2 3 is not. When any player gets rid of all his cards by melding, play ends and his side scores a bonus of 25. When the stock is exhausted each player must draw from the discard pile if by so doing he is able to play.

A game comprises two deals. The side with the higher final total score wins the difference of the totals plus a game bonus of 50.

Canasta

THERE ARE many variants of Canasta, but the original game is probably still the most widely played; and the variants merely add to Canasta a few features that are quickly grasped once the parent game is known. The most popular variants, together with some of the many local customs and special "table rules," are described at the end of this section.

The game first described is basically the four-hand partnership game.

PLAYERS. Two to six. It is best for four. (As a two-hand game, Samba is better; see page 105).

With two or three players, each plays for himself. With four or more players, there are two partnerships. With four, partners sit opposite each other at the table. With five, two partners are opposed by three, but only two of the three play at a time, rotating so that a different one of the three is idle each deal. With six players, three on each side, partners sit alternately around the table; or six may play with one player of each side inactive each deal.

CARDS. The game is played with two regular decks of 52 cards, plus four jokers, all 108 cards being shuffled together. The jokers and deuces (twospots) are wild. A wild card may be designated to be of any rank, at the pleasure of the owner. (Six players may prefer to use three packs with six jokers.)

PRELIMINARIES. Partnerships may be determined by drawing cards. Highest card has choice of seats. Jokers are void, in drawing; deuces are low.

The player drawing the highest card plays first; therefore, the player at his right deals first. Thereafter the deal rotates to the left.

DEALING. The dealer gives eleven cards to each player one at a time clockwise, beginning with the opponent at his left and ending with himself. (Three players each receive thirteen cards; two players, fifteen.) The undealt remainder of the deck is placed face down in the center of the table to form the *stock*. The top card of the stock is turned face up beside it; this is the *upcard*. All subsequent discards are laid face up in one pile started by the upcard, if the first player does not take it. Only the top discard may be seen.

RED TREYS. If the upcard is a red trey (threespot) or a wild card it must immediately be covered by another card from the top of the stock, and the discard pile is then *frozen* (see below). The red treys are bonus cards, counting for or against the side to which they fall but never forming a part of the hand. At his first turn to play, each player must withdraw from his hand each red trey dealt to him, put it face up on the table, then draw a card from the top of the stock to restore his hand to the full number of cards. On drawing a red trey from the stock, a player must immediately face the trey on the table and draw a replacement from the stock to keep in his hand. A red trey taken in the discard pile is similarly faced, but is not replaced from the stock.

THE PLAY. The opponent at left of the dealer plays first; thereafter the turn passes to the left, clockwise. Each turn comprises a draw, then a meld (optional), and then a discard.

The player in turn is always entitled to draw the top card of the stock. Subject to restrictions given in the following sections, he may instead take the top card of the discard pile and immediately use it in a meld. Having so taken the last discard, he must take the entire pile and add it to his hand or his melds.

A discard must always be made from the hand, never from a meld. The act of discarding ends a player's turn.

Melds. The principal object of play is to form *melds,* combinations of three or more cards of the same rank, with or without the help of wild cards. (Sequences are not valid melds in Canasta.) A meld is valid if it contains at least two *natural* (not wild) cards of the same rank, and not more than three wild cards. But black treys may not be melded unless the player *goes out* in the same turn. Jokers and deuces may never be melded separately from natural cards. A meld must be laid face up on the table, in some proper turn of the owner. All the melds of both partners are placed before one of them but may not be combined.

A player may add one or more cards of the same rank or wild cards to a meld previously faced by himself or his partner (not to an opponent's meld). No meld may contain more than three wild cards. A side may not make two separate melds of the same rank, but may meld in a rank also melded by an opponent.

Canastas. A meld comprising seven or more cards is a *canasta.* A canasta may be built up by an initial meld of three or more cards and addition of other cards later. Seven natural cards form a *natural canasta,* valued at 500. A canasta formed with help of one to three wild cards is *mixed* and is valued at 300. Additional cards added to a canasta do not increase the bonus. A wild card added to a natural canasta reduces it to a mixed canasta.

Minimum Count. Every card melded has a point value, as follows:

Each joker	50
Each deuce	20
Each ace	20
Each king, queen, jack, 10, 9, 8 . . .	10
Each 7, 6, 5, 4, and black 3	5

The first meld made by a side is its *initial meld.* The initial meld must have a *minimum* count that depends upon the accumulated total score of that side at the beginning of the current deal, as follows:

TOTAL SCORE	MINIMUM COUNT
Minus	0
0 to 1495	50
1500 to 2995	90
3000 or more	120

A player may make two or more different melds in the same turn to achieve the minimum count. Not even a canasta may be melded initially unless the count of its cards satisfies the minimum. The only exception is a *concealed hand* (see below).

After a side has made its initial meld, either partner may make any valid meld without reference to any minimum count.

Taking the Discard Pile. The discard pile is *frozen,* as concerns a side, until that side has made its initial meld.

Even for the side that has melded, the discard pile is *frozen* at any time that it contains a red trey (turned as upcard) or a wild card (upcard or a later discard).

At a time when the discard pile is frozen (for both sides or his side alone), a player may draw the top card only to make a meld with two natural cards of the same rank from his hand. At a time when the discard pile is not frozen, a player may draw the top card; to make a meld with two cards from his hand, either two natural cards or one natural and one wild card; or to add to a meld of his side.*

In taking the discard, a player must proceed as follows (to show his legal right to it): face two cards from his hand that form a valid meld with the discard; lift off the top discard and place it with them; in the case of an initial meld, make such additional melds from his hand as are necessary to meet the minimum requirement. Next the player must take the rest of the discard pile into his hand, and he may then make all additional melds he chooses, with the aid of these cards; but these melds do not help to fulfill the minimum count.

The discard pile may not be taken when it is topped by a wild card or a black trey.

Forcing. After the last card of the stock is drawn, play continues so long as each player in turn legally takes and melds the card discarded by his right-hand opponent. It is compulsory (when the stock is exhausted) to take the discard if it is legally possible to add it to a meld. (Making a discard that the next player must take, at this time, is called *forcing.*) The play ends when the player in turn does not take the discard, either because he cannot legally or because he does not choose to.

Going Out. A player *goes out* when he (legally) gets rid of the last card of his hand, either by discard or by meld. A player may go out only if his side has melded at least one canasta. Failing this requirement, he must keep at least one card in his hand. A player need not make a discard after going out; he may meld all of his remaining cards.

---

* By far the most widely played "table rule," adopted by agreement, is that a player may never take the top card with one natural and one matching card, or to add to a completed canasta of his side, even if the pack is not frozen. He may take it to add to a lesser meld.

Concealed Hand. A player goes out with a *concealed hand* if he melds all his cards in one turn, having previously melded not a single card. (In going out concealed he may not add a card to a meld of his partner's.) The player going out with a concealed hand must himself meld a complete canasta, but need not have any specific minimum count for an initial meld if he goes out after drawing from the stock.

Asking Permission. If able to go out before drawing, or after drawing from the stock, a player may ask his partner "May I go out?" The partner must answer "Yes" or "No" and the player is bound by the reply. Permission to go out may not be asked by a player when he has melded any card in that turn. (A player may go out without asking permission.)

When any player goes out, play ends and the deal is scored.

SCORING. The side that goes out determines its net score for the deal as follows:

(a) Total the point values of the cards in its melds.
(b) Total all bonuses under this schedule:

For going out	100
For each red trey	100
(All four red treys count 800.)	
For each natural canasta . . .	500
For each mixed canasta . . .	300
For concealed hand	100

(c) Total the point values of all cards left in the hand of the player whose partner went out.
(d) Subtract item (c) from the sum of items (a) and (b).

The opponents of the side that went out determine their net score for the deal in the same way, but with these differences: If this side has made no meld, the value of its red treys is deducted instead of added; points values of cards left in both hands are deducted.

If the last card of the stock is a red trey, plays ends; the player drawing it may not discard and has no further opportunity to meld. Play also ends when the stock is exhausted and any player in turn fails to take the top discard. In either case the net scores are determined according to the preceding paragraph.

Scoring a Game. A game is won by the first side to reach a total of 5,000 points or more. If both sides reach 5,000 in the same deal (the final deal is played out, even though it is known that one side will reach 5,000 after play ends), the side with the higher total wins. There is no bonus for winning a game.

The score should be recorded on paper, with one column for each side, and the record should show each net deal score together with the cumulative total of such scores for each side. (Minimum count for the initial meld is fixed by this cumulative total.)

IRREGULARITIES. Prepared by the Association of American Playing Card Mfrs.; based on the official laws of the National Canasta Laws Commission.

New Deal. There must be a new deal by the same dealer if he departs in any respect from the laws of correct procedure in dealing, or if he exposes a card other than the correct upcard, or if it is discovered during the deal that the cut was omitted. There must be a new deal if it is discovered, before every player has completed his first turn, that any hand was dealt an incorrect number of cards, that a card is faced in the stock, or that the deck contains a foreign card. (If the error is discovered too late for a new deal, a short hand continues short, a faced card is shuffled in the stock, or a foreign card is discarded from the deck and if it was in a hand the player draws a replacement.)

Drawing Too Many. If a player draws too many cards from the stock he must show the excess cards (if they were not placed in his hand) to all players and replace them on the stock. The next player to draw from the stock may, if he wishes, shuffle it before drawing. If excess cards drawn are placed in the hand, the player must forego drawing in enough successive turns to reduce his hand to the correct number, discarding one card in each turn. Until his hand is correct, he may not meld.

Exposed Card. If a player exposes a card from his hand except as a meld or discard, such card becomes a penalty card and must be left face up on the table. A penalty card counts as part of the hand, and may be duly melded. If not melded, it must be discarded at first opportunity. With two or more penalty cards, the owner may choose which to discard.

Insufficient Count. If a player puts down an insufficient count for an initial meld, he may correct the error by melding additional cards and may rearrange the cards melded. Or he may retract all the cards, in which case the minimum count requirement for his side (during the play of that deal only) is increased by 10 points.

Illegal Meld. Cards melded illegally, e.g., in an effort to go out when the side has no canasta or when partner has answered "No" to "Partner, may I go out?"; or excess wild cards in a meld, must be retracted. The side is penalized 100 points for the offense. The same penalty applies if a player, having put down insufficient count for an initial meld, makes it sufficient with additional cards but retracts one or more of those already exposed.

Failure to Declare a Red Three. If at the end of play a hand is found to contain an undeclared red three the side is penalized 500 points. (This does not apply if a player has had no turn, another before him having gone out on the first turn, but the red three still counts 100 minus if his side has not melded.)

Condonement. If a player makes an illegal meld and the error is not called until the next hand has drawn or indicated intention to take the pack, the penalty for illegal meld or insufficient count does not apply. An initial meld of insufficient count stands as sufficient; an incorrect combination is retracted without penalty. But excess wild cards in a meld remain, and are debited against the side (at 50 each if there is question which was the fourth wild card added).

Taking Pack Illegally. A player attempting to take the discard pile without having established his right to do so should be stopped at once. There is no penalty if he can then show a valid claim. But if he has taken the pile into his hand before doing so, the opponents may face his whole hand and reconstruct the pile from it. The offender then picks up his card and draws from the stock, and his side is penalized 100 points.

Irregularity in Asking. If a player asks "Partner, may I go out?" after melding any card or indicating intention to take the discard pile, he must if possible go out. If a player asks the question at a proper time, but melds any card before receiving an answer, he must if possible go out. If the player then cannot go out, or if he asks, receives the answer "Yes," and then cannot go out, his side is penalized 100 points.

STRATEGY. The basic approach to Canasta strategy applies in general to the variant games described on the following pages, though of course each game gives rise to some special considerations.

The object of the game is to get the pack and do a lot of melding. The more cards you have in your hand, the better your chance to get the pack. The beginner's worst mistake is melding fast and reducing his hand to a few cards. Then he probably will never get the pack, cannot complete canastas, and cannot go out.

When you need for the initial meld: 50, do not waste any cards from your hand; unless you can take the pack, do not make the initial meld. 90, reduce your hand by no more than four cards. 120, reduce your hand by no more than six cards. Only in the late stages should you use more cards.

Make mixed canastas fast rather than wait to try for natural canastas.

There are various reasons for freezing the pack (by discarding a wild card). One reason arises when an opponent has made the initial meld and your side has not. If the pack has more than a few cards in it, freeze it to equalize matters.

Don't be in a hurry to go out if you have a better chance for further scoring than the opponents.

Build up a hand of pairs (in the early stages preferably low pairs if you have some wild cards to build up your count for an initial meld). Low discards, however, are safer than high discards in the early stages.

Before your side has melded, know at all times the count of the melds you have in your hand and what discards might allow you to take the pack and meld. If you have to stop and count after the discard is made, you reveal your hand.

It pays to keep your score just under 1,500, or just under 3,000, even at the sacrifice of a few hundred points you might have scored, so as to avoid increasing the minimum you need on the next hand.

TWO-HAND CANASTA

In two-handed Canasta, each player is dealt 15 cards. When a player draws from the stock he draws two cards, but he discards only one card in each turn. To go out, a player needs two canastas instead of one. Otherwise the rules are as in the four-hand game.

CANASTA VARIATIONS

SAMBA

Samba follows the rules of Canasta except for the following:

Cards. Three decks of 52 cards each, plus six jokers, making 162 cards in all.

Deal. Each player receives 15 cards, regardless of the number of players.

Draw. A draw from the stock (instead of taking the discard pile) is two cards, but one card is discarded to end the turn.

Sequence Meld or Samba. Three or more cards of the same suit and in sequence (ace high, fourspot low) are a valid meld. Such a meld may be increased by sequential cards up to a total of seven, when it becomes a *samba* and is turned face down. No card may be added to a samba, and it may never contain a wild card. A samba ranks as a canasta for purpose of going out. The bonus for a samba in 1,500.

Melding Wild Cards. No meld may ever contain more than two wild cards.

Adding to a Canasta. The discard pile may not be taken to add its top card to a completed canasta. Only natural (not wild) cards from the hand may be added to a canasta.

Duplicate Melds. A side may meld two or more sets of the same rank. Either partner in his turn may combine melds of like rank (to build toward a canasta).

Taking the Pack. The discard pile may be taken only (a) by melding its top card with a natural pair from the hand, or (b) when it is not frozen, by adding its top card to a meld on the table. (But note that a sequence meld may not be initiated by the top of the discard pile, plus cards from the hand; it must come wholly from the hand.)

Initial Meld. Requirements for the inital meld are:

Minus	15
0 to 1495	50
1500 to 2995	90
3000 to 6995	120
7000 or more	150

Game. Game is 10,000 points.

Going Out. A side must have at least two canastas to go out and also to count its red threes plus. (A samba is a canasta.) The bonus for going out is 200. No bonus for "concealed hand."

Red Threes. If all six red threes are drawn by one side they count 1,000.

URUGUAY

Uruguay follows the rules of Canasta except for the following:

Wild Cards. Three or more wild cards, up to seven, are a valid meld. A canasta of wild cards counts 2,000.

CHILE, or CHILEAN CANASTA

Either the three-deck (162-card) Samba pack or a four-deck (208-card) pack with eight jokers is used. Sequence melds as in Samba and wild-card melds as in Uruguay are permitted.

BOLIVIA

Bolivia follows the rules of Samba except for the following:

Wild Cards. From three to seven wild cards form a valid meld. A canasta of seven wild cards is a *bolivia,* counting 2,500.

Samba. The samba (seven cards in suit and sequence) is called an *escalera.* It counts 1,500.

Game. Game is 15,000. The initial meld requirement stays at 150 from 7,000 up.

Going Out. A side must have two canastas, including an escalera, to go out.

Red Treys. Red treys count plus for the side if it has

completed two canastas of any description; otherwise they count minus.

Black Treys. A black trey left in the hand when any other player goes out counts 100 minus. A black trey melded in going out counts only 5.

BRAZILIAN CANASTA

Brazilian Canasta is not much different from Bolivia. Game is 10,000 and the special initial meld requirements are: Score 5,000-7,000, 150; 7,000-8,000, any canasta; 8,000-9,000, 200; 9,000-10,000, a natural canasta. Any canasta of wild cards counts 2,000. Five red threes count 1,000 and all six count 1,200. Black threes may never be melded. If a side has a melded sequence of less than five cards when play ends, 1,000 points are deducted from its score.

ITALIAN CANASTA

Italian canasta follows the rules of Samba except as noted:

Discard Pile. After the deal and before a card is turned each player replaces his red treys. Then the top card is turned. A number of cards equal to its rank (counting jack 11, queen 12, king 13, ace or joker 20) are counted off the stock to begin the discard pile. They are turned face down, and the upcard is placed face up on them.

The discard pile may be taken only by a natural pair from the hand (it is "always frozen").

Wild Cards. Deuces may be melded as an independent rank, with or without the aid of jokers as wild cards. A side that has melded deuces may not meld wild cards elsewhere until the canasta of deuces is completed.

Initial Meld. The initial meld must meet the required count without aid of any wild card. The requirements are:

TOTAL SCORE						MINIMUM COUNT
0 to 1,495	.	.	.	.	.	50
1,500 to 2,995	.	.	.	.	.	90
3,000 to 4,995	.	.	.	.	.	120
5,000 to 7,495	.	.	.	.	.	160
7,500 to 9,995	.	.	.	.	.	180
10,000 or more	.	.	.	.	.	200

Going Out. A wild-card canasta does not count as one of the two canastas required to go out. The bonus for going out is 300.

Red Treys. When a side has no more than three red treys, they count 100 each; four or more, 200 each.

Scoring. Seven deuces count 3,000; a mixed canasta of deuces, 2,000; but these bonuses go only to the side that goes out; opponents having deuce melds score only the point value of the cards. Extra bonuses: for five pure canastas, 2,000; for five canastas including a mixed, 1,000; for ten canastas of any kind, 2,000.

Game. Game is 12,000.

CUBAN CANASTA

Several variants of Canasta are called "Cuban." It resembles regular Canasta rather than the Samba variants. The pack (108 cards), the draw (one card at a time) and the values of cards are as in Canasta. The differences are:

Game. Game is 7,500. From 5,000 to 7,500, the initial-meld requirement is 150.

Discard Pile. The pack is always frozen. No canasta may contain more than seven cards, so the pack may not be taken to add to a five-card meld.

Canastas. In addition to natural and mixed canastas, wild cards may be melded. A canasta of seven deuces counts 4,000; four jokers and three deuces, 3,000; any other wild-card canasta, 2,000. Sequences may not be melded. A side needs two canastas to go out.

Threes. One red three counts 100, two count 300, three count 500, all four count 1,000. They count plus if the side has a canasta, otherwise minus. Black threes may not be melded. When a black three is taken in the pack it is removed from play, and if a side gets all four black threes in this way it scores 100.

JOKER CANASTA

This is a variant of Cuban Canasta with these general exceptions:

Thirteen cards are dealt to each player. A wild card may never be discarded. Black threes are played and scored the same as red threes—but scores for black and red threes are counted separately. Both are counted minus against a side that fails to complete a canasta.

THE SEVENS (JOKER CANASTA)

A canasta of sevens counts 2,000.

A player holding more than three sevens at the end of a hand subtracts 500 points from his score.

For an uncompleted canasta of sevens on the table, 1,500 points are deducted.

This variation greatly changes the strategy of the game, since a player can rarely afford to take the pack with a seven unless he knows his side can make a canasta in sevens, or the pack is worth the 1,500 points which an incomplete canasta will cost.

LOCAL OPTIONS

The following table rules are sometimes encountered in one or more of the variant games:

A player must ask partner's permission before going out.

A player cannot go out without making a discard.

A tabled meld of three wild cards may be transformed into a mixed canasta by the addition of any four natural cards put down at one turn.

No additions can be made to a completed canasta.

SIGNAL INITIAL DISCARDS

These vary greatly from one group to another, but most common is probably: Ten-spot or higher shows three or more wild cards; partner plays an eight or nine to show two; with three, melds them if he has the "count", signals with a ten or higher if he can't go down.

Contract Bridge

THIS IS THE principal scientific card game throughout the world. "Rubber bridge" is the form of the game played in clubs and at home; the side that first wins two games receives a bonus for winning the "rubber." "Duplicate bridge," described later, is the game played in tournaments; the object is to make a better score than other contestants who hold the same cards.

PLAYERS. Four, two against two as partners. Five or six may participate in a "cut-in" game, the extra players sitting out until a rubber is finished. Partners share equally in every result, and only one score is kept for each side.

CARDS. The 52-card pack. Usually two packs are used; while one pack is being dealt, the dealer's partner shuffles the other pack. Having shuffled it, he sets it down at his right. The cards in each suit rank downward in order: A (high), K, Q, J, 10, 9, 8, 7, 6, 5, 4, 3, 2. The suits rank: spades (high), hearts, diamonds, clubs.

PRELIMINARIES. Before each rubber, one pack is spread face down on the table. Each player draws a card, but not one of the four cards at either end. If more than four wish to play, those drawing the lowest cards do not play in the first rubber; at the end of the first rubber, they will replace the player or players who drew the next-lowest cards. Of the four active players, the one who drew the highest card becomes the first dealer and has choice of cards and seats; the player who drew the next-highest card becomes his partner and sits opposite him; the other two players take the other two seats.

The Shuffle and Cut. The shuffled pack is placed at the dealer's left. The dealer transfers it to his right. The player at dealer's right must cut the pack by lifting off a packet and setting it down toward the dealer. The dealer completes the cut by putting the other packet on top of this one. Each packet must be at least five cards.

ROTATION. The rotation is always clockwise, the turn passing from each player to the player at his left, in dealing, in bidding, and in play.

DEALING. The dealer distributes the cards one at a time face down, in rotation, beginning with the player on his left, until all have been dealt and each player has received thirteen cards. No player should touch or intentionally look at the face of any card dealt to him until the deal is completed.

THE AUCTION, OR BIDDING. When the deal is completed, each player picks up and looks at his hand. Then each player in rotation, beginning with the dealer, may continue to *call* until the auction closes. A *call* may be a pass, a bid, a double or a redouble.

Pass. A player who does not wish to make any other call says "Pass."

Bid. A bid is an offer to undertake to win a stated number of *odd-tricks* (tricks in excess of six, the first six tricks being called "the book") with a named suit as trump, or with no-trump. The lowest possible bid is a bid of one and, since there are thirteen tricks in all, the highest possible bid is seven. The form of a bid is: "One diamond," "One no-trump," "Four spades," etc.

A bid must be *sufficient* to *overcall* the preceding bid if any. To be sufficient it must name a greater number of odd-tricks, or the same number of odd-tricks in a higher-ranking denomination (suit or no-trump), the rank being: No-trump (high), spades, hearts, diamonds, clubs. Thus, one spade will overcall one heart; two or more clubs will overcall one spade.

Double. A player in turn may double the last preceding bid if it was made by an opponent and has not previously been doubled. The effect of a double is to increase the scoring values of tricks. A double does not affect the sufficiency of bids; if a three-spade bid has been doubled, any player in turn may still overcall it with a bid of three no-trump, or four clubs, or anything higher.

Redouble. A player in turn may redouble the last preceding bid if it was made by himself or his partner, has been doubled by an opponent, and has not been redoubled. The redouble further increases the scoring values, but, like the double, does not affect the sufficiency of bids.

A double or redouble applies only to the last preceding bid. If a four-club is doubled, and there is a subsequent bid of four hearts, the four-heart bid counts at its usual, single, value unless it also is doubled.

Opening the Auction. The auction is said to be opened when any player makes a bid. If all four players pass originally, the deal is *passed out*, the cards are thrown in and the next dealer in turn deals. Once the auction has been opened, it must continue until it closes and the cards must be played.

Closing the Auction. When a bid, double or redouble is followed by three consecutive passes, the auction is closed. Every card of the suit named in the final bid becomes a trump; or, if the final bid was in no-trump, the cards will be played without a trump suit. Of the side which made the final bid, the member who first named the suit (or no-trump) specified in that bid becomes the *declarer*. The number of odd-tricks named in the final bid becomes his *contract*. The play period commences.

THE PLAY. The player at declarer's left selects any card from his hand and places it face up in the center of the table; that is the *opening lead*. Declarer's partner then places his hand face up on the table in front of him, grouped in suits with the trumps, if any, to his right; this hand, and declarer's partner are each called the dummy. Declarer's partner will take no further part in the play of the cards; declarer will select the plays from the dummy hand as well as from his own, but each in proper turn.

The object of play is to win tricks. A *trick* consists of four cards, one from the hand of each player in rotation, the first card played to a trick generally being called the *lead*. A player is required to follow suit to the card led if he can; if he cannot follow suit, he may play any card. A trick containing any trump is won by the highest trump it contains; a trick not containing trump is won by the highest card of the suit led. The hand that wins a trick leads to the next.

When a trick is complete (contains four cards) a member of the side that won it takes in the cards, turns them face down, and places them in front of him. One partner takes in all the tricks won by his side. A player may look back at the last trick until he or his partner has led or played to the next; after that, he may not look at any previous trick.

Play continues in this way until thirteen tricks have been played.

SCORING. Any player may keep score; one player for each side should keep score; and at least one player at the table must keep score.

The Contract Bridge score sheet is divided by a vertical line in columns headed "we" and "they" and the scorekeeper enters all scores made by his side on the "we" side and all scores made by his opponents on the other side. Midway of the score sheet there is a horizontal line; scores designated as *trick score* go *below the line;* all other scores (usually called the *honor score*) go *above the line.*

Trick Score. If declarer fulfils his contract by winning as many or more odd-tricks than his contract calls for, he scores below the line for every odd-trick named in the contract:

Score for Each ODD-TRICK BID AND MADE If Trumps Were	If the contract was undoubled	If the contract was doubled	If the contract was redoubled
♠ or ♡	30	60	120
◇ or ♣	20	40	80
N T, first odd-trick	40	80	160
N T, each additional odd-trick	30	60	120

No trick not included in the contract is scored below the line. If declarer wins more tricks than his contract calls for, their value is scored above the line (see *overtricks,* below).

Game. When a side has scored 100 or more points below the line, it has won a *game.* The scorekeeper draws a horizontal line across the entire sheet, below the score which ended the game, to signify that a game is beginning. A game may be made in more than one hand: A side may score 60, then its opponents may score 40, then the first side may score 40, giving it 100 points and ending the game. The opponents' trick score of 40 does not carry over to the next game, however. Each side begins the next game at zero.

Vulnerability. A side that has won a game is said to be vulnerable. A vulnerable side receives increased bonuses in some cases, and is subject to increased penalties when it does not fulfill its contract.

Overtricks. Any trick won by declarer in excess of his contract is called an overtrick, and is scored above the line to the credit of his side, as follows:

Score for Each Odd-Trick MADE BUT NOT BID If Trumps Were	If the contract was				
		Doubled		Redoubled	
	Undoubled	Vulnerable	Not Vulnerable	Vulnerable	Not Vulnerable
♠ or ♡	30	200	100	400	200
♢ or ♣	20	200	100	400	200
N T	30	200	100	400	200

Doubled Contract. If declarer makes any doubled or re-doubled contract, with or without overtricks, he adds 50 points to his score above the line.

Honors. When there is a trump suit, the ace, king, queen, jack, and ten of trumps are honors. If a player holds four trump honors in his hand, his side scores 100 above the line; if he holds all five trump honors, his side scores 150 above the line; if he holds all four aces at a no-trump contract, his side scores 150 above the line. The player holding the honors may be declarer, dummy, or either *defender* (opponent of declarer).

Slams. If declarer fulfills a contract of six odd-tricks (called a *little slam,* or *small slam*), his side scores 500 above the line if not vulnerable, and 750 if vulnerable. If declarer fulfills a contract of seven odd-tricks (*grand slam*), his side scores 1000 points above the line if not vulnerable, and 1500 if vulnerable.

Undertrick Penalties. If declarer fails to fulfill his contract—that is, if he *goes down* or is *set* one or more tricks —his opponents score above the line, as follows:

IF DECLARER "Goes Down"	Undoubled		If the contract was Doubled		Redoubled	
	Not Vulnerable	Vulnerable	Not Vulnerable	Vulnerable	Not Vulnerable	Vulnerable
1 trick	50	100	100	200	200	400
Each add'l trick }	50	100	200	300	400	600

Rubber. A rubber ends when either side has won two games. The side which has won two games wins the rubber and adds to its score 500 points if its opponents have won a game; and 700 points if its opponents have not won a game.

All points scored by both sides, both above the line and below the line, are then added up. The side that has scored the greatest number of points wins the difference between its score and its opponents' score.

IRREGULARITIES IN CONTRACT BRIDGE

These excerpts from the Laws of Contract Bridge, © 1963 by the American Contract Bridge League, have been prepared with the permission of the National Laws Commission, a standing committee of the League, which promulgates the laws in the Western Hemisphere. The present laws represent the first change since 1948.

There are some provisions of the laws that apply to many other laws and to which frequent reference is or could be made in the following pages. They are:

LEAD PENALTY. If a defender leads out of turn declarer may accept the lead; treat the card led as a penalty card; require the lead of that suit from the proper leader, or forbid him to lead that suit for as long as he holds the lead at that turn.

There are some other cases in which declarer has some control over a defender's lead, but not so much. In such cases, the exact penalty has been specified.

BARRED PLAYER. A player who is barred once, or for one round, must pass the next time it is his turn to bid; a player who is barred throughout must pass in every turn until the auction of the current deal is completed.

WAIVER OF PENALTY. When a player calls or plays over an illegal call or play by his right-hand opponent, he accepts the illegal call or play and waives a penalty. The game continues as though no irregularity had occurred.

RETENTION OF THE RIGHT TO CALL. A player cannot lose his only chance to call by the fact that an illegal pass by his partner has been accepted by an opponent. The auction must continue until the player has had at least one chance to call.

PENALTY CARD. A card illegally exposed by a defender must be left on the table, face up, until it is played; and it must be played at the first legal opportunity, whether in leading, following suit, or trumping. When a defender has a penalty card and his partner has the lead, declarer may require or forbid the partner to lead the suit of the penalty card; but if declarer does so, the card may be picked up and ceases to be a penalty card.

NEW SHUFFLE AND CUT. Before the first card is dealt, any player may demand a new shuffle and cut. There must be a new shuffle and cut if a card is faced in shuffling or cutting.

DEAL OUT OF TURN. The correct dealer may reclaim the deal before the last card is dealt; thereafter, the deal stands as though it had been in turn and the correct dealer loses his right to deal in that round.

REDEAL. There must be a redeal if the cards are not dealt correctly; if the pack is incorrect; if a card is faced in the pack or elsewhere; if a player picks up the wrong hand and looks at it; or if at any time during the play one hand is found to have too many cards and another too few (and the discrepancy is not caused by errors in play). When there is a redeal, the same dealer deals (unless the deal was out of turn) and with the same pack, after a new shuffle and cut.

INCORRECT HAND. If a player has too few cards and the missing card is found (except in a previous trick), it is considered to have been in the short hand throughout. If it cannot be found, there is a redeal. If it is found in a previous trick, see *Defective Trick*.

ENFORCING A PENALTY. Either opponent (but not dummy) may select or enforce a penalty. If partners consult as to selection or enforcement, the right to penalize is canceled.

CARD EXPOSED DURING THE AUCTION. No penalty for exposing a single card lower than a ten. If the exposed card is an honor, or any card prematurely led, or more than one card, each exposed card must be left face up on the table; the partner of the offender must pass at his next turn; and each exposed card becomes a penalty card if the other side plays the hand.

CHANGE OF CALL. A player may change a call without penalty if he does so without pause. Any other attempted change of call is canceled. If the first call was an illegal call, it is subject to the applicable law; if it was a legal call, the offender may either:

(a) allow his first call to stand, whereupon his partner must pass at his next turn; or

(b) substitute any legal call (including a pass, double, or redouble) whereupon his partner must pass at every subsequent turn.

INSUFFICIENT BID. If a player makes an insufficient bid, he must substitute either a sufficient bid or a pass (not a double or redouble). If he substitutes:

(a) The lowest sufficient bid in the same denomination, there is no penalty.

(b) Any other bid, his partner must pass at every subsequent turn.

(c) A pass, his partner must pass at every subsequent turn, and declarer (if an opponent) may impose a lead penalty (page 1). A double or redouble illegally substituted is penalized the same as a pass and is treated as a pass.

The offender need not select his final call until the law has been stated; previous attempts at correction are canceled.

INFORMATION GIVEN IN CHANGING CALL. A denomination named, then canceled, in making or correcting an illegal call, is subject to penalty if an opponent becomes declarer: If a suit was named, declarer may impose a lead penalty (page 1); if notrump was named, declarer may call a suit, if the offender's partner has the opening lead; if a double or redouble was canceled, the penalties are the same as when a pass is substituted for an insufficient bid.

CALL OUT OF ROTATION (OR "OUT OF TURN"). Any call out of rotation is canceled when attention is drawn to it. The auction reverts to the player whose turn it was. Rectification and penalty depend on whether it was a pass, a bid, or a double or redouble, as follows:

A call is not out of rotation if made without waiting for the right-hand opponent to pass, if that opponent is legally obliged to pass; nor if it would have been in rotation had not the left-hand opponent called out of rotation. A call made simultaneously with another player's call in rotation is deemed to be subsequent to it.

PASS OUT OF TURN. If it occurs (a) before any player has bid, or when it was the turn of the offender's right-hand opponent, the offender must pass when his regular turn comes; (b) after there has been a bid and when it was the turn of the offender's partner, the offender is barred throughout; the offender's partner may not double or redouble at that turn; and if the offender's partner passes and the opponents play the hand, declarer may impose a lead penalty (page 1).

BID OUT OF TURN. If it occurs (a) before any player has called, the offender's partner is barred throughout; (b) after any player has called and when it was the turn of the offender's partner, the offender's partner is barred throughout and is subject to a lead penalty (page 1) if he has the opening lead; (c) after any player has called and when it was the turn of the offender's right-hand opponent, the offender must repeat his bid without penalty if that opponent passes but if that opponent bids the offender may make any call and his partner is barred once.

DOUBLE OR REDOUBLE OUT OF TURN. If it occurs (a) when it was the turn of the offender's partner, the offender's partner is barred throughout and is subject to a lead penalty (page 1) if he has the opening lead, and the offender may not in turn double or redouble the same bid; (b) when it was the turn of the offender's right-hand opponent, the offender must repeat his double or redouble without penalty if that opponent passes but may make any legal call if that opponent bids, in which case the offender's partner is barred once.

IMPOSSIBLE DOUBLES AND REDOUBLES. If a player doubles or redoubles a bid that his side has already doubled or redoubled, his call is canceled; he must substitute (a) any legal bid, in which case his partner is barred throughout and if he becomes the opening leader declarer may prohibit the lead of the doubled suit; or (b) a pass, in which case either opponent may cancel all previous doubles and redoubles, the offender's partner is barred throughout, and if he becomes the opening leader he is subject to a lead penalty (page 1).

If a player doubles his partner's bid, redoubles an undoubled bid, or doubles or redoubles when there has been no bid, he must substitute any proper call, and his partner is barred once.

OTHER INADMISSIBLE CALLS. If a player bids more than seven, or makes another call when legally required to pass, he is deemed to have passed and the offending side must pass at every subsequent turn; if they become the defenders, declarer may impose a lead penalty (page 1) on the opening leader.

CALL AFTER THE AUCTION IS CLOSED. A call made after the auction is closed is canceled. If it is a pass by a defender, or any call by declarer or dummy, there is no penalty. If it is a bid, double or redouble by a defender, declarer may impose a lead penalty at the offender's partner's first turn to lead.

DUMMY'S RIGHTS. Dummy may give or obtain information regarding fact or law, ask if a play constitutes a revoke, draw attention to an irregularity, and warn any player against infringing a law. Dummy forfeits these rights if he looks at a card in another player's hand.

If dummy has forfeited his rights, and thereafter

(a) is the first to draw attention to a defender's irregularity, declarer may not enforce any penalty for the offense;

(b) warns declarer not to lead from the wrong hand,

either defender may choose the hand from which declarer shall lead;

(c) is the first to ask declarer if a play from declarer's hand is a revoke, declarer must correct a revoke if able but the revoke penalty still applies.

EXPOSED CARDS. Declarer is never subject to penalty for exposure of a card, but intentional exposure of declarer's hand is treated as a claim or concession of tricks.

A defender's card is exposed if it is faced on the table or held so that the other defender may see its face before he is entitled to do so. Such a card must be left face up on the table until played and becomes a penalty card.

PENALTY CARDS. A penalty card must be played at the first legal opportunity, subject to the obligation to follow suit or to comply with another penalty.

If a defender has two or more penalty cards that he can legally play, declarer may designate which one is to be played.

Declarer may require or forbid a defender to lead a suit in which his partner has a penalty card, but if declarer does so the penalty card may be picked up and ceases to be a penalty card.

Failure to play a penalty card is not subject to penalty, but declarer may require the penalty card to be played and any defender's card exposed in the process becomes a penalty card.

LEAD OUT OF TURN. If declarer is required by a defender to retract a lead from the wrong hand, he must lead from the correct hand (if he can) a card of the same suit; if it was a defender's turn to lead, or if there is no card of that suit in the correct hand, there is no penalty.

If a defender is required to retract a lead out of turn, declarer may either treat the card so led as a penalty card, or impose a lead penalty on the offender's partner when next he is to lead after the offense.

PREMATURE PLAY. If a defender leads to the next trick before his partner has played to the current trick, or plays out of rotation before his partner has played, declarer may require the offender's partner to play his highest card of the suit led, his lowest card of the suit led, or a card of another specified suit. Declarer must select one of these options, and if the defender cannot comply, he may play any card. When declarer has played from both his hand and dummy, a defender is not subject to penalty for playing before his partner.

INABILITY TO PLAY AS REQUIRED. If a player is unable to lead or play as required to comply with a penalty (for lack of a card of a required suit, or because of the prior obligation to follow suit) he may play any card. The penalty is deemed satisfied, except in the case of a penalty card.

REVOKE. A revoke is the act of playing a card of another suit, when able to follow suit to a lead. Any player, including dummy, may ask whether a play constitutes a revoke and may demand that an opponent correct a revoke. A claim of revoke does not warrant inspection of turned tricks, prior to the end of play, except by consent of both sides.

CORRECTING A REVOKE. A player must correct his revoke if aware of it before it becomes established. A revoke card withdrawn by a defender becomes a penalty card. The nonoffending side may withdraw any cards played after the revoke but before attention was drawn to it.

ESTABLISHED REVOKE. A revoke becomes established when a member of the offending side leads or plays to a subsequent trick (or terminates play by a claim or concession). When a revoke becomes established, the revoke trick stands as played (unless it is the twelfth trick—see below).

REVOKE PENALTY. The penalty for an established revoke is two tricks (if available), transferred at the end of play from the revoking side to the opponents. This penalty can be paid only from tricks won by the revoking side after its first revoke, including the revoke trick. If only one trick is available, the penalty is satisfied by transferring one trick; if no trick is available, there is no penalty.

There is no penalty for a subsequent established revoke in the same suit by the same player.

A transferred trick ranks for all scoring purposes as a trick won in play by the side receiving it. It never affects the contract.*

REVOKES NOT SUBJECT TO PENALTY. A revoke made in the twelfth trick must be corrected, without penalty, if discovered before the cards have been mixed together. The nonoffending side may require the offender's partner to play either of two cards he could legally have played. A revoke

---

* For example, if the contract is 2♥ and declarer wins 8 tricks plus 2 tricks as a revoke penalty, total 10 tricks, he can score only 60 points below the line and the other 60 points go above the line.

not discovered until the cards have been mixed is not subject to penalty, nor is a revoke by any faced hand (dummy, or a defender's hand when faced in consequence of a claim by declarer). A revoke by failure to play a penalty card is not subject to the penalty for an established revoke.

DEFECTIVE TRICK. A defective trick may not be corrected after a player of each side has played to the next trick. If a player has failed to play to a trick, he must correct his error when it is discovered by adding a card to the trick (if possible, one he could legally have played to it). If a player has played more than one card to a trick, he does not play to the last trick or tricks and if he wins a trick with his last card, the turn to lead passes to the player at his left.

DECLARER CLAIMING OR CONCEDING TRICKS. If declarer claims or concedes one or more of the remaining tricks (verbally or by spreading his hand), he must leave his hand face up on the table and immediately state his intended plan of play.

If a defender disputes declarer's claim, declarer must play on, adhering to any statement he has made, and in the absence of a specific statement he may not "exercise freedom of choice in making any play the success of which depends on finding either opponent with or without a particular unplayed card."

Following curtailment of play by declarer, it is permissible for a defender to expose his hand and to suggest a play to his partner.

DEFENDER CLAIMING OR CONCEDING TRICKS. A defender may show any or all of his cards to declarer to establish a claim or concession. He may not expose his hand to his partner, and if he does, declarer may treat his partner's cards as penalty cards.

CORRECTING THE SCORE. A proved or admitted error in any score may be corrected at any time before the rubber score is agreed, except as follows: An error made in entering or failing to enter a part-score, or in omitting a game or in awarding one, may not be corrected after the last card of the second succeeding correct deal has been dealt (unless a majority of the players consent).

EFFECT OF INCORRECT PACK. Scores made as a result of hands played with an incorrect pack are not affected by the discovery of the imperfection after the cards have been mixed together.

Contract Bridge Strategy

SKILLFUL BIDDING at Contract Bridge requires use of a bidding system, agreed upon between the partners and fully revealed to their opponents. (The use of private understandings is unethical.)

The first such system was the Vanderbilt Club System, devised by Harold S. Vanderbilt, who introduced the modern game of Contract Bridge in 1926. From 1930 into the 1940s the most popular bidding system throughout the world was the Culbertson System, devised by Ely Culbertson, whose publicity genius did most to make Contract Bridge the most widely played card game. Since the 1940s the bidding system of Charles H. Goren has been favored by the vast majority of American players.

It is the Goren system that is described below.

VALUING THE HAND. Every player, upon picking up his hand, makes some rough estimate of its value. Using the point-count method, a player values his hand as follows:

> 4 points for each ace
> 3 points for each king
> 2 points for each queen
> 1 point for each jack

There are 40 points in all. The average hand is 10 points. Usually the two partners together must hold 20 points to make any contract, 26 points to make a game, 33 points to make a small slam, and 37 points to make a grand slam.

For no-trump bidding, only high-card points are counted. For opening suit-bids, a player adds the following points based on the distribution of his hand:

> 3 points for a void suit
> 2 points for each singleton
> 1 point for each doubleton

CORRECTION POINTS. Neither the point-count method nor any other valuation method is entirely accurate. There are several cases in which experts advocate adjustment of the point-count to fit a particular hand. Among these cases are:

Add one point when holding all four aces.

Deduct one point for an aceless hand.

Deduct one point for an insufficiently guarded honor, such as a singleton king.

BASIC REQUIREMENTS FOR OPENING BIDS. An opening bid is the first bid made. Thereafter, a bid is termed an *overcall* (of the opponent's bid), a *response* (to partner's bid), or a *rebid* (by a player who has previously bid).

Most hands, if opened at all, should be opened with a bid of one.

Opening No-trump Bids. Bid one no-trump with 16 to 18 points (high-card count only). No fewer than 16 points, no more than 18. The distribution of the hand should be 4-3-3-3 (ideal), 4-4-3-2, or 5-3-3-2. The high cards should be distributed among at least three suits and preferably all four. A doubleton should not be weaker than Q-x.

An opening bid of two no-trump requires 22 to 24 points with no suit weaker than K-x or Q-10-x. This bid is not forcing.

An opening bid of three no-trump requires 25 to 27 points with no suit weaker than K-x or Q-J-x.

Opening Suit-bids of One. For opening suit-bids count both high-card and distributional points.

14 or more points make an opening bid obligatory.

13 points usually justify an opening bid, but a 13-point hand distributed 4-3-3-3 is sometimes passed.

12 points justify an opening bid only in a strong trump suit (five cards headed by A-K or a six-card or longer suit).

Hands weaker than 12 points should usually be passed.

The opening bid is made in a *biddable suit,* as described below.

Honor-tricks. A hand should not be opened unless it contains at least two *honor-tricks,* or *quick tricks:*

2 Honor-tricks	A-K
1½ Honor-tricks	A-Q
1 Honor-trick	Ace or K-Q
½ Honor-trick	K-x

BIDDABLE SUITS. No suit is *biddable* which does not contain at least four cards including some minimum number of high cards. No suit is *rebiddable* which does not contain at least five cards.

Regular biddable suits: Four cards headed by 4 points, such as A-x-x-x or K-J-x-x; five cards headed by Q or J-10. May be bid once; should not be rebid unless partner has raised.

Rebiddable suits: Five cards headed by Q-J-9, K-J, or

better; or *any* six cards. May be bid and then rebid once without support.

Choice of Suits. With two biddable suits of different lengths, bid the longer suit first; if they are of the same length, bid the higher-ranking. *Exception:* With clubs and hearts or spades, prefer to bid one club.

HIGHER OPENING BIDS. *Opening Suit-bids of Two.* Requirements are:

With a good 5-card suit	25 points
With a good 6-card suit	23 points
With a good 7-card suit	21 points

With a second good 5-card suit, one point less is needed; if the game is to be in a minor suit, 2 points more will be needed. This bid is forcing to game.

Opening Suit-bids of Three or Four. These are preëmptive bids made to shut out the opponents (discourage them from bidding). The bidder must have a reasonably good suit and must be able to win without support within two tricks of his contract if vulnerable; within three tricks if not vulnerable. Such bids indicate weakness in high-card strength and should not be made if the hand contains more than 10 points in high cards. In other words, do not preëmpt with a hand which qualifies as an opening one-bid.

RAISES OF OPENING BIDS. *Adequate Trump Support.* No raise should be given to partner's suit without at least Q-x-x, J-10-x, K-x-x, A-x-x or any four trumps, unless partner has rebid the suit, in which case a raise may be given with Q-x, K-x, A-x or any three trumps.

Valuation for Raises. Add the points assigned for: (a) high cards at their face value; (b) short suits, as follows:

Add 1 point for each doubleton.
Add 3 points for each singleton.
Add 5 points for a void.

Deductions must be made when the dummy hand contains defects. The most common defects are possession of only three trumps and possession of a 4-3-3-3 distribution. In either instance 1 point must be deducted.

When to Raise. With adequate trump support and 7 to 10 points, raise partner's one-bid to two. With four or more trumps and 13 to 16 points, raise to three (forcing to game). At least 10 of these points must be in high cards. A raise to four is a preëmptive bid, showing at least five trumps, a 5-card or longer side suit, and 6 to 8 points in high cards.

OTHER RESPONSES. *No-trump Takeouts*. Count high-card points only. Respond one no-trump with 6 to 9 points; two no-trump (forcing to game) with 13 to 15 points; three no-trump with 16 to 18 points (a hand that would justify an opening bid of one no-trump).

Suit Takeouts. Count points as for an opening suit-bid. Bid one (the "one-over-one") in a biddable suit higher-ranking than partner's with 6 or more points. Bid two in a biddable suit lower-ranking than partner's with 11 or more points. These responses are forcing for one round.

Forcing Takeouts. With a sure game and possible slam (usually at least 19 points) bid one trick more than necessary in a new suit, as two spades over partner's one diamond, or three clubs over partner's one spade. These responses are forcing to game.

Responses to Opening Suit-bids of Two. To make a positive response (any response but two no-trump) responder's hand must have at least 7 points including high cards and distribution; with less than one trick responder should have 8 points. If the hand contains less than one-half quick trick, responder must make the negative bid of two no-trump.

Responses to Preëmptive Bids. Raise a major-suit three-bid to four (game) with three winners.

Responses to Opening No-trump Bids. On a balanced hand (no singleton or very long suit) raise a one-no-trump bid as follows, counting high cards only:

8 or 9 points	Two no-trump
10 to 14 points	Three no-trump
15 to 16 points	Four no-trump
17 to 18 points	Five no-trump
19 to 20 points	Six no-trump
21 points or over	Seven no-trump

Raise a two-no-trump bid to three with 4 to 8 points. With 9 or more points make a slam try. With 6 or more points make a slam try over partner's opening three-no-trump bid. The slam try may be a suit takeout or a raise beyond three no-trump.

A takeout of an opening one-no-trump bid to two diamonds, two hearts or two spades shows less than 8 points. The opening no-trump bidder is expected to pass.

A takeout to two clubs is an artificial bid* and requires

---

* Known as the Stayman Convention.

the opening one-no-trump bidder to show any biddable major suit. This bid is forcing and should not be made with less than 8 points. The opening bidder must show any 4-card major suit as good as Q-x-x-x.

When responder has a good 5-card major suit including 10 or more points, he may jump to three of that suit.

REBIDS. *Revaluation for Rebids.* When opening bidder's suit has been raised, opener revalues his hand by adding 1 additional point for the fifth trump and 2 additional points for the sixth and each subsequent trump.

Rebids by Opening Hand. If partner gives a single raise, usually pass with 16 points or less and rebid with 17 or more points. If partner's response is one no-trump game is unlikely unless the opener has 18 or more points, but with unbalanced distribution or a 6-card suit opener should usually rebid in a suit.

If partner makes a suit takeout of the opening bid, it is forcing and the opening bidder must rebid at least once. In rebidding: With a near-minimum hand (usually, 14 or 15 points), rebid a rebiddable suit; show a new biddable suit; raise partner's suit with adequate trump support; bid *one* no-trump (but a non-jump rebid of *two* no-trump requires 15 points). With a stronger hand (usually, 18 or more points), rebid two no-trump, give partner a double raise, bid a new suit, or jump to three in a strong rebiddable suit. *Do not pass if partner's response was a jump bid.*

The principle in rebidding is: If the combined hands are likely to hold 26 points or more, continue to bid. Whenever it is apparent that the combined hands do not hold as many as 26 points, pass unless a better part-score contract seems available.

Blackwood Slam Convention. A four-no-trump bid is forcing, provided either member of the bidder's side has previously made any bid in a suit. The bidder of four no-trump tells nothing about his own hand, but requires his partner to respond as follows: Five clubs holding no ace or all four aces; five diamonds holding any one ace; five hearts holding any two aces; five spades holding any three aces.

If the four-no-trump bidder, after the response, bids five no-trump, he requires his partner to respond: Six clubs holding no king; six diamonds holding any one king; six hearts holding two kings; six spades holding any three kings; six no-trump holding all four kings.

Gerber Convention. An immediate response of four clubs to an opening bid of one, two or three no-trump requests the opening bidder to show aces as follows: he bids four diamonds holding no ace, four hearts with one ace, four spades with two aces, etc. If the four-club bidder wishes to ask for kings, he bids the next ranking suit over his partner's response to four clubs.

DEFENSIVE BIDDING. *Rule of Two and Three.* Defensive bids, made when the other side has bid and when partner has not bid, are based on a count of winners. The bidder must be able to win, in his own hand, within two tricks of his bid if vulnerable; within three tricks if not vulnerable.

Overcalls of Opponents' Bids. Overcall if holding the required winners, including at least 1½ honor-tricks and a 5-card or longer suit. An overcall at the one-level may occasionally be made in a 4-card suit.

Takeout Doubles. An informatory or takeout double, (see below) requires 13 or more points and the doubler must be prepared to support any suit his partner bids, or to rebid safely.

No-trump Overcalls. To overcall an opponent's one-bid with no-trump shows approximately the same sort of hand as an opening one-no-trump bid, including a sure stopper in the opponent's suit.

Preëmptive Overcalls. A jump overcall (as, two or three spades over an opponent's one heart) is a preëmptive bid equivalent to an opening preëmptive bid.

Overcalling in the Opponent's Suit. To bid the opponent's suit shows the ace or a void in that suit, together with a powerful hand. If partner has not yet bid, this overcall acts as a gigantic takeout double, and is a force to game; partner must respond. If partner has previously bid, the overcall is forcing to game and suggests a possible slam.

DOUBLING. A double may be either *informatory* or for *business*.

Informatory Doubles, also called *Takeout Doubles,* are conventional bids. A double is for a takeout provided (a) partner has not made any bid; (b) the doubled bid is a suit-bid of one, two or three; (c) it is the doubler's first opportunity to double.

The takeout double announces that even though the opponents have opened the bidding, the doubler has a strong hand. He does not want his partner to pass the double, but requests his partner to take out the double by showing his best suit.

Penalty or "Business" Doubles. Any double other than an informatory double simply announces that the doubler wishes to have the opponents play at the last bid they made, where he believes he can defeat the contract. The doubler's partner is supposed to pass a business double, unless there is some more profitable bid he feels he can make.

ARTIFICIAL BIDS. *Cue-bids.* A bid in a suit an opponent has already bid is called a cue-bid. It is an artificial bid, showing a strong hand together with "first-round control" (that is, ability to win a trick the first time the suit is led) in the opponents' suit, but not actually implying any intention or desire to play the hand in the suit named.

Another kind of cue-bid is made to show the ace of a previously unbid suit. For example, a partnership reaches a contract of four hearts, then one partner bids five clubs. He shows the ♣A.

Any cue-bid is forcing. In almost all cases a cue-bid suggests an eventual slam.

Two-club Bid. Many players do not use the opening two-bid as a forcing bid as described on page 124. With a similarly strong hand, an opening bid of two clubs is made. The two-club bid may and may not contain a club suit; it merely shows partner a game-going hand and requires him to keep the bidding open. If partner has a good hand (usually, about 1½ honor-tricks) he responds as though he were responding to a one-bid. If partner has a weak hand, he makes an artificial response of two diamonds, whether or not he has a diamond suit. The opening bidder then proceeds to show his genuine suit, or to bid no-trump, and the bidding proceeds normally thereafter.

Vanderbilt Club Bid (see page 122). Many players use an opening one-club bid as an artificial opening bid, in the same manner that the two-club bid described in the preceding paragraph is used. Usually, the opening one-club bid shows 3½ quick tricks and does not necessarily promise any strength in clubs; the partner must respond one diamond if he has less than 2 quick tricks, and if he has 2 quick tricks

he responds normally, bidding two diamonds if his suit
happens to be diamonds.

OPENING LEADS. The following table shows the proper
card to lead from any given suit holding, the selection
varying in some cases depending on whether the contract
is a trump or no-trump one.

HOLDING IN SUIT	LEAD AT SUIT BID	LEAD AT NO-TRUMP
A-K-Q alone or with others	K, then Q	K, then Q
A-K-J-x-x-x-x	K, then A	A, then K
A-K-J-x-x or A-K-x-x (-x)	K, then A	Fourth best
A-Q-J-x-x	A	Q
A-K-x	K	K
A-Q-10-9	A	10
A-Q-x-x (-x)	A	Fourth best
A-J-10-x	A	J
A-10-9-x	A	10
A-x-x-x (-x)	A	Fourth best
A-K alone	A	K
K-Q-10 alone or with others	K	K
K-Q-x-x (-x-x)	K	Fourth best*
K-Q alone	K	K
K-J-10 alone or with others	J	J
K-10-9-x	10	10
Q-J-10 or Q-J-9 alone or with others	Q	Q
Q-J-x or Q-J	Q	Q
Q-J-8-x (four or more)	Q	Fourth best*
Q-10-9 alone or with others	10	10
J-10-9 or J-10-8 alone or with others	J	J
J-10-x or J-10	J	J
J-10-x-x or more	J	Fourth best
10-9-8 or 10-9-7, alone or with others	10	10
10-9-x-x (-x)	10	Fourth best
K-J-x-x (-x-x)	Fourth best	Fourth best
And other four-card or longer suit not listed above	Fourth best	Fourth best
Any two cards	High card	High card
Three small cards.	Highest	Highest
A-J-x, A-x-x, K-J-x, K-x-x, Q-10-x, Q-x-x, J-x-x of partner's suit	Highest	Lowest

* Lead the highest if partner has bid the suit.

The opening lead of an ace against a no-trump contract calls upon partner to play his highest card of the suit led. The opening lead of a king against a no-trump contract calls upon partner to play his second-highest card of the suit led. This rule is not followed at suit contracts, nor is it followed at no-trump contracts with the partner can see that he might risk a trick by so playing.

THE RULE OF ELEVEN. When the leader has led his fourth-highest card, subtracting the card led from 11 will give the number of higher cards in the other three hands. This is the "rule of eleven."

SIGNALS IN PLAY. *The High-Low.* When a player unnecessarily discards or follows suit with a card that is not the lowest one available to him, and later plays or discards a lower card in the same suit, the series of plays acts as a signal that asks his partner to continue leading that suit.

Encouraging and Discouraging Signals. When at any time a player discards what seems to be an unusually high card, the presumption is that he wants a lead in the suit in which his high discard is made. The play of such a card is therefore called "encouraging."

Likewise, the play of one's lowest card is considered to discourage a lead of that suit.

Plays from Sequences. When one leads from a sequence of cards, he leads the highest card in the sequence (except that K is led from A-K). When he is following suit to someone else's lead, however, he always plays the lowest card in sequence.

Duplicate Bridge

DUPLICATE BRIDGE is a method of eliminating the luck of the deal. It is virtually the only form of Contract Bridge played in tournaments.

NUMBER OF PLAYERS. Four players in two partnerships may play Replay Duplicate. Eight or more players may play a pair game, an individual game, or a team-of-four match.

EQUIPMENT. A set of duplicate boards, or trays, and one pack of cards for each board. Each tray has four pockets, corresponding to the compass points, for holding the hands of the respective players. The face of each tray is marked with an arrow pointing toward one pocket, and with an indication of the dealer and vulnerability. There should be at least 16 boards to a set, numbered consecutively, with dealer and vulnerability as follows:

DEALER	VULNERABILITY
N—1, 5, 9, 13	Neither—1, 8, 11, 14
E—2, 6, 10, 14	N-S only—2, 5, 12, 15
S—3, 7, 11, 15	E-W only—3, 6, 9, 16
W—4, 8, 12, 16	Both—4, 7, 10, 13

Boards numbered 17 to 32, if used, correspond to boards 1 to 16 respectively except in their identifying numbers.

SHUFFLE AND DEAL. Any player, in the presence of an opponent or of the tournament director, prepares a board by shuffling the pack of cards and dealing it, one card at a time face down, into four packets, each of which he inserts in a pocket of the duplicate board.

THE AUCTION. The arrow on the board is pointed in the direction of the room designated as North. Each player takes the hand from the pocket nearest him, and counts his cards to make sure he has thirteen. The player designated as dealer calls first, and the auction proceeds as described on page 111 until the contract is determined. There is no redeal when a hand is passed out.

THE PLAY. The opening lead, exposure of dummy, and subsequent play are as described on page 112, except:

After a trick is completed, each player retains possession of his card and places it face down on the table directly in front of him, pointed lengthwise toward the partners who won the trick. Declarer plays dummy's cards by naming or touching them, and dummy turns them and keeps them in front of him.

SCORING. The score of each board is independent of the scores of the other boards, and trick points scored on one board cannot count toward game on a subsequent board. No rubber premium is scored. Instead the following premiums are scored:

	DECLARER'S SIDE	
	VULNERABLE	NOT VULNERABLE
For bidding and making a game contract	500	300
For making a contract of less than game	50	50

If match-point scoring is used to determine the winner of the game, there is no premium for holding honors in one hand.

In other respects the scoring of each board follows the schedule shown on pages 113–114.

DETERMINING THE WINNER. Match-point scoring is always used in individual games, is most often used in pair games, and may be used in team-of-four games. Cumulative (or "total-point") scoring may be used in pair and team-of-four games.

Cumulative or Total-Point Scoring. All the points scored by a pair on all hands it played are totalled at the end of the game and compared with the scores of other pairs that played the same boards *in the same direction* (N-S or E-W). The highest total wins.

Match-Point Scoring. Match-point scoring is the most popular and the most equitable method for duplicate play. In this method all scores made by N-S pairs on a given deal are tabulated in a vertical column for purposes of comparison. Each score receives one match-point for each other N-S score it beats and ½ match-point for each N-S score it ties. For example, in a section of 9 tables, there would be 9 scores; the highest score would have beaten 8 others and would therefore receive 8 match-points; the second highest score would have beaten 7 others and would receive 7 match-points, etc. The E-W scores are similarly tabulated and compared among themselves.

Contract Bridge Variations

GOULASHES

Strictly speaking, the "goulash" hand (also called Mayonnaise, or Hollandaise) is not a game, but only a way of creating freak hands in a regular Bridge game. It is played only by special agreement, for example to have a goulash after a hand has been passed out.

Every player assorts his cards into suits. Dealer places his sorted hand, face down, in the center of the table; on top of this is placed the hand of the player on his left, then his partner's hand, then the hand of the player on his right. The cards may now be dealt with or without a cut; it is preferable to have them cut. Dealer gives five cards at a time to each player, then another five cards at a time to each player, then three cards at a time to each player. The resultant hands are bid, played and scored as in Auction or Contract Bridge. The assortment of the cards almost always results in freakish hands.

CUTTHROAT CONTRACT

This is a four-hand Contract Bridge game in which the partnerships are not fixed in advance but are determined by the bidding. It is the invention of S. B. Fishburne. The name Cutthroat Contract is also used for three-hand Bridge (page 135).

THE AUCTION. After the same preliminaries as in Contract Bridge, with the 52-card pack, the four players proceed to bid as in Contract Bridge except: (1) a player is subject to penalty if he makes the opening bid without having at least three honor-tricks or 13 points and at least four cards in the suit bid; (2) the first bid may be any legal bid, from one club up, but the second bid may be no lower than three no-trump (in some games, four no-trump).

If the final bid is not sufficient for game, the cards are

thrown in and a goulash is dealt. No doubling is permitted during the auction, so a player is always safe in making a part-score bid, no matter how unprepared he may be to play it.

If the final bid is sufficient for game, the player who made it becomes the declarer and selects any of the other players as his partner. Unless that player is already in the seat opposite declarer, he exchanges places with the player in that seat.

The partner selected may now accept the partnership, in which case the scoring will be as in Contract Bridge; or may reject the partnership, in which case declarer will collect from all three other players if he makes his contract and will pay all three other players if he is defeated.

When the partnership has been accepted or rejected, the defender on declarer's left may double, and if he does not, the other defender may double. If doubled, declarer may redouble (or dummy may redouble if he has accepted).

THE PLAY proceeds as in Contract Bridge.

SCORING. A separate score is kept for each player, who may score both above and below the line. A player holding honors receives the only score for them. If a vulnerable declarer makes his contract and neither defender is vulnerable, declarer scores 700 points as a rubber bonus; if either defender is vulnerable he scores only 500. If dummy has accepted the partnership and is not vulnerable, he gets only 300 points for game even though declarer wins the rubber; but if he and declarer are both vulnerable, both score the rubber bonus.

If declarer is defeated, and he is vulnerable (or dummy is vulnerable and has accepted) the defenders score the under-trick penalties at vulnerable rates.

When a player has won two games, the rubber ends; all scores are totalled up and each player settles with each other player on the difference in their scores.

IRREGULARITIES. If a player passes out of turn, each of the other three players scores 50; if he bids or doubles out of turn, each of the other players scores 300. An insufficient bid must be corrected unless the player next in turn has called, but is not subject to any other penalty.

If declarer made the opening bid, and does not have the requirements, he may announce this fact before selecting his partner and in that case there is no penalty; if it is discovered after he has selected his partner, declarer pays 300 points to each player. If declarer's partner opened the bidding without the requirements, declarer may call the deal off and he and the other two players each score the 300-point penalty; or declarer may condone the offense, in which case there is no penalty.

STRATEGY. Every player tries to doublecross every other player. Fake bids that misrepresent the hand are frequent, the idea being to induce one's selection as a partner, and then, by rejection, to collect undertrick penalties.

VARIANT. Many players play the following rules: (1) When an opening bid is made, the next player in turn must bid four no-trump (or any higher bid), regardless of his hand. (2) A player who opens without the minimum in honor-tricks (or points) must always pay the penalty of 300 points per player.

THREE-HAND BRIDGE (CUTTHROAT BRIDGE)

Any three-hand Bridge game may be played with either Auction or Contract Bridge scoring.

CUTTHROAT BRIDGE. Three players, but the preliminaries and deal are as in Contract Bridge. The hand between dealer's two opponents is left on the table untouched until the auction is completed. Dealer has the first turn to call, and the auction proceeds as in Contract Bridge until two successive passes following any call close the auction. The player at the left of the high bidder than leads, and the high bidder sorts the dummy and spreads it opposite himself and between his two opponents. Play proceeds as in Contract Bridge.

SCORING. A separate score is kept for each player. If declarer fulfills his contract, he scores the proper points; if he is defeated, each of his opponents scores the penalty points in full. If a defender holds honors, both defenders score them.

If Contract Bridge scoring is used, the winner of the rubber scores 500 points bonus if either opponent has a game, and 700 points if neither has a game. If Auction Bridge scoring is being used, the winner of a game scores 125 points bonus and the winner of the rubber scores 250 points in addition.

IRREGULARITIES. The Laws of Contract Bridge should be followed for all irregularities occurring or continuing after the auction ends. During the auction there is no penalty for a bid out of turn or an insufficient bid, but either opponent may demand that an insufficient bid be made sufficient. A bid out of turn is void unless both opponents condone it. A double out of turn may be cancelled by the player who is doubled, and thereafter neither opponent may double him at any contract.

EXCHANGE DUMMY. This is no different from regular Three-hand Bridge except that, at the close of the auction, declarer puts his own hand down as dummy and takes the unexposed fourth hand as his own.

TRIO. This is the best of all three-hand Bridge games. It was developed by George S. Coffin.

The three players are designated as South, North, and East, occupying those compass positions. Four hands are dealt. The dummy always belongs to East. The entire dummy is arranged and exposed before the bidding begins. The turn to deal passes from player to player, but South always bids first and North-South are always partners against East.

The turn to bid is South, North, East, and so on; dummy has no turn to bid. Any player may become declarer and the opening lead is always made by the hand at his left, but no hand except dummy (West) is ever exposed.

Scoring is exactly as in Contract Bridge. At the end of the rubber the players change places so that a different player sits East and gets the dummy.

TWO-HAND BRIDGE

Nearly all two-hand Bridge games are called "Honeymoon Bridge." There are several different ways of playing.

DOUBLE DUMMY. Four hands are dealt, as in Contract Bridge. The two players sit in adjoining positions at the table, not opposite each other. The hand opposite each player is that player's dummy.

Without looking at their dummies, the players bid as in Contract Bridge, dealer first, until a pass following any call closes the auction. Each player then looks at his dummy.

In one variant, the opening lead is made from the hand at declarer's left, then both dummies are exposed and the cards are played out, each hand playing in turn, each player choosing the card to play from his dummy.

In the other variant, neither player exposes his dummy to his opponent. Racks for holding the cards can be obtained and placed on the table in such position that a player cannot see his opponent's dummy but can see his own.

When the play is finished, the result may be scored as in either Auction or Contract Bridge.

SEMI-EXPOSED DUMMY. After the four hands have been dealt, six cards of each dummy are placed face down in a row, and the other seven cards of that dummy are turned up, one being placed on each of the face-down cards. The bidding ended, play proceeds with six cards of each dummy still face down; a player must play as he can from his dummy's exposed cards, and when a play from dummy uncovers a face-down card, that card is turned up.

DRAW BRIDGE. The players face each other across the table. Thirteen cards are dealt to each, one at a time, and the other twenty-six cards are placed face down to form the stock. Non-dealer leads first, and the cards are played as at no-trump, two cards constituting a trick. After each trick, each player draws a card from the stock, the winner of the trick drawing first. The first thirteen tricks do not count. When the stock is exhausted, there is an auction as in Contract Bridge, dealer bidding first; then the last thirteen tricks are played and a record is kept of them, the result being scored as in Auction or Contract Bridge.

FOUR-DEAL BRIDGE (Chicago)

The Laws of Contract Bridge are followed, except as modified by the following rules.

THE RUBBER. A rubber consists of a series of four deals that have been bid and played. If a deal is passed out, the same player deals again and the deal passed out does not count as one of the four deals.

A fifth deal is void if attention is drawn to it at any time before there has been a new cut for partners or the game has terminated; if the error is not discovered in time for correction, the score stands as recorded. A sixth or subsequent deal is unconditionally void and no score for such a deal is ever permissible.

In case fewer than four deals are played, the score shall stand for the incomplete series unless attention is drawn to the error before there has been a new cut for partners or the game has been terminated.

When the players are pivoting, the fact that the players have taken their proper seats for the next rubber shall be considered a cut for partners.

VULNERABILITY. Vulnerability is not determined by previous scores but by the following schedule:

First Deal. Neither side vulnerable.

Second and Third Deals. Dealer's side vulnerable; other side not vulnerable. (In some games, this is reversed.)

Fourth Deal. Both sides vulnerable.

PREMIUMS. For making or completing a game (100 or more trick points) a side receives a premium of 300 points if on that deal it is not vulnerable or 500 points if on that deal it is vulnerable. There is no additional premium for winning two or more games, each game premium being scored separately.

THE SCORE. As a reminder of vulnerability in Four-Deal Bridge, two intersecting diagonal lines should be drawn near the top of the score pad.

The numeral "1" should be inserted in that one of the four angles thus formed that faces the first dealer. After play of the first deal is completed, "2" is inserted in the next angle in clockwise rotation, facing the dealer of the second deal. The numerals "3" and "4" are subsequently inserted at the start of the third and fourth deals respectively, each in the angle facing the current dealer.

A correctly numbered diagram is conclusive as to vulnerability. There is no redress for a bid influenced by the scorer's failure to draw the diagram or for an error or omission in inserting a numeral or numerals in the diagram. Such error or omission should, upon discovery, be immediately corrected and the deal or deals should be scored or rescored as though the diagram and the number or numbers thereon had been properly inserted.

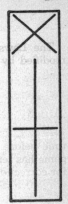

PART-SCORES. A part-score or -scores made previously may be combined with a part-score made in the current deal to complete a game of 100 or more trick points. The game premium is determined by the vulnerability, on that deal, of the side that completes the game. When a side makes or completes a game, no previous part-score of either side may thereafter be counted toward game.

A side that makes a part-score in the fourth deal, if the part-score is not sufficient to complete a game, receives a premium of 100 points. This premium is scored whether or not the same side or the other side has an uncompleted part-score. There is no separate premium for making a part-score in any other circumstances.

DEAL OUT OF TURN. When a player deals out of turn, and there is no right to a redeal, the player who should have dealt retains his right to call first, but such right is lost if it is not claimed before the actual dealer calls. If the actual dealer calls before attention is drawn to the deal out of turn, each player thereafter calls in rotation. Vulnerability and scoring values are determined by the position of the player who should have dealt, regardless of which player actually dealt or called first. Neither the rotation of the deal nor the scoring is affected by a deal out of turn. The next dealer is the player who would have dealt next if the deal had been in turn.

Pinochle

PINOCHLE is an American game based on the French Bézique and the German Sixty-six. In popularity it ranks fourth among American games, after Rummy, Bridge, and Poker. The most popular forms are the four-hand partnership game and the game generally called Auction Pinochle, devised for three players but usually played by four; nevertheless, two-hand Pinochle, the original game, is described first.

TWO-HAND PINOCHLE

PLAYERS. Two.

CARDS. The Pinochle pack of 48 cards, two each of the A, 10, K, Q, J, 9 (ranking in that order) in each suit; in the variant known as Goulash, or 64-card Pinochle, a pack of 64 cards, including two 7's and 8's of each suit.

PRELIMINARIES. Nondealer may shuffle, then dealer shuffles last and nondealer cuts, leaving at least five cards in each packet. The winner of each hand deals next, if each hand is played as a separate game; when the game of 1,000 points is played, the deal alternates.

DEALING. Dealer gives twelve cards to each player, three at a time face down (in the 64-card game, sixteen cards each, four at a time). He turns the next card up; it is the trump card and every card of its suit is a trump. The undealt cards are placed so as to partly cover the trump card, which is face up in the center of the table; this forms the *stock*.

OBJECTS OF THE GAME. The object is to score points, either by melds or by winning tricks containing counting cards.

A player melds by placing the necessary cards face up on the table before him, immediately after winning a trick in the play, and before drawing from the stock. The following are the combinations that constitute melds:

140

SEQUENCES

A-K-Q-J-10 of trump (flush)	150
K-Q of trump (royal Marriage)	40
K-Q of any other suit (Marriage)	20

GROUPS

♠A-♡A-◇A-♣A (100 aces)	100
♠K-♡K-◇K-♣K (80 kings)	80
♠Q-♡Q-◇Q-♣Q (60 queens)	60
♠J-♡J-◇J-♣J (40 jacks)	40

SPECIAL

♠Q-◇J (pinochle)	40
9 of trumps (*dix*, pronounced deece)— in the 64-card game, 7 of trumps	10

The following rules apply to melding:

1. Only one meld may be made in each turn.

2. For each meld, at least one card must be taken from the hand and placed on the table, but a card or cards may be taken from the hand and combined with one or more cards already on the table;

3. The same card may not be used twice in the same meld, nor in any two melds of the same class except that K-Q of trumps may be melded for 40 and A-J-10 added for 150.

It should be noted that there are two identical cards of each suit and rank, and though one of them has been used in a meld, the other may be used in an identical meld composed, however, entirely of cards not used in the first meld.

Values of Tricks. Each ace taken in on a trick counts 11; each ten, 10; each king, 4; each queen, 3; each jack, 2. The winner of the last trick counts 10. Lower cards count nothing in tricks.

The Dix. After winning a trick, a player may exchange the dix for the trump card (or for a dix previously exchanged for it), taking the trump card into his hand and leaving the dix there, and counting 10 points. If dealer turns the dix as a trump card, he scores 10 immediately.

THE PLAY. Nondealer leads any card to the first trick and dealer plays any card to the lead, the two cards constituting a trick; thereafter the winner of each trick leads next. The card led loses the trick to a higher card of the same suit, or to a trump if the lead was not a trump; but otherwise wins.

After each trick, until the stock is exhausted, each player draws a card face down from the stock, nondealer drawing first. When the stock is exhausted, the winner must show the card he draws, while the loser takes the trump card or the dix exchanged for it.

After the stock is exhausted, the last cards are played and it is necessary to follow suit to the card led if able to do so; to win the trick if possible when a trump is led; and to trump if possible when unable to follow suit to a lead of any other suit.

SCORING. *Use of Chips.* Each player may be supplied with a stack of chips, and as he scores points he removes chips from the stack. It is just as effective and almost as convenient to keep score with pencil and paper.

Count of Cards. The points for cards won in tricks are not scored until the last trick has been played. The winner of the last trick counts the points he has won in cards and adds 10 for last trick. If his opponent disputes the count, his opponent's tricks are also counted. The total of points must be 250. Scores are always entered in even tens, and a fraction of 6 points or less does not count. A fraction of 7 points or more counts as a full 10.

Declaring Out (when game is 1,000). At any point in the game, a player who believes he has scored 1,000 points, including melds and cards won to that point, may declare himself out. Play ceases and his cards are counted and their total added to his previous score. If he has 1,000 points, he wins the game. If he has less than 1,000 points, he loses.

Inconclusive Game. If neither player declares himself out, and at the end of the play each player has 1,000 points or more, the game is undecided and becomes 1,250. Play continues until one player reaches 1,250, or declares himself out at 1,250 under the rule given above. If the game is undecided at 1,250, the winning total becomes 1,500; if undecided at 1,500, it becomes a game of 1,750; and so on. Whatever the number of points required for game, a player may declare himself out at any time he claims to have reached that total.

IRREGULARITIES. *Misdeal.* A misdeal does not lose the deal. If the dealer exposes one of his opponent's cards in dealing, the opponent may demand a new deal or may let the deal stand. If either player was dealt too many or too few cards, either player may call for a new deal before he has led or played to the first trick; thereafter, it stands.

Exposed Card in Stock. If a card is found exposed in the stock, dealer shuffles the stock (except for the trump card or dix), nondealer cuts and play is resumed.

Wrong Number of Cards. A player with the wrong number of cards may not meld until he has corrected his number of cards and then won a trick. If he has too few cards, he draws enough cards to restore his hand to the proper number; if he has too many cards, he does not draw until, at the end of any trick, his hand has been reduced to eleven cards.

Drawing Out of Turn. When a player draws out of turn, his opponent may let the draw stand as regular, but in that case it does not change the lead to the next trick; or may demand the card illegally drawn, in which case the offender must show the card he next draws from the stock.

Drawing More Than One Card. If a player draws more than one card at a turn, he keeps the top card but must show it, and each other card he drew, to his opponent. Each card illegally drawn must then be replaced on top of the stock.

Stock Incorrect. If at any time it is found that the number of cards in the stock is odd when it should be even, both hands being correct, and the pack being correct, play continues. When only two cards remain in the stock, the player whose turn it is to draw may elect to take the trump card or the other. If he takes the trump card, the other is then exposed. The rejected card in either case does not count.

Revoke. A player who, during the last twelve tricks, fails to observe the rules regarding following suit, trumping and winning a trump trick, has revoked. If each deal is a game, he loses the game. When game is 1,000 points, the offender may score nothing for cards; but play continues to determine the winner of last trick and the nonoffender's points.

THREE-HAND PINOCHLE

The 64-card pack is used, and the rotation is to the left. Each player is dealt twelve cards. Each plays to every trick, and when identical cards are played the one played first outranks the other. Only the winner of the trick may meld, then all three in rotation draw from the stock, the winner first. Each player has a separate score. The first to reach 1,000 wins the game. Other rules are as in two-hand Pinochle.

Auction Pinochle

PLAYERS. There are three players in each deal. The game is better for four, the dealer taking no cards; five often play in the same game, and sometimes even six.

CARDS. 48 cards, two each of A, K, Q, J, 10 and 9 in each of four suits, spades, hearts, diamonds and clubs. The cards in each suit rank A (high), 10, K, Q, J, 9.

DEALING. When there are four players, dealer receives no cards; when there are five players, dealer and the player second from his left receive no cards; when there are six players, these players and the player at dealer's right receive no cards. Players who receive no cards are *inactive* and may give neither advice nor information to the active players.

Dealer gives cards to each active player in turn, either three at a time throughout or four at a time for the first three rounds and three at a time for the last round. After the first round of dealing, dealer must give three cards face down in the center of the table to the *widow*. The whole pack being dealt, each player has fifteen cards.

OBJECTS OF THE GAME. The objects of the game are to score points by melding and by winning in tricks cards having scoring values.

SEQUENCES

A-K-Q-J-10 of trump (flush)	150
K-Q of trump (royal Marriage)	40
K-Q of any other suit (Marriage)	20

GROUPS

♠A-♡A-◇A-♣A (100 aces)	100
♠K-♡K-◇K-♣K (80 kings)	80
♠Q-♡Q-◇Q-♣Q (60 queens)	60
♠J-♡J-◇J-♣J (40 jacks)	40

SPECIAL

♠Q-◇J (pinochle)	40
9 of trumps (*dix*, pronounced deece)	10

A card which is part of a meld under one heading may be counted as part of a meld under another heading but may not be counted as part of another meld under the same heading.

The scoring values of cards taken in tricks, and of the last trick, are: Each ace, 11; each ten, 10; each king, 4; each queen, 3; each jack, 2; last trick, 10. The nines have no scoring value when taken in tricks. Some players simplify the count by counting aces and tens 10 each, kings and queens 5 each, jacks and nines nothing. Other players count aces, tens and kings 10 each, queens, jacks and nines nothing. In any case, the last trick counts 10 and the total of points scored in each deal is 250.

BIDDING. Each active player in turn, beginning with the player at dealer's left, must make a bid or must pass. A bid is expressed in points only, in multiples of 10 points, and each bid must be higher than the last preceding bid. The player at dealer's left must bid 300 or more; though in some games a minimum bid of 250 is permitted, in other games a minimum bid of 200, and in still other games the first player is not required to bid, whereupon a deal may be passed out.

Having passed, a player may not thereafter bid. When two players have passed, the auction is closed. The highest bid becomes the contract, and the player who made the highest bid becomes the Bidder. The other two players jointly are the *opponents*.

THE KITTY. A separate score, or a separate pile of chips, is maintained for an imaginary extra player called the *kitty*, which is the joint property of all players in the game. If the kitty has a deficit, they must supply it equally. When any player leaves the game, each player takes his proportionate share of the kitty's score or chips.

In all games, the kitty solely collects when the Bidder concedes defeat without exposing the widow. In most games, the kitty pays or collects the same as any other player when the bid is 350 or more, and in many games the kitty collects if a bid of less than 350 is played and not made (double bete).

THE WIDOW. If the Bidder obtained the contract at 300 (or such other minimum bid as is determined by the rules of the game), the Bidder may decline to expose the widow and pay to the kitty a forfeit equivalent to the value of a 300 or other minimum bid, after which the deal passes to the next player in turn.

In any other case, the Bidder, immediately after the bidding is closed, turns the three cards of the widow face up on the table so that all players may see them. After this he takes them into his hand.

MELDING. Only the Bidder may meld. He shows on the table any combinations of cards that have melding values. Having shown his melds, the Bidder takes them back into his hand; but, on demand, he must show his melds again at any time before either opponent has played to the first trick.

The Bidder may change his meld at any time before he has led to the first trick.

BURYING. After melding, and preferably before picking up any cards he shows on the table, the Bidder must *bury* or lay away, face down, any three cards that he has not melded, to reduce the number of cards in his hand to fifteen. The cards laid away count as though they were a trick won by the Bidder. It is not necessary for the Bidder to announce the fact when he lays away a trump, an ace, or any other card.

At the same time, the Bidder announces the trump suit. He may change his meld, the cards he buries and the trump suit as often as he wishes before he leads to the first trick, but not thereafter. If the Bidder names the trump suit and both opponents concede, he may not then change the trump suit.

THE PLAY. The Bidder always leads to the first trick. He may lead any card.

The card led and two cards, one each played in turn by the other two active players, constitute a *trick*. Any trick containing a trump is won by the player who played the highest trump; any other trick is won by the player who played the highest card of the suit led. Of two cards of identical suit and rank, the one played first is the higher. The winner of each trick leads to the next, and may lead any card.

If the card led is a trump, each player must, if able, play a higher trump than any previously played to the trick. This is called *playing over*.

Each player must follow suit to the card led if able. If he is unable to follow suit, but holds a trump, he must play a trump. If another player has previously played a trump to the same trick, he may play any trump—he need not win the trick.

CONCESSION. The Bidder may concede defeat without leading to the first trick, whereupon he pays to each other active and inactive player the basic unit value of his bid. This is a *single bete*.

Either opponent may propose that the Bidder's contract be conceded to him, and if the other opponent agrees, the contract is made; but if the other opponent declines to concede the Bidder must commence play.

If the Bidder scores, in melds and tricks, at least as many points as he named in the contract, his contract is made. If he scores fewer points, he is *double bete*.

SCORING. It is most convenient to use chips, so that each player pays or collects after each deal, settling separately with each other player. A satisfactory score may also be kept with pencil and paper.

In settlement, the Bidder pays to or collects from every other player, *active or inactive,* and including the kitty if the contract was 350 or more. If the Bidder made his contract, he collects by any one of the following schedules, each of which is in use in one or another locality:

	BASIC UNIT VALUES			
Contract	A	B	C	D
300–340	3	3	1	1
350–390	5	5	2	3
400–440	10	10	4	7
450–490	15	20	6	10
500–540	20	40	8	13
550–590	25	80	10	16
600 or more	30	160	12	19

If the Bidder leads to the first trick and then does not fulfill his contract, he is double bete and pays twice the basic unit values shown in whichever schedule is adopted.

In nearly all circles, the basic unit values are doubled if spades are trumps. In some circles, the basic unit values are tripled if hearts are trumps.

In no case does the Bidder score more than the amount of his contract, regardless of how many points he actually scores.

Play for 1,000 Points. Some do not play each deal as a separate game, but play until any player has scored 1,000 points, when that player wins the game. If a Bidder fails to fulfill his contract, the amount of the bid is subtracted from his score, even if it gives him a net minus score.

OPTIONAL LAWS. *290 or 320.* In some games, when the minimum bid for the first two players is 250, the third player, after two passes, may not make any bid in the 250 range of less than 290; nor any bid in the 300 range of less than 320.

Bonus Payments. In some games, bonuses are paid for special melds. The most usual bonus is called "in the mitt": If the Bidder melds 100 aces without the help of the widow, he receives an additional chip from each other player if he makes his contract.

IRREGULARITIES. The following laws concerning irregularities are condensed, by permission, from the Laws of Auction Pinochle, copyright 1946.

Misdeal. There must be a new deal by the same dealer if, in dealing, the dealer exposes more than one card of any player's hand or any card of the widow.

Exposure of the Widow. If at any time before the auction closes a player handles the widow and in so doing exposes a card, there must be a new deal by the next dealer in turn, and (penalty) the offender must pay to each other player, including the kitty and every inactive player, the unit value of the highest bid last made prior to his offense.

Incorrect Hand. If any player or the widow has too few cards and another player, or the widow, has too many: If it is discovered before the widow has been properly exposed by the Bidder, the hand with too few cards draws the excess, face down, from the player or widow having too many; if it is discovered at any later time, and if the Bidder's hand (including the widow) contains the correct number of cards, the Bidder's contract is made; if the Bidder's hand contains an incorrect number of cards, he is single or double bete, depending on whether or not he has led to the first trick.

If the widow has too few cards, there must be another deal by the same dealer.

Exposure of Cards. If an opponent drops, or names, or otherwise exposes his possession of any *one* card, except in leading or playing it: When first he can legally lead or play that card he must so announce and the Bidder may either require or forbid him to play it. Pending such time the card must be left face up on the table. If the opponents, or either of them, expose more than one card, the Bidder's contract is made.

Bid Out of Turn. A bid out of turn is void without penalty; but the other two players (or either of them, if the other has passed) may treat it as a correct bid by bidding or passing over it.

Insufficient Bid. If a bid in turn is not high enough to overcall the last preceding bid it is considered a pass; except that the other two players (or either of them, if the other has passed) may treat it as a correct bid by bidding over it.

Improper Burying. If the Bidder leads before burying, or buries a card he has melded, or buries too many or too few cards and as a result has an incorrect number of cards in his hand, he is double bete.

Information as to the Auction and Meld. Until an opponent has played to the first trick, the opponents may ask or state the number and nature of the cards melded by the Bidder, the trump, the point value of the meld, the amount of the bid, and the number of points the Bidder needs to win in cards. After either opponent has played to the first trick, any player may ask only what the trump suit is; if an opponent asks or gives any other information, play ceases and the Bidder's contract is made.

Looking at Turned Card. Any player may turn and look at a trick until his side has played to the next trick. If the Bidder turns and looks at a trick thereafter, he is double bete; if an opponent does so, the contract is made.

Revoke (Renege) A player revokes, if, when able to play as required by law, he fails to do so. A revoke may be corrected before a member of the revoking side has led or played to the next trick, and if the offender is the Bidder, the opponents may withdraw any cards played to the next trick, but there is no other penalty; if the offender is an opponent, play continues but the Bidder does not pay if he fails to fulfill his contract.

A revoke becomes established when either member of the revoking side has led or played to the next trick, and if the offender is the Bidder, he is double bete; if the offender is an opponent, the contract is made.

If both sides revoke, the penalty applies to the offense to which attention is first called; if attention to both revokes is drawn simultaneously, the penalty applies to the offense which was committed first.

Lead Out of Turn. If the Bidder leads when it was an opponent's turn to lead, there is no penalty; the opponent whose lead it was may choose to treat the lead as a correct one, or may require that the card be withdrawn. If an opponent leads when it is not his turn to lead, it is treated as a revoke.

Claim or Concession. If at any time after the first lead is made: (a) The Bidder concedes that he is bete, or an opponent exposes or throws in his cards or expressly concedes that the contract is made, play ceases and the concession is binding; (b) An opponent suggests concession, as by saying to his partner, "Shall we give it to him?", the concession is not valid, and play must continue unless said partner agrees; (c) The Bidder claims that the contract is made, or an opponent claims that the Bidder is bete, play ceases and all unplayed cards are taken by the side which did not make the claim.

Error in Count of Meld. (a) If, after the Bidder leads to the first trick, he is found to lack a card essential to a meld he announced but did not show, he is double bete. (b) If an incorrect point value was agreed upon for the Bidder's meld, correction may be made at any time before settlement is completed.*

STRATEGY. *Bidding.* Conservatism in bidding is the primary requirement for winning at Auction Pinochle. Except in unusual cases, a player should bid only upon values already held in his hand. He can count on adding about 20 points in playing strength. It is almost invariably bad tactics to stretch a sure 300-hand to a doubtful 350, or a sure 350-hand to a doubtful 400.

Altogether there are 5,465 possible three-card buys. The following table gives the figures on the various chances:

---

* *Example:* The contract is 350. Bidder shows ♠A K Q J 10 9 and ◇K Q J. The agreed value is 210; Bidder plays and takes in 134. Before paying, he recalls that his melds as shown actually totalled 220. The contract is made.

PLACES OPEN	FAVORABLE CASES	ODDS
1	961	5 to 1 against
2	1802	2 to 1 against
3	2531	23 to 20 against
4	3156	1½ to 1 for
5	3685	2 to 1 for
6	4126	3 to 1 for

When to Play. Assuming that spades are double: If spades are trumps, play if you have at least an even chance to make the contract. If any other suit is trumps, play even if the odds are as much as 2 to 1 against your making it.

Suppose diamonds are trumps and you figure that the odds are 2 to 1 against your making it. That is, if you play the hand three times you would make it only once and be double bete twice. The bid is 300. Here is how it works out:

If you concede all three times you lose 3 x 9, or 27 chips in all.

If you play all three times you collect 9 chips the time you make it, but lose 18 + 18 the two times you are double bete. You will have taken in 9 and paid out 36, losing 27 chips in all.

When spades are trumps you should have an even chance to make the contract because if you decide not to play you can name another suit as trumps and lose only a single bete, whereas if you play at spades and are double bete it costs you four times the value of the contract.

Play. The Bidder's first lead may be any card, and it is usually neither necessary nor desirable to lead trumps. Sometimes, however, trumps should be led first. From a flush (A-10-K-Q-J-9) the best first lead to limit the trump loss to two tricks is the queen. Occasionally it is necessary to play such a trump suit to lose only one trick. In such a case the ace should be led first, followed immediately by another trump lead—the nine if the ten fell on the first round (for then the only hope is that one opponent held A-10 alone), and otherwise the queen, unless the queen dropped on the first round.

Partnership Pinochle

IN THE OLDEST FORM of Partnership Pinochle, there is no bidding; a turned card establishes the trump. This basic form of the game is not described, because it has been largely superseded by bidding games—Partnership Auction Pinochle, Double-Pack Pinochle, and other variants.

PARTNERSHIP AUCTION PINOCHLE

PLAYERS. Four play in two partnerships, each player facing his partner and having an opponent at each side.

CARDS. The pack of 48 cards, as described on page 140, with the cards in each suit ranking: A (high), 10, K, Q, J, 9.

DEALING. The dealer distributes the cards in rotation, beginning with the player at his left, three at a time face down.

BIDDING. Each player in turn may bid or pass. Eldest hand bids first. The lowest possible bid is 100, and each bid must at least overcall the last previous bid. Bids must be in multiples of 10 points. Once having passed, a player may not again bid.

The highest bidder names the trump, after which melding and play proceed.

MELDING. Each player then places on the table his melds, in accordance with the table on page 141.

A side loses the melds of both its members unless either member wins a trick during the play of the cards. Winning a trick is said to make the melds "official." The trick need not contain a scoring card.

THE PLAY. When all melds have been shown, each player restores the cards to his hand. The highest bidder then leads to the first trick; he may lead any card. Each player in turn thereafter must play a card to the trick, and must observe the following rules: If holding a card of the suit led, he must follow suit; having no card of the suit led, but having a trump, he must play a trump but need not try to win the trick; if the card led was a trump, each player in turn must try to win the trick by playing a higher trump than any previously played to that trick, if he has one. If unable to play according to these rules, a player may play any card.

The four cards so played constitute a trick. A trick is won by the highest-ranking card of the suit led; or, if it contains a trump, by the highest trump it contains. Of identical cards played to the same trick, the first ranks higher. A member of the side winning the trick gathers it in and turns it down in front of him. The winner of each trick leads to the next.

SCORING. The non-bidding side always scores whatever it makes in melds and cards. The bidding side scores whatever it makes, provided this is at least as much as it bid; if it makes less than it bid, the entire amount of the bid is substracted from its score, which may give it a net minus score.

Values of Cards. When the play is completed, each side counts 10 points for each ace or ten it won in a trick, and 5 points for each king or queen it won in a trick. Jacks and nines have no scoring value. The side winning the last trick scores 10. (Some further simplify the count by making all aces, tens and kings count 10 each and no other cards count anything.) The total score by cards, including last trick, is 250.

Game is 1,000 points, as in Partnership Pinochle, but the score of the bidding side is always counted first and if it equals or passes 1,000 it wins the game even though its opponent's score, if it were counted, would be more. There is no declaring out.

IRREGULARITIES. *New Deal.* If more than one card is exposed in dealing, there must be a new deal. If dealer neglects to turn the trump card, either opponent may call for a new deal. If no new deal is demanded, a trump card is drawn, face down, from the dealer's cards before melding begins. When there is a new deal, it is by the same dealer.

Wrong Number of Cards. If one player has too many cards and another too few, and if it is discovered before these players have looked at their hands, the player with too few cards draws the extra cards from the player with too many. If the irregularity is not discovered before the players have looked at their hands, they proceed to meld, after which the player with too few cards draws the excess from the unmelded cards of the player with too many.

If it is discovered, after the play of the cards has begun, that any player has an incorrect number of cards, play continues unless it is found that the pack is incorrect; the side of the player with the incorrect hand may not score any points for cards in that deal, but does not necessarily lose its melds; a player with too few cards does not play to the last trick, while any card remaining in the hand of a player after the last trick is dead.

Insufficient bid or bid out of turn counts as a pass.

Revoke. If a player fails to follow suit, trump, or play over on a trump lead, when able, his side may not score anything for cards in that deal, but does not necessarily lose its melds.

Exposed Card. If a player illegally exposes a card, he must leave it on the table and play it at his first legal opportunity to do so; and either opponent may call a lead from the offender's partner the next time it is his turn to lead. (Many, however, penalize an exposed card as a revoke.)

Lead or Play Out of Turn. The penalty is the same as for an exposed card.

Error in Count or Scoring. A player is entitled to the full value of any melds he shows on the table, even if he announces their value incorrectly, but no correction may be made after the final score of the deal has been agreed upon by both sides and entered on the score sheet (or settled in chips). The same rule is followed when a player overstates the value of his melds or of cards won in play.

PARTNERSHIP AUCTION PINOCHLE WITH A WIDOW

Only eleven cards are dealt to each player, three at a time on the first three rounds and two at a time on the last round; the four other cards are placed face down in the center of the table. There is bidding as in Partnership Auction Pinochle. The highest bidder picks up the widow, takes one card for himself, and gives one card to each of the other players, without showing the cards. Melding and play then proceed as in Partnership Auction Pinochle.

SIX-HAND PARTNERSHIP PINOCHLE

Three play as partners against the other three. Members of the opposing sides are seated alternately, so that each player has an opponent at his right and at his left. Two 48-card Pinochle packs are mixed together to make a 96-card pack, of which each player receives sixteen cards, dealt four at a time.

The rules of Partnership Auction Pinochle, in any variant, may be followed; but it is customary to add the following bonus melds to the table shown on page 141.

Two kings and two queens of same suit	300
Three kings and three queens of same suit	600
Four kings and four queens of same suit	1200
Triple pinochle	600
Quadruple pinochle	1200
12 aces	2000
12 kings	1600
12 queens	1200
12 jacks	800
Triple royal sequence	3000
15 of same denomination, as 15 aces, etc.	3000

Eight-Hand Partnership Pinochle is the same as the six-hand game except that only twelve cards are dealt to each player, three at a time.

DOUBLE-PACK PINOCHLE

This game is virtually the only form of Partnership Pinochle played in the United States Army.

PLAYERS. Four, two against two as partners.

CARDS. 80 cards, four each of A, 10, K, Q, J (the cards ranking in that order) in each suit. Mix two regular Pinochle packs together, discarding all nines.

DEALING. All the cards are dealt out, no more than 5 and no fewer than 4 cards at a time, so that each player holds 20 cards.

BIDDING. (a) Beginning with the player at dealer's left, each player in turn must make a bid, announce a meld, or pass. Having once passed, a player may not reënter the auction.

(b) The minimum bid is 500. Each bid must be higher than any previous bid. Bids are in multiples of 10 points. When a player bids, he may announce that he has a trump sequence, or a long trump suit, but may not name a suit, may not say that he has more than one strong suit, and may give no information about his playing strength.

(c) A player in turn may announce a meld in points; he may have more than he announces. Before any player has bid, a player announcing a trump sequence or long suit is deemed to have bid 500, but announcement of a meld in points does not constitute a bid. After a bid has been made, any announcement constitutes an overcall of 10 points for each 100 points (or fraction thereof) of meld announced. (Thus: over a bid of 500, announcing a meld of 140 constitutes a bid of 520.)

(d) If no one bids in the first round, the hands are thrown in and the next player deals.

As some play, only bids and passes are allowed, no announcement of melds or long suits.

MELDING. The high bidder names the trump before melding begins. (If he does not, the first card he melds, or the bottom card—the one touching the table—of several cards melded at once, fixes the trump suit.) All players then meld, according to the following values:

SEQUENCES

A-K-Q-J-10 of trumps (flush)	150
K-Q of trumps (royal marriage)	40
K-Q of any other suit (marriage)	20

(No extra score for duplicated sequences; *e.g.*, double flush counts 300.)

GROUPS

♠A-♡A-◇A-♣A (100 aces)	100
Double aces	1000
Triple aces	1500
♠K-♡K-◇K-♣K (80 kings)	80
Double kings	800
Triple kings	1200
♠Q-♡Q-◇Q-♣Q (60 queens)	60
Double queens	600

Triple queens	900
♠J–♡J–◇J–♣J (40 jacks)	40
Double jacks	400
Triple jacks	600

(A quadruple group counts as two doubles;
e.g., sixteen aces count 2000.)

SPECIAL

♠Q–◇J (pinochle)	40
Double pinochle	300
Triple pinochle	450
Quadruple pinochle	3000

Each partner melds separately; the melds of partners
may not be combined.

A side's meld does not count unless it wins at least one
scoring card in the play.

THE PLAY. The high bidder leads, and the play follows
the rules of Partnership Pinochle. A player must follow
suit if able, play over if a trump is led, and trump if unable
to follow suit. Of duplicate cards, the one played first ranks
higher.

SCORING. Cards won in tricks count 10 each for aces,
tens, and kings; nothing for queens and jacks. (Some count
aces and tens 10 each, kings and queens 5 each, jacks 0.)
Last trick counts 20. The total score in cards is 500.

If the bidding side, in melds and cards, makes at least
the amount of its bid, it scores whatever it makes; if it
makes less than it bid, the amount of the bid is subtracted
from its score. The non-bidding side in any case scores
whatever it makes.

Game is 3,550 and the score of the bidding side is counted
first.

IRREGULARITIES. Follow the rules of Partnership Pinochle
for Misdeal and Incorrect Hand (page ???); except that
any player may demand a new deal if two players have
incorrect hands and have looked at their hands.

Revoke. A revoke may be corrected (by withdrawing
such cards as are necessary) until the revoking side has
led or played to the next trick. If it is too late for correction: the bidding side is set back the amount of its meld.
Its opponents score their meld. No points are scored for
cards.

Illegal Information. During the bidding, if a player names his suit, or says he has two suits, or gives any other illegal information, the opponents may call it a misdeal.

WIPE-OFF

This is Double-Pack Pinochle with the proviso that a side must score 200 or more points in cards to count either its meld or its cards.

FIREHOUSE PINOCHLE

This is Partnership Auction Pinochle with the following special rules: The minimum bid is 200. The high bidder must meld a marriage (or flush) in the trump suit he names. (Therefore no player may bid without a marriage.) Eldest hand bids first and leads first. Game is 1,000 and the score of the bidding side is counted first.

CHECK PINOCHLE

Rules of Partnership Auction apply (page 152), with the following additions or amendments:

Minimum bid is 200. None of the first three players may bid unless he holds a marriage. If first three players pass, dealer must assume the contract with a bid of 200; may bid more if he holds a marriage.

Game is 1,000; score of bidding side is counted first; high bidder leads first; a side loses its meld if it fails to win a trick.

CHECK AWARDS: Each partner collects from one opponent the following checks (chips):

Melding: Round trip, 5; flush, 2; 100 aces, 2; 80 kings, 60 queens, 40 jacks, 1; double pinochle 2. *Making contract*: 200–240, 2 checks; 250–290, 4; 300–340, 7; 350–390, 10; thereafter, 5 checks more for each series of 50 points. *Defeating opponents*: twice the number of checks for making contract. *Slam* (winning all 12 tricks): 5. *Winning the game*: 10, plus 1 for each 100 or fraction of their victory margin; plus 5 checks if losers have net minus score.

IRREGULARITIES: *Bidding without a Marriage*: Opponents may elect to a) abandon the deal; b) assume the contract at the highest or lowest bid they made during the auction; or c) require offending side to play at highest bid it made. *Revoke* (established when offending side leads or plays to the next trick): previous tricks stand, but all others go to offender's opponents.

Bézique

THIS IS THE original game of a family that includes all the popular American games called Pinochle. Bézique is relatively young among games, dating probably from the early 1860's. Some forms of Bézique (Rubicon, Chinese or Six-pack) are still very popular, but the original game (described next) is little played now.

PLAYERS. Two.

CARDS. The pack of 64 cards, consisting of two 32-card packs shuffled together. The cards in each suit rank: A (high), 10, K, Q, J, 9, 8, 7.

PRELIMINARIES. Each lifts a portion of the shuffled pack and shows the bottom card; if the cards are of the same rank the players cut again and continue to do so until the lower of the two cards determines the first dealer. Either player may shuffle, the dealer last. Nondealer must cut the pack.

DEALING. Each player receives eight cards, dealt 3-2-3, nondealer first. The next card is turned face up as the trump card; every card of its suit becomes a trump. The remaining cards are placed face down so as partly to cover the trump card, and become the *stock*.

OBJECT OF THE GAME. The first player to amass 1,500 points wins the game.

SCORING CARDS. Each ace or ten (called a *brisque*) taken in a trick counts 10; dealer counts 10 if he turns a seven as the trump card, and thereafter either player, upon winning a trick, may exchange a seven of trumps for the trump card, or merely show a seven of trumps and score 10 for it; and winning the last trick counts 10.

Declarations. Upon winning a trick, a player may place on the table in front of him any of the following combinations of cards and score for them as indicated:

159

Marriage (K-Q of the same suit), in trumps 40
        in any other suit...................... 20
Sequence (A-K-Q-J-10 of trumps).......250
Bézique (♠Q and ◇J).................... 40
Double bézique 500
Any four aces............................100
Any four kings........................... 80
Any four queens......................... 60
Any four jacks........................... 40

THE PLAY. Nondealer leads first. He may lead any card
and (until the stock is exhausted) his opponent may play
any card. The card led and the card played by opponent
constitute a trick, which is won by the higher card of the
suit led, or by the higher trump; when identical cards are
played to the same trick, the one led wins the trick. The
winner of each trick leads to the next, after declaring and
after drawing from the stock to restore his hand to eight
cards, the winner drawing first and his opponent next.

A declaration is made after winning a trick and before
drawing, by placing the required combination of cards face
up on the table. Once declared, the cards remain there until
the stock is exhausted, unless the holder wishes to lead or
play them, which he may do as though they were in his
hand. Only one declaration may be scored in each turn.

A card may be used in different declarations, but not
twice in the same declaration; for example, ♠Q may be
used in a marriage, sequence, bézique, and four queens; but
if four queens have been declared and one of them has
been played, another queen may not be added for the same
score. Four different queens would be required.

A king or queen of trumps which has been declared in a
sequence may not be later declared in a royal marriage.

Bézique may be declared as 40, and a second bézique
added for 500, but if double bézique is declared at the same
time it counts only 500.

The Final Play. When only one face-down card and the
trump card remain in the stock, there may be no more declaring. The winner of the next trick takes the face-down
card, and his opponent the trump card; each picks up all
declared cards he has on the table, and the last eight tricks
are played. In this play, a player is required to follow suit
to the card led, and to win the trick, if he is able to do so.

GAME. If one player reaches 1,500 points before his opponent has 1,500 points, he wins the game. If both players reach or pass 1,500 points on the same deal, the higher score wins; if they have exactly the same score, they continue play and game becomes 2,000.

IRREGULARITIES. *Incorrect Deal.* It may be rectified by mutual agreement, but either player may demand a new deal. There must be a new deal if either player is dealt too many cards and it is discovered before a card is played.

Incorrect Hand. If it is discovered at any time that each player has too many cards, there must be a new deal. If it is discovered, after both players have drawn from the stock, that a player has too few cards, play continues and the player with fewer cards than his opponent cannot win the last trick. If one player has too many cards and his opponent the right number, the opponent may either demand a new deal or permit the offender to rectify his hand by not drawing.

Illegal Draw. If a player, in drawing, sees a card he is not entitled to, his opponent at his next draw may look at the two top cards of the stock and select either.

Lead Out of Turn. It must be withdrawn on demand, but may not be withdrawn without permission.

Odd Number of Cards in Stock. The last card of the stock (trump card) is dead.

Revoke. If a player fails to play according to law after the stock is exhausted, his opponent scores last trick.

RUBICON BÉZIQUE

Two play, using a 128-card pack (four 32-card packs shuffled together). Each player receives nine cards in the deal, three at a time. No trump is turned, the first marriage (or sequence) declared establishing the trump suit.

Carte Blanche. When a player's hand as originally dealt to him does not contain any face card (that is, is composed entirely of sevens, eights, nines and aces), he may show it and declare *carte blanche,* scoring 50. Each time thereafter that he draws he may show the card drawn and if it is not a face card he may score 50 again. Once he has drawn a face card, he may not thereafter declare carte blanche.

Declarations. In addition to the declarations listed on page 160, a sequence in a nontrump suit (called a "back door") counts 150; triple bézique counts 1,500, quadruple bézique counts 4,500. There is no count for the seven of trumps.

Method of Declaring. The same cards may be used more than once in the same declaration, as follows: A declaration is made and scored exactly as in Bézique. If a card of that declaration is then played from the table, and the player (after winning a trick) adds a card which restores the declaration, he counts in full for the declaration again.

To score a declaration, all cards required for the declaration must be on the table at the time the score is made.

The Play. It is customary to let the cards played accumulate in the center until any brisque is played, whereupon the winner of that trick takes in all the cards. Brisques are not counted except to determine whether or not there is a rubicon, explained below. The last trick counts 50 for the winner.

Rubicon. Each deal is a game. If the loser (player with the lower score for that deal) has less than 1,000 points, including his brisques, he is *rubiconned;* the winner receives all the points scored by both players, plus 320 for all the brisques.

Bonus for winning game is 500; or, in a rubicon, 1,000.

The rubicon counts even though the winner himself has less than 1,000 points; if he wins by 800 to 600, his margin for the game is 2700 points (2720 in all, but in settlement fractions of 100 are disregarded).

SIX-PACK BÉZIQUE
or CHINESE BÉZIQUE

This is a development of Rubicon Bézique and is the most popular form of the game. The rules are similar to those of Rubicon Bézique, with the following exceptions:

Six 32-card packs are used, shuffled together to make a pack of 192 cards. It does not matter if the packs used differ in back design or color.

Twelve cards are dealt to each player.

Declarations. In addition to all the declarations used in Rubicon Bézique, four aces of trumps count 1,000; four tens of trumps, 900; four kings of trumps, 800; four queens of trumps, 600; four jacks of trumps, 400.

Carte blanche counts 250.

Winning the last trick counts 250.

Brisques are never counted, and all the played cards accumulate in the center, untouched.

Players are permitted to look back at played cards, and to count the stock to see how many cards remain.

The Béziques. Most people play that cards making up the bézique vary in accordance with the trump suit: ♠Q and ◇J are bézique if spades are trump; ◇Q and ♣J if diamonds are trump; ♡Q and ♣J if hearts are trump; ♣Q and ♡J if clubs are trump. However, there are many who play with ♠Q and ◇J always serving as bézique.

Dealer's Pack. Before dealing, dealer lifts off a portion of the total pack, trying to lift off exactly 24 cards. Without touching or counting the cards lifted off, his opponent tries to guess how many he took. If dealer took exactly 24 cards he scores 250; if his opponent guessed the number correctly, his opponent scores 150.

Game. Each deal is a game, the winner adding 1,000 to his score. If the loser has failed to reach 3,000, he is rubiconned and the winner scores the total of both players. Fractions of 100 points are disregarded except to determine the winner of the game.

Klaberjass or Belotte

THIS IS A POPULAR game in several European countries and has a large following in the United States. In Central Europe it is Klaberjass, in France it is Belotte, in some American circles it is Clabber, and it is variously called also Klob, Klab, Clob, Clab, and (by confusion with other games) Kalaber or Kalabriás.

PLAYERS. TWO.

CARDS. The pack of 32. In the trump suit, the cards rank: J (high) 9, A, 10, K, Q, 8, 7. The jack of trumps is called *jasz* (pronounced yahss), and the nine is menel'. In plain suits the rank is: A (high), 10, K, Q, J, 9, 8, 7.

DEALING. Cards are dealt three at a time, beginning with nondealer. Each player receives six cards. The thirteenth card is turned face up and placed partly underneath the stock.

BIDDING. The turned card, often called *the trump*, proposes the trump suit for the deal. Nondealer begins the bidding by making one of three declarations: *take, schmeiss* (or, in France, *valse*), or *pass*. To take is to accept the suit of the turn-up for trump. To schmeiss is to propose that the deal be abandoned; if the opponent refuses, the turn-up is trump and the schmeisser (not the refuser) is the *maker* of trump. Refusal of a schmeiss is therefore usually expressed by saying "Take it."

If nondealer passes, dealer has the option of the same three declarations. If he too passes, there is a second round of bidding. Nondealer may then schmeiss, pass, or name a suit for trump (other than that rejected). If he declares schmeiss, and dealer refuses, nondealer must name the trump suit and become the maker. If nondealer passes again to commence the second round, dealer may name the trump or abandon the deal.

The player who voluntarily or by compulsion (refusal of his schmeiss) accepts the turn-up or names the trump suit is the trump *maker*.

ADDED CARDS. The trump suit being fixed, dealer gives three more cards to each hand from the top of the stock. The bottom card of the stock is then exposed and placed face down on top. The exposed card does not enter into the play.

SEQUENCES. The hands being filled to nine cards each, any *sequences* held are declared. A sequence is a group of three or more cards of adjacent rank in the same suit, with the rank (for this purpose alone) fixed as: A (high), K, Q, J, 10, 9, 8, 7. A sequence of three cards counts 20; of four or more cards, 50.

Only the player holding the best sequence may score it. One worth 50 beats any worth 20; one of higher rank beats one of lower rank when both count the same; of two equal in the foregoing respects, a trump sequence beats a plain, and if both are plain, nondealer's beats dealer's. There is no tie.

If nondealer holds a sequence, he announces "Fifty" or "Twenty." Dealer responds "Good," "Not good," or "How high?" and so on, pursuing inquiry only until he has received enough information to pronounce "Good" or "Not good." The object of making comparison in this way is to protect the nonscorer from divulging anything more than is necessary to settle who may score. The hand entitled to score for best sequence may also score any additional sequences he holds. All sequences that score must be exposed to the opponent, after the first trick is complete.

THE PLAY. Nondealer makes the opening lead. The other hand must follow suit to a lead, if able, and if unable must play trump if able. On a trump lead the other must play higher if able. A trick is won by the higher trump if any, otherwise by the higher card of the suit led. The winner of a trick leads next.

The combination of the king and queen of trumps in one hand is *bella,* and it scores 20 if the holder announces "Bella" on playing the second of the two cards. (The holder may keep silent, and avert the extra loss, if he sees that he must go *bete.*)

If the turn-up card is accepted for trump, either player holding the seven of trumps (called *dix,* pronounced deece) may exchange it for the turn-up, provided that he does so before playing to the first trick. There is no score for the dix.

The Objects in Play are to win cards of counting value, and to win the last trick, which counts 10.

SCORING. The high cards have *point values* as follows:

Jasz (trump jack)	20
Menel (trump nine)	14
Each ace	11
Each ten	10
Each king	4
Each queen	3
Each other jack	2

After the play, each player totals what he has scored in sequences, bella, last trick, and points for cards won in tricks. If the trump maker has the higher total, both players score their totals in the running record. If the totals are the same, the maker scores nothing, while nonmaker scores his own total. If the nonmaker has the higher total, he scores both his own and the maker's total. In the last case, the maker is said to go *bete*.

The first to reach 500 points wins the game. The usual practice is to play out every deal, and if both players reach 500 in the same deal the higher total wins. But by agreement "counting out" during the play may be allowed.

IRREGULARITIES. *Misdeal.* Before bidding, nondealer may either require a new deal or require correction if any of his cards is exposed in dealing, if a card is exposed in the pack, or if either player has the wrong number of cards. When correction is demanded, a hand with too many cards is offered face down to the opponent, who draws the excess; a short hand is supplied from the top of the pack.

Incorrect hand, if discovered after the bidding has started, must be corrected.

A revoke is: failure to follow suit, to trump, or to play over on a trump lead, when required by law to do so; announcing a meld not actually held (as, for example, by saying "how high?" when not holding a sequence of equal value); having too few or too many cards after leading or playing to the first trick. The nonoffender receives all points for melds and cards on that deal.

A player may not exchange the dix for the turned-up card after playing to the first trick, nor score 20 for the trump king-queen if he does not announce "Bella."

Skat

SKAT is one of the most popular German card games and has retained its popularity among Americans of German origin. The North American Skat League, founded at a congress held in St. Louis, Mo., on January, 1898, has codified the game as described below.

PLAYERS. Skat is a game for three. More than three frequently participate in a game, but only three hands are dealt. With four, the dealer does not give cards to himself. With five, dealer omits himself and the third player at his left.

CARDS. The pack of 32 is used, A, K, Q, J, 10, 9, 8, 7 in each suit. The suits rank: clubs (high), spades, hearts, diamonds. The four jacks are always the four highest trumps, ranking: ♣J (high), ♠J, ♡J, ♢J. The remaining cards of the trump suit rank: A (high), 10, K, Q, 9, 8, 7. This is also the rank of the cards in each plain suit. When there is no trump suit, the cards in every suit rank: A (high), K, Q, J, 10, 9, 8, 7.

DEALING. Each active player is dealt ten cards, in rounds of 3-4-3. After the first round of the deal, two cards are dealt face down for the skat (widow).

DESIGNATION OF PLAYERS. In order to left of the dealer, the three active players are known as Vorhand (forehand or leader), Mittelhand (middlehand), and Hinterhand (endhand or rearhand). The highest bidder, who names the game to be played, is called the Player, and the other two, who combine against him, are the opponents.

BIDDING. The first declaration is made by Mittelhand, for the reason that Vorhand is entitled to name the game unless another player makes a bid which he is unwilling to meet. If Mittelhand wishes to try for the contract, he makes his bid, and Vorhand may either pass or say "I stay," "I retain," "Yes," or similar words indicating that he is willing to name a game of value at least as great as Mittelhand's bid. When Vorhand stays, Mittelhand may increase his bid,

until one of the two eventually drops out. The survivor then
settles in the same way with Hinterhand for the right to
name the game.

If Mittelhand and Hinterhand both pass without a bid,
Vorhand MUST name the game, but in this case he has the
additional option of naming *ramsch.*

A bid is for a number of points, without reference to any
intended game or trump suit. The lowest possible bid is 10.
Mittelhand, if he bids at all, starts with 10 and increases no
more than he has to in order to force out Vorhand, if he can
do so at all. The rules state that each bid must be for a number of points that can be scored in some game, e.g., 10 and
12 are possible, but 11 is not. The bidding is very largely in
even numbers.

THE GAMES. The high bidder, now the Player, forthwith
names the game he will play. As Skat is played today, there
are fifteen different "games" from which a bidder may
choose. They are classed in four categories, as follows:

Tournee. A card is turned up from the skat to determine
the trump suit.

Solo. The Player names the trump suit, and plays without
use of the skat.

Grand. Only the four jacks are trumps. In some grand
declarations, the skat is used; in others, it is not.

Null. There are no trumps. The skat is not used.

Full explanation of the games is given in succeeding sections. The *base value* of all games is given in the following
table.

TRUMPS	$\diamond$	$\heartsuit$	$\spadesuit$	$\clubsuit$	JACKS TRUMPS		NO TRUMPS	
Tournee	5	6	7	8	Tournee grand	12	Simple null	20
Solo	9	10	11	12	Gucki grand	16	Null ouvert	40
					Solo grand	20		
					Grand ouvert	24		
					Ramsch	10		

Tournee. If the Player names *tournee,* he looks at the top
card of the skat without showing it to the opponents. Should
it satisfy him as the trump suit, he faces it, then picks up
both skat cards without showing the second. Then he discards two cards face down to restore his hand to ten cards.
His discards are counted toward his point score after the
play.

If dissatisfied with the first card of the skat, the Player may place it in his hand without showing it. The second card is then faced and fixes the trump suit. Rejection of the first card is called *passt mir nicht*—"It does not suit me"—or Second Turn. If the Player loses the game at Second Turn, his loss is double what he would have won had he made it. In Second Turn, as when the first card is accepted, the Player picks up both skat cards and discards two.

If either card turned up from the skat is a jack, the Player may either accept its suit as trump or declare grand—in which only jacks are trumps. The game *tournee grand* thus can arise only through the accident that a jack is turned after a declaration of simple tournee.

Solo. The Player forthwith names the trump suit, or declares grand (jacks trumps), and play begins. The skat cards are not touched, but are added to the Player's tricks at the end of the hand.

Gucki Grand. This is also called *guckser*. The Player declares grand (jacks trumps) and forthwith picks up the skat. (Taking both cards of the skat, without any remark, is equivalent to declaring gucki grand.) He discards two cards, which will be added to his tricks after the play. When a gucki contract is not fulfilled, the loss is doubled.

Simple Null. There are no trumps, and the cards rank as at Bridge. The Player contracts to win no tricks at all. The skat is set aside untouched.

Ouvert. In declaring ouvert (open), the Player contracts to play with his entire hand exposed to inspection by the opponents. Such exposure must be made before the opening lead. Declaration of ouvert may be made only at grand or null, and the skat is set aside untouched.

Null ouvert is the same as simple null with the addition that the Player faces his hand.

Grand ouvert is a contract to win *all the tricks,* with jacks trumps and the Player's hand exposed.

Ramsch. This game may be declared only by Vorhand, if he so chooses, when Mittelhand and Hinterhand pass without a bid. Jacks are trumps, and the object of play is to take in as few points as possible. Each hand plays for himself. The skat is not touched, but is added to the last trick and goes to the winner thereof.

THE PLAY. Vorhand invariably makes the opening lead. He may lead any card. A lead calls upon the other two hands to follow suit if able. When unable to follow suit, a player may play any card in his hand, trumping or discarding as he pleases. Each trick is won by the highest card of the suit led, or by the highest trump if it contains one. The winner of a trick leads to the next.

Except at ramsch, the Player is opposed by the two others acting in partnership. Their object is to prevent the Player from taking the number of points or tricks called for by his game.

The object in play is described below.

Point Values of Cards. The higher cards have a *point value* as follows:

Each ace	11	Each queen	3
Each ten	10	Each jack	2
Each king	4	(No count for 9, 8, 7)	

There are 30 points in each suit, and 120 in the pack.

In any tournee, solo, or gucki, the Player contracts to win in tricks (plus the skat or his discards) cards that total at least 61 points. If he fails, he loses the value of his game (doubled in case of gucki and Second Turn). If he succeeds, and also if the value of his game is at least equal to his bid, he wins this value.

Schneider and Schwarz. If the Player wins 91 or more points in play, he is said to *schneider* the opponents and the value of his game is increased. If he wins all the tricks, he wins a further increase for *schwarz*.

If the Player fails to win 31 points in play, he is schneidered and his loss is increased. Similarly he loses more if he suffers schwarz, by taking no trick.

Prediction. The Player may, in an effort to increase his winnings, announce that he will schneider or schwarz. Such announcement is permitted only in solo games (skat not used), and it must be made before the opening lead. Of course he loses if he does not fulfil the prediction.

Matadors. The Player who holds the ♣J is said to be "*with*" so many *matadors*—as many top trumps as he holds in unbroken sequence from the ♣J down. For example, a top holding of ♣J, ♠J, ◊J is "with two," because the ♡J is missing.

The Player who lacks the ♣J is said to be "without" as many matadors as there are trumps outstanding higher than his highest. For example, if his highest trump is ◊J, the Player is "without three."

COMPUTING THE GAME. The *value of a game* is the product of two factors, of which the first is the base value of the game as given in the table under *The Games*. The second factor is the sum of all applicable *multiples,* and can never be less than 2. (Hence 10 is the lowest possible bid.)

The first item reckoned under the multipliers is the number of matadors that the Player is either "with" or "without." This number can vary from 1 to 11. The usual way of reckoning is then to count "1 for game," plus any increments for schneider, schwarz, and prediction. A less confusing way is: To the number of matadors ("with" or "without"), add *one* item below.

Player makes "game" (61-90 points in play)	**1**
Schneider made, without prediction (91 up by Player; 90 up by opponents)	2
Schwarz made (by either side) without prediction	3
Schneider predicted and made by Player	3
Schneider predicted, schwarz made, by Player	4
Schwarz predicted and made by Player	5

At either null game, no multipliers apply. The base values are invariable. Therefore a player is not permitted to declare simple null if he has bid more than 20, nor null ouvert if he has bid more than 40.

Ramsch has a special scoring as described below.

SCORING. If the Player makes his contract, and if the value of his game is at least equal to his bid, he wins the full value.

If the Player fails to win the required number of points in play, he loses the value of his game. If the game was gucki grand or Second Turn in a tournee, the loss is doubled.

If the value of the Player's game is less than his bid, he is said to have *overbid* and he loses regardless of whether he wins the required number of points in play. The amount he loses is that multiple of the base value of his game which is the first higher than his bid. For example, a player bids 18 and plays a spade tournee; he makes game but not schneider and is found to be "without one." His game is worth only $2 \times 7 = 14$. He loses 21, the next multiple of 7 higher than 18. If the tournee was a Second Turn, his loss would be 42.

Ramsch has a special scoring. The player who gathers the least points in tricks wins 10, or 20 if he takes no tricks at all, and the others score nothing. If each player takes 40 points in tricks, Vorhand is deemed the winner and scores 10. If two players tie for low score, the one who did not take the last trick as between these two scores 10. If one player takes all the tricks, he loses 30 points and the others score nothing.

SETTLEMENT. The score kept for each player is the running net of his winnings and losses. Some or all of these nets can be minus.

At the end of a session, the final scores are added (algebraically) and divided by the number of players, to determine the average. Those who are minus pay out, and those who are plus collect.

For example, suppose the final scores to be

A	B	C	D	E
119	92	76	35	—12

The total is $322 - 12 = 310$. Dividing by 5 gives the average as plus 62. The differences from average are:

A	B	C	D	E
+57	+30	+14	—27	—74

IRREGULARITIES. Condensed from the official rules of the North American Skat League, copyright 1947. The spirit of the Skat laws differs from that of other games in one important respect: When an opponent of the player violates a law, he must usually pay the full cost himself; his partner does not suffer, though the Player may profit. Generally, any error gives the game to the other side but the error is corrected if possible and play continues to determine the extent of the offender's loss.

Misdeal. If a card is exposed in dealing, the same dealer deals again.

Incorrect Hand. If the Player has the correct number of cards, he wins; if the Player's hand is incorrect he loses, even if an opponent also had an incorrect hand.

The Skat. (a) If a player picks up a skat card, a card is drawn from his hand to restore the skat and the offender is fined 25 points. (b) If a player illegally looks at the skat, he is fined 10 points and barred from further bidding; and if he showed a skat card to another player, the skat is shuffled before a card is turned and *Passt mir Nicht* is barred. (c) A dealer looking at the skat is fined 100 points. (d) If the Player sees both skat cards when turning the first, he must accept the top card. (e) If the Player of a Solo game looks at a card of the skat, he loses. (f) If an opponent looks at a card of the skat before it is turned by the Player, the Player wins.

Revokes, Leads and Plays Out of Turn. Any such play loses the game; except that if play continues and the other side makes a similar error, it condones the first error. If the Player's error is thus condoned by an opponent's later error, and the Player makes his game, the amount of the game is charged against the offending opponent.

Claims. When a player exposes his hand, he claims the game. Play stops and the cards are counted. If the claimant has not won at that point, he loses; if the claimant was an opponent, the full loss is charged to him.

Ramsch. If a player at Ramsch revokes or plays out of turn, he may not score in that hand and the points made by the other players are charged to him; but a similar error made later by another player cancels this penalty and leaves the new offender subject to the same penalty.

Looking Back at Tricks. If a player looks at a turned trick after a card is played to the next trick, the opposing side may claim the game.

STRATEGY. *Solo.* The minimum trump length normally required for a solo is five, plus two side aces or a side ace and a ten (in a different suit) if the hand has some "plus" value, such as a king with the ace. Each extra trump over five may be deemed to take the place of a side card.

Tournee. The object in declaring tournee, in preference to solo, is twofold: (a) to obtain an additional trump card; (b) to be able to lay away some cards. The chance of buying a valuable card in the skat, as an ace or ten, is slight.

ODDS AGAINST BUYING ONE CARD

When only one card will serve	10 to 1
When either of two cards will serve	5 to 1
When any of three cards will serve	3 to 1
When any of four cards will serve	2 to 1
When any of five cards will serve	3 to 2
When any of six cards will serve	even

The general rule is that a hand must be ready to play any of three suits.

Grand. A convenient rule for weighing the merits of a hand for a grand is to reckon each jack or ace as one, and position as Vorhand as one; grand should not be bid with less than 5 of these possible 9 points.

Null. A bid to take no tricks is naturally possible only with a hand liberally supplied with low cards. Such a holding as K-J-9-7 is unassailable, since it can always underplay any lead and remain with the lowest card of the suit. A holding of 10-7 doubleton is fairly safe, but J-10-8 or any other combination of three or more cards lacking the 7 is risky.

RÄUBER SKAT

In the original game of Skat, the Player may not pick up the skat cards unless he is willing to let them fix the trump suit, or to declare only jacks trumps. The essential idea of the variant Räuber (*German:* pirate, brigand) is to let the Player pick up the skat and then name any game he chooses, after the manner of Pinochle. The differences from the original game are given below.

THE GAMES. Any one of the four suits as trump; grand (only jacks trumps); null or nullo (no trump); ramsch or reject (a grand in which the object is not to win points).

All rules for ramsch are as in Skat. Any other game may be played either with use of the skat cards or without. Playing solo without the skat is called *handplay.* In handplay with a trump, the Player has the right to try for increased score by announcing that he will win *little slam* (same as schneider) or *grand slam* (same as schwarz). If he chooses to use the skat cards, the Player need not name the trump until he has seen them.

At nullo, the Player may try for increased score by playing *open* (same as ouvert), either with or without use of the skat. Nullo is a contract to lose all the tricks.

BASE VALUES

TRUMPS		NULLO		HANDPLAY	
◇	9	Simple	23	(open)	59
♡	10	Open	46		
♠	11				
♣	12	Ramsch	10		
Jacks	20				

MULTIPLIERS. Following is the list of all possible multipliers.

Matadors	from 1 to 11
Game	1
Handplay	1
Little Slam	1
Big Slam	1
Announced Little Slam	1
Announced Big Slam	1

As in Skat, matadors are counted whenever there is a trump and "1 for game" is always counted (except ramsch).

The multipliers for slams are cumulative, that is, having earned any one of the four listed, the Player is entitled to all preceding it. For example, if he announces and makes little slam, he adds 3 for it to matadors and game.

SCORING. If the Player fails to make his game he loses the value of his game at handplay, or double the value if he has used the skat. The opponents may count slams, if made by them, but of course may not announce slams. If the Player picks up the skat and believes he cannot make game, he has the right to abandon his cards in order to save slam. When he does so he must name some game, so that the amount of his loss can be computed.

When the Player is found to have overbid, the value of his game is fixed at the multiple of the base value next higher than his bid. (As in Skat.) The value is then doubled if he has picked up the skat.

Booray or Bouré

THIS GAME, combining features of Écarté and Poker, is most popular with Creoles of the Louisiana region and French-Canadians of that and other regions.

PLAYERS. Two to seven. Each plays for himself.

THE PACK. 52 cards, ranking A (high), K, Q, J, 10, 9, 8, 7, 6, 5, 4, 3, 2, in each suit.

THE ANTE. For each deal there is a pot to which each player antes. The current dealer decides the amount of the ante to be contributed by each player (the same for all including the dealer), but usually a maximum is placed on the ante by agreement.

THE DEAL. Players draw or cut for first deal; after that, turn to deal passes to the left. Only the dealer shuffles and the player at his right cuts. Five cards are dealt to each player, one at a time, face down, in rotation to the left. The dealer turns up the next card, which fixes the trump suit, and must announce the suit.

THE DRAW. After looking at his cards, each player may discard his hand and forfeit his ante, or may stay in and have a chance to win the pot but also be subject to additional losses. Each active player in turn to dealer's left may then discard one or more cards and receive replacements from the deck, as in Draw Poker. A player may stand pat. A limit may be placed on the number of cards drawn, three or four cards, depending on the number of players who stay in.

THE PLAY. When the draw is completed, the player at dealer's left leads and the cards are played out in tricks (one card from each player in turn). The leader must lead his highest trump if he has the ace, king and/or queen. To each trick a player in turn must follow suit if able, "play over" (play a higher card than any previously played) if able, and play a trump if unable to follow suit; but a player unable to follow suit need not overtrump; and if unable to follow suit or trump, a player may play any card. A trick is won by the highest card of the suit led unless a trump is played, in which case the highest trump wins. The winner of a trick leads to the next trick and may lead any card in his hand, except that if he holds the ace, king and/or queen of trumps he must lead his highest trump.

OBJECT OF PLAY. To win the most tricks; and to win at least one trick.

THE SCORING. The player who wins the most tricks wins the pot. If two players win two tricks each, or if five players win one trick each, they divide the pot equally. A player who stays in but fails to win a trick must contribute an amount equal to the current pot, which however is added to the next pot and not to the winnings of the winner of the current pot.

Casino

EARLY writers state that Casino is of Italian origin, and that its name means precisely what it says—a public gaming hall. The word appears as *Cassino* in most English manuals, the extra *s* having been inserted, it is said, by a whimsical printer.

PLAYERS. Two. Casino can be played by three, each for himself (not a very good game), or by four, two against two in partnerships (described later).

CARDS. The pack of 52. Ace counts 1, other cards from 2 to 10 count as their index numbers; jacks, queens and kings have no numerical value.

PRELIMINARIES. Dealer has the right to shuffle last. Opponent cuts; the cut must leave at least four cards in each packet. The right to deal alternates unless each deal is a separate game, in which case the winner of each hand deals the next.

DEALING. In the first deal, dealer gives two cards to his opponent, then two face up to the table, then two to himself; then he deals a second round in the same manner as the first. Each player thus receives four cards, and four are placed face up on the table. The hands are played; then dealer gives each player four more cards, in rounds of two at a time. And so on following: the hands of four cards are dealt and played until the pack is exhausted. After the first deal, no more cards are dealt to the table. The dealer must announce "Last" on commencing the last deal.

THE PLAY. Each hand in turn, beginning with nondealer, must play a card to the table and thereby *take in, build,* or *trail.*

Taking In. The general object of play is to win or to take in cards from the table. A card from the hand my be used to take in another of the same rank on the table. *Example:* A player may use ♣8 from his hand to take ◇8 on the table.

(Suits are immaterial.) Such *pairing* is the only way face cards (kings, queens and jacks) can be taken in.

Building. A card from the hand may be used to take in two or more cards of the same total of pips. *Example:* A player may use ♠9 to take ♡4 and ♣5.

A card from the hand may be placed on another on the table, to be taken later by a second card from the hand. *Example:* A player may place ♣7 from his hand on ◇2, and later take them with ◇9 from his hand.

Such a play is a *build,* and on placing the first card the player must announce "Building (nin)." The announcement prevents the opponent from splitting the build and using any of the cards separately. *Example:* Nondealer puts ♡5 on ♡3 and says "Building eight"; dealer may not then take in either of the cards by pairing.

No build may be made unless the player holds in hand a card of the rank necessary to take it. When a build is left on the table (as it has to be when it includes a card from the hand), the opponent of the builder may take it in. *Example:* Nondealer plays ♣A on ♡5, building six. Dealer may take the build with any six.

If a player has made a build, and it is not taken by opponent, the player at his next turn may not *trail;* he must *duplicate* or *increase the build* or *take in.* But he need not take in that build; if he prefers and can, he may instead take in a pair or take an adverse build.

Duplicating a Build. The same card from the hand may be used to take in two or more groups of cards, each of which totals the like number of pips. *Example:* ♣9 from the hand may be used to take in ♡6, ♣3 and ♠A, ◇8, and ◇9, all at the same time.

A build left on the table may be duplicated as many times as there are cards available. *Example:* Dealer builds seven with ♡4 and ♣3; at his next turn, he finds ♠5 and ♡2 also on the table; he may take them with his build. Or suppose that at his next turn only ♠5 is on the table besides his build; he may add ♡2 from his hand and ♠5 from the table to his build, to be taken in at his following turn.

Single cards, of rank ten or lower, can be built in the same way. *Example:* A player holds ♣9, ♠9, while ♡9 is on the table; he may place ♣9 on ♡9, saying "Building nines," and take the build later with ♠9. All four cards of a rank can thus be gathered in one build. Note that *face cards* may never be built, but only paired.

Increasing a Build. A player may increase a build so that it requires for capture a higher card than originally announced. *Example:* Nondealer places ♣3 from his hand on ♣6 on the table and says "Building nine"; dealer may add ♡A and say "Building ten," provided the he has a ten in hand with which to take the increased build.

A player may increase either his own or his opponent's build. But a build that is duplicated may never be increased. *Example:* A player puts ♡4 from his hand on ♠3 on the table, and adds ◇7 from the table, building sevens; the build may not be increased.

Note that the same limitation applies to builds of pairs. *Example:* A player puts ♣4 on ♠4, and says "Building fours"; his opponent may not add ♡A and say "Building nine," because the original announcement overrides, and marks the build as double.

A build may be increased only by a card from the hand, *not* by a card from the table. (Consequently such a build cannot be taken in on the same turn when it is increased, but must be left on the table for one turn. The opponent always has an opportunity to take an increased build, or to increase it yet again.)

Trailing. If unable or unwilling to *take in*, the player in turn simply places a card from his hand face up on the table. This is called *trailing*. A player may trail if he wishes, even if able to take in by pairing. *Example:* The table shows ♡J and ♠5. Nondealer with ◇5 may trail instead of taking in ♠5. (The object may be to avert the chance of a sweep or to leave a combination of ten in case he is dealt ◇10 in the last deal.)

COUNTING CARDS. The object of play is to take in cards and combinations of cards of scoring value. The points to be scored are as follows:

Cards, majority of the 52 cards	3
Spades, majority of the 13 spades	1
Big Casino, the ◇10	2
Little Casino, the ♠2	1
Aces (each counting 1)	4
Total	11

Sweeps (optional) count 1 each.

A player makes a *sweep* when he takes in all the cards on the table. (In some localities sweeps do not count.)

Each player places the cards he *takes in* in a pile face down. A sweep is recorded by turning a card of this pile face up.

After the last card is played out, any cards remaining on the table go to the player who was last to *take in* any card. Gathering cards by virtue of this rule does not count as a sweep.

If each player takes in 26 cards, there is no score for *cards*.

SCORING. After the whole pack is played out, each player counts the number of points in his cards. If desired, each deal may be treated as a separate game for the majority of the 11 (or more) points. Much more common, however, is the fixing of game at 21 points. If during a deal a player claims correctly that he has reached a total of 21 points, he wins, even though his opponent has "gone out" earlier (but failed to claim the game).

If "counting out" is not allowed, and if both players reach 21 in the same deal, the points are counted in the order given under *Counting Cards* to determine the winner.

IRREGULARITIES. In two-hand play, when each deal constitutes a game, any irregularity loses the game. If any card is exposed in dealing before the first four cards are dealt to the table, that card goes to the table and is replaced from the top of the pack. If a card is exposed in dealing after the table has its four cards, dealer must take the exposed card and give the opponent another card. If dealer gives any player too many cards, and the player has looked at his hand, he may put the excess among the cards on the table, choosing the cards he will put there, and on the next round of dealing the dealer plays with fewer cards than his opponent.

If on the final round there are not enough cards to give every player four, the dealer receives fewer cards than the opponents (unless the pack is shown to be imperfect, in which event the entire deal is void).

Counting or Looking Back at Cards. If a player counts or looks back at any cards taken in and turned, except at cards taken in since he last played, his opponent may either add one point to his own score or deduct one point from the offender's score.

Not Taking in Builds. If a player trails when he has a build standing on the table, he must on demand take the build; but the card with which he trailed remains on the table, and he does not play in his next turn. If a player has not the appropriate card with which to take in a build he made, his opponent may add one point to his own score or deduct one point from the offender's score.

Play Out of Turn. A card played out of turn (or, in partnership play, illegally exposed) must remain on the table, as though the offender had trailed with it, and the offender does not play in his next turn; in partnership play, his partner may not take in that card.

THREE-HAND CASINO

Each player receives four cards on each deal, as in two-hand; four cards are dealt to the table on the first round, but no cards thereafter. Eldest hand plays first and the turn to play passes in rotation. If there is a tie for the most cards or spades, the respective points do not count for anyone. Usually a game of 11 points is played; if it is attempted to make each deal a game, there are too many ties. Three-hand Casino is not often played because eldest hand and dealer have a great advantage over the player "in the middle."

PARTNERSHIP CASINO

Four play, in two partnerships, partners being seated alternately. The dealing, turn to deal, and turn to play rotate to the left. Cards taken in by each pair of partners are combined and counted together, and partners try to help each other, but each player must observe the rules of the game. *Example:* One partner is known to hold a nine. The other partner has a four and there is a five on the table; but he has no nine in his hand. Therefore he cannot build a nine, even though he knows the first partner could take it in.

A game of 21 points may be played, or each deal may represent a game.

ROYAL CASINO

This variant, in the opinion of many experts, is superior as a test of skill.

In Royal Casino, face cards are used in building and duplicating builds, as the lower cards are. Jack is counted as 11, queen as 12, king, as 13, while the ace may be used as 1 or 14 at the option of the player.

SPADE CASINO

In this variant, there is no count for majority of spades. but each spade taken in is itself worth 1 point, except jack and two, which are each worth 2. The rest of the count is the same, so that there are 24 points to be won, exclusive of sweeps. Scoring is best done on a cribbage board, with game fixed at 61. First player to "count out" during play wins the game.

DRAW CASINO

After the first deal of twelve cards (four to each hand and four to the table), the rest of the pack is placed face down to form the *stock*. After each play, the player restores his hand to four cards by drawing the top of the stock. After the stock is exhausted, the hands are played out as usual.

Card Games for Children

THE GAMES in this section are recommended for children because they are simple enough to be understood by the very young, not because they are without interest to adults.

Each of the games is played with one pack of 52 cards. Except where otherwise specified, the rank of cards in each suit is: A (high), K, Q, J, 10, 9, 8, 7, 6, 5, 4, 3, 2.

SLAPJACK

Age Group. Four to nine.

Players. Two to eight.

Dealing. The cards are dealt out one at a time as far as they will go. It does not matter if some players have more cards than others.

The Play. Each player keeps his cards in one pile face down. Each in turn beginning with eldest hand turns up one card from the top of his stock and places it in a common pile in the center of the table. Whenever a jack is turned, the first player to slap it takes all the cards in the common pile, and the next hand begins a new pile. The object of play is to win all 52 cards.

Cards won by slapping are put by the winner at the bottom of his stock.

If a player loses all his stock, he stays in the game until the next jack is turned. If he slaps it first, he continues in play with the cards won, but if he fails, he is out of the game.

Rules important to enforce are:

1. Cards must be turned up from the stock *away* from the owner, so that he does not get a peek before the others.

2. Turning cards and slapping must be done with the same hand.

3. When several slap at once—and they always do!—the lowermost hand, nearest to the jack, wins.

4. If a player slaps a card that is not a jack, he must give one card from his stock, face down, to the player of the card. The penalty card is placed at the bottom of the receiver's stock.

OLD MAID

AGE GROUP. Five to ten.

PLAYERS. Two or more.

DEALING. One queen is first discarded from the pack. Then the pack is divided into packets approximately equal, one for each player. It does not matter if the distribution is unequal.

DISCARDING. Each player spreads his packet of cards and picks out all pairs, which he discards face up in the center of the table. There is no necessity for concealing the hand from the other players; it can be placed face up on the table, and players can help each other pick out the pairs.

THE PLAY. When all hands have been reduced to non-paired cards, each player mixes his cards behind his back. Then one player presents his cards face down to his left-hand opponent, who draws out one card. If it pairs with a card in his hand, he discards the pair, then shuffles his hand and presents it face down to his left neighbor. Play continues in the same way, each player drawing a card from the hand at his right, paired cards being discarded, until only the odd queen remains.

The player stuck with the queen is "Old Maid" and loses the game.

PIG

AGE GROUP. Six to ten.

PLAYERS. Three to thirteen. Best for four to seven.

DEALING. The pack comprises sets of four cards of a kind, as many sets are there players. *Example:* Four players use 16 cards, which may be face cards or aces, or any other four ranks.

Four cards are dealt to each player, one at a time. Each looks at his hand. Then, simultaneously, each places one card face down to the left, then picks up the card discarded from the right. Play continues by such simultaneous exchanges, the object of each player being to get the four cards of any one rank. As soon as any player so collects a *book*, he stops exchanging and puts his finger to his nose.

Each other player, on noticing this action, must stop play and likewise put his finger to his nose. The last to do so is the Pig, and loses the game.

AUTHORS

Authors is the name of a proprietary game for which special cards are manufactured, but it can as well be played with regular playing cards.

AGE GROUP. Eight to sixteen. But it is also played by adults, sometimes for high stakes.

PLAYERS. Three to six. Best for four or five.

DEALING. The cards are dealt out, one at a time, as far as they will go. It does not matter if some players receive more cards than others.

THE PLAY. Each player in turn, beginning with eldest hand, calls another by name and requests a card, by suit and rank, as "John, give me the six of clubs."

The card requested must be in a rank of which the asker holds at least one card, but must be of a different suit. (That is, a player may not ask for a card that he himself holds.)

If the player addressed has the card specified, he must give it and the asker has another turn. He may continue asking so long as he is successful in getting cards. When he fails, the turn passes to his left.

As soon as any player gets all four cards of one rank, he must show them and place the book on the table before him. The one who collects the most books wins the game.

When the game is played for a stake, a player on completing a book collects one chip from each other player.

GO FISH

This is a simpler form of Authors, suitable to a younger age group.

AGE GROUP. Six to ten.

PLAYERS. Two to six.

DEALING. Cards are dealt one at a time. Each player receives: in two-hand, seven cards; with more players, five cards. The rest of the pack is placed face down in the center of the table to form the *stock*.

THE PLAY. Commencing with eldest hand, each player in turn calls another by name and requests cards of a specified rank, as "David, give me your aces."

The card requested must be of a rank in which the asker holds at least one card. Having one or more cards of the specified rank, the player addressed must give up *all* of them. With none of the specified rank, the player replies "Go fish!" and the asker draws the top card of the stock.

A player's turn to ask continues so long as he is successful in getting the cards specified. If he is told to *go fish*, and he chances to draw a card of the rank he named, he may show this card, and his turn continues.

As soon as any player gets a book (all four cards of one rank), he must show them and place the book on the table before him. The one who collects the most books wins the game.

If the draw from the stock completes a book in the hand, the book must at once be shown. Strictly, the player's turn does not continue unless the book is of the rank he last asked for, but among younger children this distinction is best eliminated.

STEALING BUNDLES

This game is essentially Casino with the builds left out. It forms an easy introduction to Casino.

AGE GROUP. Six to ten.

PLAYERS. Two.

DEALING. Cards may be dealt one or two at a time. Each player first receives four cards, and four are dealt face up on the table. Thereafter, each time the hands are played out four more cards are dealt to each player, but none to the table. The game ends after the pack is exhausted.

THE PLAY. Nondealer plays first, and thereafter the hands play alternately. The player may either *trail* by placing a card face up on the table, or *take in* a card from the table with a card of the same rank from the hand. Cards taken in must be placed in a pile face up, forming the *bundle*. A player may *steal* his opponent's bundle by taking it in with a card of the same rank as its top card.

The player who has the greater number of cards in his bundle by the time the pack is exhausted wins the game.

BEGGAR-YOUR-NEIGHBOR

AGE GROUP. Eight to twelve.

PLAYERS. Two.

DEALING. Each player receives half the pack. It is not necessary to deal the cards one by one. It is simpler to shuffle thoroughly, then count off the first 26 cards for the nondealer.

THE PLAY. Each player holds his packet face down. Nondealer turns up a card from the top and places it on the table. Dealer then turns a card from his packet and places it upon the other. Play continues in the same way, by alternate contributions to the common face-up pile, until interrupted by the appearance of a face card or ace.

When one player turns such a high card, the other must place upon it: four cards for an ace, three for a king, two for a queen, one for a jack. If the high card draws its quota in *lower* cards (ten or lower), the player of the high card takes up the entire common pile, places it face down under his packet, and leads for a new series of plays. But if a face card or ace appears in the course of playing the quota upon an adverse high card, the obligation is reversed, and the adversary must give a quota. The excitement of the game comes when high cards follow each other in close order, so that the last in effect "captures" all the rest.

The player who gets the entire pack into his hands wins. Naturally there is no opportunity for skill. The outcome is decided by the chance of the shuffle, and a game may end in one "run through" or may continue for a long time.

I DOUBT IT

AGE GROUP. Nine to ninety. This is one of the easiest of games to "play at," and at the same time it offers as much opportunity for skill as Poker—and of the same character.

PLAYERS. Four to twelve. Best for six to nine.

CARDS. Four or five players should use one pack of 52 cards. Six or more should use two packs shuffled together. The game is much better with two packs than with one.

DEALING. The cards are dealt out as far as they will go. It does not matter if some players receive more cards than others. Dealing should be in packets of convenient size, from two to four cards, except in the last round or two, when they should be dealt one at a time.

THE PLAY. Eldest hand begins by placing any number of cards from one to eight (four with a single pack) face down in the center of the table, saying "Three aces"—or whatever the number of cards happens to be. Each hand in rotation thereafter must discard cards face down on the same pile, announcing the number of cards and their rank.

The rank is rigidly fixed: eldest hand must commence with aces, next hand must play kings, and so on in descending rank to deuces, then aces again, kings again, and so on in circular sequence.

The player must state correctly the number of cards he puts out, but none need be of the announced rank. The object of play is to get rid of one's entire hand; it is often advisable or necessary to add some cards not of the specified rank to the packet played.

Following a play, any other player may say "I doubt it!" Then if the last player discarded any card other than the specified rank, he must take all the cards on the table into his hand. But if the discard was strictly in accord with the announcement—as is proved by turning the last discard face up—the doubter must take up the whole discard pile.

It often happens that several players doubt the same discard. Paradoxically, this is most likely to occur when the discard is correct, the object of doubting being to obtain cards of certain ranks. The following rules as to precedence in doubting should be rigidly enforced:

1. "I doubt it" *may not be declared until the player's hand has quitted his discard.* A premature doubt is void, and the doubter loses his right to doubt that discard. (Announcement should be made before the cards are placed on the discard pile, to give due notice to would-be doubters.)

2. *The first to doubt takes precedence when his lead over the second doubter is clear.*

3. *When none has a clear lead in being the first to doubt,*

the doubter nearest the player's left in rotation has prece- dence.

SCORING. The first player to get rid of all his cards wins the deal. Each deal should be treated as a separate game. Or the number of cards left in the hands may be charged against the owners, and the player with lowest score when another reaches 100 may be deemed the winner of a game.

CONCENTRATION (MEMORY, PELMANISM)

AGE GROUP. Nine to ninety. With children under sixteen, the contestants should be of nearly the same age or the older will have a pronounced advantage.

PLAYERS. Any number up to six can play; but the best game is for two.

THE LAYOUT. A pack of 52 cards is shuffled and then dealt face down on a table so that no two cards touch. No effort should be made to put the cards into orderly rows and files; the greater the irregularity, the better.

THE PLAY. Each player in turn turns two cards face up, one at a time, without moving either away from its position in the layout. If the two cards are a pair, he removes them to his own pile of pairs won, and turns up two more cards. When he turns up two cards which are not a pair, he turns the cards face down, and the turn passes to his left.

The player who gathers a plurality of the cards wins the game.

While there is some luck in the game, victory goes con- sistently to the player who more accurately remembers the location of unpaired cards previously turned.

Each card turned should be left on the table, face up, in its original position, for a few seconds at least before it is either taken by the player or turned down again.

Solitaire

BY SOLITAIRE or Patience is meant any card game that can be played by one person. There are probably more Solitaires than all other card games together. Only a few have achieved universally-known names, as Canfield and Klondike.

CARDS. Almost every Patience uses one or two packs of 52 cards each, the cards ranking: K (high), Q, J, 10, 9, 8, 7, 6, 5, 4, 3, 2, A. Sometimes the sequence is continuous, the ace and king being of adjacent rank.

To WIN. the game is to get the entire pack into a certain prefixed order, such as: the four suits segregated and each suit in sequence. This is also called *making* the game, or *breaking* it.

THE LAYOUT is the array of cards first dealt on the table, comprising usually the tableau, and sometimes a stock and some foundations also.

THE TABLEAU is dealt in some distinctive arrangement; many Patience games differ only in the form of the tableau. Horizontal lines of cards are *rows*, while lines extending vertically away from the player are *columns*.

THE FOUNDATIONS are usually all the cards of a certain rank. The object in play is to build cards onto the foundations, and the game is won when all foundations are completely built up.

THE STOCK is a special pile of cards, a part of the layout in some games.

THE HAND is the rest of the pack, if the layout does not use all the cards.

THE TALON is a pile into which cards turned up from the hand are placed, when they cannot be immediately built onto the tableau or foundations.

AVAILABLE CARDS are those of the tableau, stock, etc., which may be transferred to other parts of the layout.

Usually, certain cards of the tableau are not available until *released* by the transfer of covering cards.

A SPACE in the tableau, created by transferring all cards of one pile elsewhere, is often very helpful in building.

BUILDING is playing cards to the tableau so as to release additional cards or save cards from being buried in the talon.

WASTE PILES or discard piles are talon piles; usually they may be spread so that all cards are visible, while the talon proper must usually be kept squared up so that only the top card is visible.

ACCORDION
One pack

Deal cards one by one in a row from left to right, not overlapping. Whenever a card matches its immediate neighbor to the left, or matches the card third away to the left, it may be moved onto that card. Cards match if they are of the same suit or same rank. After making a move, look to see if it has made additional moves possible. Deal out the whole pack, combining piles toward the left when possible. The game is won if the pack is reduced to one pile.

KLONDIKE
(Erroneously called Canfield)
One pack

Tableau. Deal one card face up, then six face down in the same row toward the right. Deal one face up on the card just to the right of the first face-up, then add another face down on each card to the right. Continue in the same manner, dealing one less card each round, turning the first face up, the rest face down. The result is seven piles, comprising 1, 2, 3, 4, 5, 6, 7 cards in order left to right. The top card of each pile is face up; the rest are face down.

Foundations. Aces, which must be put in a row above the tableau as they become available. Each foundation must be built up in suit and sequence to the king. A card once placed on a foundation may not thereafter be moved.

Building. On the uppermost card of a tableau pile may be placed a card of next-lower rank and opposite color. (The sequence of rank ends with the king, high.) All face-up cards on a tableau pile must be moved as a unit (onto a card of next higher rank and opposite color to the bottom card of the unit). When such a transfer is made, the top face-down card of the pile is turned face up, and becomes available. The top card of the talon is always available. The top card of a tableau pile or of the talon may be played onto a foundation. It is not compulsory to build on a foundation when able, except that aces may not be built or built upon in the tableau.

Spaces may be filled only by kings.

The Hand is turned up one card at a time and is run through only once. Any card that cannot be built or played to a foundation is placed face up on the talon.

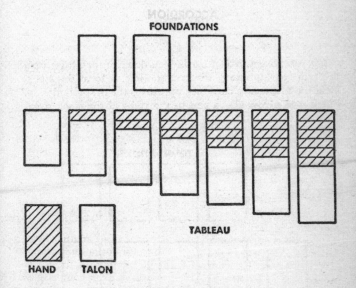

FOUNDATIONS

TABLEAU

HAND   **TALON**

DOUBLE KLONDIKE
(Usually called Double Solitaire)
Two players, two packs

Many solitaires can be played as games by two players. Klondike is a favorite for this purpose. Each player has a pack and makes his own Klondike layout. If one has an ace showing and the other has not, the former plays until he cannot use a card turned from his hand, whereupon the turn passes to his opponent, and so on. When neither original layout shows an ace, the player with the lowest card at the left of his tableau has precedence; if these are tied, the next card to the left decides. All aces are placed between the two players and form common foundations.

The first to get rid of all his cards onto the foundations wins the game. Or, if play comes to a standstill, the one with the more cards played to the foundations wins. It is not compulsory to play on a foundation when able; withholding a card may block the opponent from getting rid of a greater number of cards.

CANFIELD

One pack

Layout. Deal thirteen cards face down in one pile; turn the pile face up and place it at the left to form the stock. Deal the fourteenth card face up; this is the first foundation. Place it in a row above and to the right of the stock. Deal

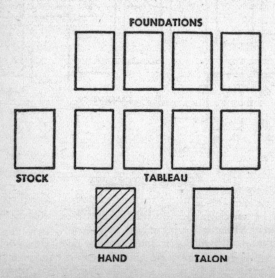

four cards face up in a row to right of stock, forming the tableau.

Foundations. All cards of the same rank as the first foundation. Such cards must be placed in the foundation row as soon as available: they may not be built or built upon in the tableau. Each foundation must be built up in the same suit and ascending sequence, the sequence in the suit being continuous, ace going on king, and so on.

Building. On the uppermost card of a tableau pile may be placed a card of next-lower rank and opposite color. A tableau pile must be moved as a unit (onto a card of the next-higher rank and opposite color to the bottom card of the unit). The top card of the talon is always available. The top card of a tableau pile or of the talon may be played onto a foundation.

(Some play the rule that the top card of a tableau pile is always available. *Example:* ♡7 ♣6 ◇5 may be moved as a unit, under the regular rule, or ◇5 may be moved onto ♠6, and then ♣6 onto ◇7.)

Spaces must be filled by cards from the top of the stock, which should always be kept squared up so that only the top card is identifiable. After the stock is exhausted, spaces may be filled from the talon.

The Hand is turned up in packets of three cards at a time. Each packet is placed face up on the talon. The top card is available, and others below as released. After the hand is exhausted, turn over the talon, without shuffling, to form a new hand. The hand-talon may be run through any number of times, so long as any plays can be made. (Some play that the hand may be run through only three times.)

SPIDER

Two packs

Tableau. Deal ten cards face down in a row. Deal three more rows face down on the first. Next deal one card face down on each of the first four piles at the left. Finally deal a row of ten cards face up on the piles. The tableau thus comprises 54 cards.

Building. All building is done in the tableau, there being no separate foundations. On the uppermost card of a pile

may be placed a card of next-lower rank, regardless of suit.
Available for transfer is the top card of a pile, together with
any or all below it which form an ascending sequence in
the same suit. *Example:* The top cards is ♡5, and below it
in order are ♡6, ♡7, ♣8. The first one, two or three cards
may be moved as a unit. But if the second card is ♢6, then
♡5 must be moved before ♢6 can be moved.

When all face-up cards have been removed from a pile,
the top face-down card is turned up and becomes available.

Spaces may be filled by any available cards or units. All
spaces must be filled before additional cards are dealt.

The Hand. When building on the original tableau comes
to a standstill, an additional row of ten cards is dealt face
up on the tableau piles. Similarly, each time all possible or
desired plays are completed, an additional row is dealt, until
the hand is exhausted. There is no redeal.

The Object of Play is to assemble thirteen cards of a suit,
in sequence from ace to king (top to bottom). When a suit
is so assembled, at the top of a tableau pile, thirteen cards
may be lifted off and discarded from play. It need not be
discarded at once, however; it may be used to aid in further
operations on the tableau. The game is won if the pack is
discarded in eight sequences of suits.

NAPOLEON AT ST. HELENA
(Forty Thieves, Big Forty)
Two packs

Tableau. Deal ten cards in a row, face up. Deal three
more face-up rows overlapping the first, making 40 cards
in all.

Foundations. Aces, which must be placed in a row above
the tableau as soon as available. Each foundation must be
built up in suit and sequence to the king.

Building. Only the uppermost card of a tableau pile is
available. An available card may be played on a foundation,
or on a tableau card of next-higher rank in the same unit.

Spaces may be filled by any available cards. Note that a
king on a tableau pile may be moved only to a space or to
a foundation.

Hand cards are turned up one at a time, and are placed in

a talon pile which may be spread out so that all cards are identifiable. The top card of the talon may be played onto foundations or tableau. The hand is run through only once.

CALCULATION

One pack

Foundations. Place in a row one ace, one two, one three, and one four, regardless of suits. Each foundation must be built up in arithmetic sequence as follows:

A, 2, 3, 4, 5, 6, 7, 8, 9, 10, J, Q, K
2, 4, 6, 8, 10, Q, A, 3, 5, 7, 9, J, K
3, 6, 9, Q, 2, 5, 8, J, A, 4, 7, 10, K
4, 8, Q, 3, 7, J, 2, 6, 10, A, 5, 9, K

Suits are ignored throughout the play.

Hand cards are turned up one by one. A card that cannot be played on a foundation must be placed in one of four *waste piles* in a row below the foundations. Waste piles may be spread so that all cards are identifiable. Once on a waste pile, a card may be removed only if it can be played on a foundation. The uppermost card of a pile alone is available. The hand is run through only once.

CLOCK

One pack

Tableau. Deal the entire pack in thirteen packets of four cards, face down. Place the first twelve packets in a circle; consider them to be numbered like the face of a clock. The thirteenth packet goes in the center.

The Play. Turn over the top card of the 13-pile. Suppose it to be a seven. Place it face up, halfway underneath the 7-pile, and turn up the top of that pile. Suppose this card to be a three; place it partially under the 3-pile and turn up the top card of that pile—and so on. A jack counts as 11, queen as 12, king as 13, ace as 1.

The game is won if all other cards are turned face up before the fourth king is reached. The game ends when the fourth king turns up, because then the 13-pile does not furnish a card with which to continue play.

GOLF

One pack

Tableau. Deal a row of seven cards face up. Deal four more rows face up on the first, spread so that all cards are identifiable. The tableau thus comprises 35 cards.

The Play. Turn up the first card from the hand and place it to start the talon. Any card at the top of the tableau pile may be removed and placed on the talon if it is in sequence with the top card there—*either up or down.* A series of cards may be played off the tableau talon, in one turn, provided that each pair of adjacent cards is in sequence, either way. *Example:* Top card of talon is a 4; this may be built 4, 5, 6, 5, 4, 3, or 4, 3, 2, 3, 2, A, etc. Suits are ignored. But the sequence is not continuous; only a two may be placed on an ace, and a king *stops* the sequence (no card may be played on a king).

Cards are turned up from the hand and put on the talon, one at a time, until the stock is exhausted. There is no redeal.

The Object of Play is to remove all cards from the tableau into the talon. Since a tableau card may be moved only into the talon, a space has no special use.

A game is won if the tableau is completely cleared. Another way of scoring is to try to beat "par" of 36 "strokes" in nine "holes." Each deal is a hole; each card left in the tableau at the end of a deal is a stroke; par is a total of 36 in nine deals. If the tableau is cleared, any cards remaining in the hand count one "minus stroke" each, and are subtracted from the running score.

MULTIPLE GOLF

Golf Solitaire may be played as a contest among several participants. It is especially popular for two. Each is provided with a pack. Each plays nine "holes" of Golf Solitaire, and the "strokes" required for each hole are recorded on paper. A player wins 1 point for each hole he beats his opponent ("match play"), and the player with the smaller total for the nine scores 5 points ("medal play"). "Minus strokes" are duly subtracted from the final total.

POKER SOLITAIRE

One pack

Tableau. Deal the first 25 cards one by one, placing them in five rows of five cards each, with columns aligned. Each card may be placed anywhere with respect to those previously placed, so long as all remain within the limits of a "square" 5 x 5. (Some play that each card must be adjacent, if only at a corner, to some card previously placed.) Once put in position, a card may not be moved.

The Object of Play is to score as high a total as possible when each row and each column of the tableau is reckoned as a Poker hand.

Scoring. The English system of scoring is in accord with the relative difficulty of making the hands in Poker Solitaire. The American system preserves the ranking of the hands at Poker, ignoring the conditions of Solitaire play.

HAND	ENGLISH SYSTEM	AMERICAN SYSTEM
Royal Flush	30	100
Straight Flush	30	75
Four of a Kind	16	50
Full House	10	25
Flush	5	20
Straight	12	15
Three of a Kind	6	10
Two Pairs	3	5
One Pair	1	2

Variant Game. Count off 25 cards, examine them at leisure, and make the best possible count by placing them in a 5 x 5 square.

POKER SQUARES

This is a multiple way of playing Poker Solitaire. Any number of players may participate. Each is provided with one pack.

One player is appointed *caller* in each round (or the caller may be a non-player). Caller shuffles his pack, then turns up the first 25 cards one by one, announcing each aloud. All other players sort their packs into suits. When a card is called, each player finds it in his pack and places it in his own tableau. The player with the tableau of highest count wins the round or game.

As Poker Squares is intended to be a game of skill, the English system of scoring should be used.

CRIBBAGE SOLITAIRE (DOMINO)

One pack

Deal three cards to hand, two cards to crib, then three to hand. Look at the hand and lay away two cards to the crib. Turn up the top card of the stock for the starter. Using a cribbage board, score the hand as in Cribbage (see page 72), then discard it. Turn up the crib, score it, and discard it. Place the starter on the bottom of the stock. Deal again in the same way, and repeat until the stock is exhausted. At the end, there will be four cards left; turn them up and score them as a hand.

A jack turned as starter counts 2 for his heels. A jack in hand or crib or same suit as starter counts 1 for his nobs.

This Solitaire is recommended to beginners at Cribbage as an excellent way to learn scoring, and strategy of laying away. Average score for a game is said to be 85. A score of 121 may be considered to "win."

CRIBBAGE SOLITAIRE (SQUARE)

One pack

Deal the first 16 cards one by one, placing them in four rows of four cards each. A card may be placed anywhere with reference to those previously placed, so long as all remain within a square 4x4. Turn up the 17th card as the starter. Count each row and column of the tableau, with the starter, as a Cribbage hand. (See page 72.) A jack turned as starter counts 2 for his heels; a jack in the tableau of same suit as starter counts 1 for his nobs (once only, not once for the row and once for the column).

The game may be considered "won" if the total is 61 or more.

Russian Bank or Crapette

THIS POPULAR pastime for two players is often called a "game," but is really a double solitaire.

CARDS. Two packs of 52, with different backs. Each of the two players has his own pack. The cards in each suit rank: K (high), Q, J, 10, 9, 8, 7, 6, 5, 4, 3, 2, A.

PRELIMINARIES. One pack is spread face down and each player draws a card. The lower card has choice of packs and seats, and plays first. Each player then shuffles the pack to be used by his opponent.

Each deals cards from his own pack to make the *layout*. First, twelve cards are dealt face down in a pile at the player's right; these are his *stock*. Next, four cards are dealt face up in a column above the stock, extending toward the opponent. The two columns are the *tableau*. The rest of the pack, called the *hand*, is placed face down at the player's left.

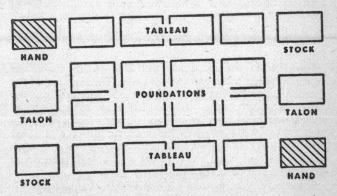

The players sit at left and right of this diagram. Each has his *stock* at his right and *hand* at his left. The stock (as well as hand) is dealt face down, but the top card remains face up after the player has begun his first turn.

THE PLAY. The first player must begin by moving all available aces, if any, into the space between the columns of the tableau. At the outset, only the tableau cards are *available* (for play). Later, any card turned up from the stock or the hand is available. When any build has been placed on a tableau card, only the uppermost card is available.

FOUNDATIONS. The eight aces are the *foundations*. When any ace becomes available it must be moved to the *center* before any other play is made.

Foundations must be built up in suit and sequence, from ace to king. If any available card can be played on a foundation, this play must be made before any other. In short, a play to the center has priority over all others.

PLAYS IN THE TABLEAU. On a tableau pile may be placed a card of next-lower rank and opposite color to the uppermost card, e.g. either red seven may be placed on ♣8. Into a *space* created in the tableau, by removal of one entire pile, the player may move any uppermost card of a tableau pile, or (before turning a card from the *hand*) a card turned up from his stock.

Before playing in the tableau, the player is entitled to turn up the top card of his stock, as a possible guide to his play. After his first turn, he may do this even before satisfying the center (from the tableau). A play to the center from the stock takes priority over a play from the tableau.

Cards from the stock are available to be played on foundations or built onto the tableau. Having come to a standstill, and having filled all spaces in the tableau, the player next turns up a card from his hand. This card likewise is available for play on foundations or tableau. If its play makes the stock card playable, or allows additional moves in the tableau, all such plays may be made, but an unplayable card must show on top of the stock before another card is turned from the hand.

If the card from the hand is unplayable, it is laid face up directly before the player, on the *talon* or wastepile. The act of placing the card there ends the player's turn.

LOADING. The first player having concluded his first turn, the second player turns up the top of his stock and commences play under the foregoing rules, but now there is an added possibility. He may build available cards (from tableau, his stock, or his hand) *upon the adverse stock and hand.* The building here is in suit and sequence, but the sequence may go up or down. For example, if ◇9 lies on a player's stock, his opponent may cover it successively with ◇8, ◇9, ◇10, ◇J, ◇10, etc. Of course there is no object in *loading* the opponent with uppermost cards from the tableau, unless some change is made therein which prevents his returning the cards at his next turn.

Each player in turn makes all possible or desirable plays until compelled to place an unplayable card from his hand upon his talon, or until *stopped* as below. When a hand is exhausted, the talon is turned over and becomes a new hand. When a stock is exhausted, the player may fill spaces from his hand. Play continues until one player gets rid of all his cards from stock and talon and thereby wins the game.

STOPS. If a player violates a rule, his opponent is entitled to call "Stop!" and the offender's turn ends. The rules are as follows:

1. Play to the center takes priority above all else. (There is no compulsion to make playable tableau cards available by manipulations to remove covering cards.)

2. Among possible plays to the center, play from the stock takes priority over play from the tableau or hand. There is no priority among plays from the tableau. Play from the hand takes precedence over play from the tableau.

3. All spaces in the tableau must be filled, from the stock, before a card is turned from the hand. After the stock is exhausted, spaces may be filled from the hand.

SCORING. The winner scores 30 points for the game, plus 1 point for each card left in his opponent's hand and talon and 2 points for each card in his stock.

IRREGULARITIES. Any cards may be touched for the purpose of arranging, if expressly stated; otherwise, a player who touches one card when another should be played first under the rules may be stopped.

A stop may not be called for a move not in priority, if the offender has been allowed to complete another play thereafter. But attention may be drawn to the error, and the omitted play (if still possible) thereafter takes its due priority.

If a player makes an incorrect build, as ♡7 on ♣9, the move must be retracted on demand, but the player may not be stopped.

If a player exposes or sees a card of his hand or stock, other than one regularly turned, he may complete a move unless his opponent calls "Stop."

A player may spread his talon for the purpose of examining the cards, but may not spread his opponent's talon without permission. When a talon is so examined, both players are entitled to see the cards.

When a stop is called for a play out of order, the play must be retracted. When a stop is called for turning a card from stock or hand out of order, the opponent may direct whether such card shall be left up or turned down.

Black Jack or Twenty-one

NEARLY two hundred years ago a French book commented, speaking of a game called "The Farm," that the game was *very ancient.* Yet The Farm was almost identical with the game called Black Jack in American homes. The same game is almost the only card game played in American gambling houses, where it is called Twenty-one; the French know it as Vingt-et-un ("twenty-one"); and the English as Van John, an obvious corruption of Vingt-et-un.

PLAYERS. Any number can play, but five to nine make the best game.

CARDS. The pack of 52 cards is used, often with a joker or blank card which does not figure in the play. It is desirable and permissible to use a double pack of 104 cards, consisting of two 52-card packs shuffled together, plus one joker or blank card.

Values of Cards. The cards have no rank, but have numerical value as follows: Any ace counts 1 or 11, at the option of the holder. Any face card or ten counts 10. Any other card counts its index number.

PRELIMINARIES. There may be a permanent dealer, or the right to deal may pass from player to player. When it does, any player picks up a shuffled pack and deals the cards out face up, one at a time to each player, until a jack shows up. The player to whom the jack falls is the first dealer.

If a joker or blank card is used, dealer places this face up at the bottom of the pack to mark the end of the shuffled cards. If no such card is used, dealer turns up the top card of the pack, shows it to all players and (unless it is an ace) places it face up at the bottom of the pack. This is called *burning* a card. If the card so turned up is an ace, the pack must be reshuffled.

DEALING. Dealer gives one card face down to every player in rotation, beginning at his left and including himself. He then gives each other player, in the same rotation, one card face down; and gives himself a card face up.

BETTING. If there is a permanent dealer, each player must

place a bet, at least one chip and no more than the maximum established by the dealer at the beginning of the game, *before* any card is dealt.

If the game is played with a changing dealer, each player may look at the first card dealt to him and then place a bet from one chip up to the maximum; the dealer may then look at his card and, if he wishes, double all such bets; and then each other player may redouble, which ends the betting.

Each player bets only with the dealer.

THE PLAY. When each player, including the dealer, has two cards, each player in turn, beginning with the eldest hand and including the dealer, has the right to draw additional cards one at a time.

Object of the Game. Each player's object is to have cards whose numerical values total 21, or as close to 21 as possible without exceeding 21.

Naturals. If a player's first two cards count exactly 21— that is, if they are a face card or ten and an ace—he has a *natural* or *black jack* and wins immediately, unless dealer also has a natural.

If there is a permanent dealer, he pays such a player one and one-half times the player's bet, but if the dealer has a natural he collects only singly from each other player. If a permanent dealer and any other player both have naturals, the bet between them is a stand-off.

If there is a changing dealer, and any other player has a natural, the dealer pays that player twice the amount of that player's bet, doubled or redoubled as the case may be; if only the dealer has a natural, he collects from each other player twice the amount of that player's bet, doubled or redoubled as the case may be; and if the dealer and any other player both have naturals, dealer collects the amount of the bet, but only singly.

When there is a changing dealer, the first player opposed to the dealer who gets a natural becomes the next dealer (after all bets of the current deal have been settled) unless the dealer also has a natural, in which case he remains the dealer.

The dealer may not look at his face-down card to see if he has a natural unless his face-up card is an ace, face card, or ten.

Hitting. If dealer has no natural, when all bets on naturals have been settled, each player in turn, beginning with eldest hand, may draw additional cards until he chooses to *stand*, which means that he has a count of 21 or less and does not desire any more cards; or until he *busts*, which means that he has a count of more than 21. In the latter case, he pays the amount of his bet to dealer immediately.

A player who wishes an additional card says "Hit me." Dealer then gives him one card face up. There is no limit to the number of cards a player may so draw, except that he may not draw a card after his count equals or passes 21.

When a player wishes no more cards, he says "I stand," whereupon dealer proceeds to serve the next player to his left.

Play of Dealer's Cards. When all other players have been served, dealer turns up his face-down card. A permanent dealer must now stand if his count is 17 or more, and must hit himself if and so long as his count is 16 or less. A changing dealer may choose whether to stand or to take another card at any count.

If dealer goes over 21, he pays the amount of each bet not previously settled. If dealer stands at a figure of 21 or less, he settles with each other player who has stood. A permanent dealer pays any higher count, collects from any lower count, and is at a stand-off with any player having the same count; a changing dealer pays any higher count but collects from any player having the same or a lower count.

REDEALING. As each bet is settled, dealer takes the cards that are thus put out of play and places them face up on the bottom of the pack. When the deal brings the dealer to a face-up card, all face-up cards in the pack are shuffled by the dealer, any player in the game cuts them, and the deal continues. Dealer may also choose at the beginning of any deal to shuffle all cards, if in his opinion there will not be enough to complete the deal.

Whenever the dealer changes, there is a new shuffle of all the cards for the next deal.

PLAYER'S OPTIONS. *Splitting a Pair.* If a player's first two cards are the same—as two sixes, or two queens—he may place the same bet on each card that he placed originally on his single hand, and play them as two different hands. When his turn comes, he announces this, whereupon he exposes both cards and dealer gives him one card face down to go with each of them. He then plays each as a separate hand, hitting or standing independently of the other. Dealer settles with each hand separately, as though they were played by different players.

*One Down for Eleven.** If a player's first two cards have a numerical value of eleven, as a six and a five, or a seven and a four, he may turn them both face up when his turn comes, double his bet, and receive one card from the dealer face down. He may not ask for an additional card. Later dealer will settle with him on the total count of the three cards.

BONUS PAYMENTS. When there is a permanent dealer, as in a Twenty-one game played in a gambling house, bonus payments are not made. In the game played less formally, any of the following bonus payments, by agreement among the players, may be adopted:

Five and Under. If a player has a total of five cards and his total is still 21 or under, he may show his cards and collect double his bet, and cannot be beaten by dealer even if dealer later gets a total closer to 21; or the player may draw another card and try to get six cards with a total of under 21.

If a player gets six cards and his total is under 21, he collects four times the amount of his bet, and cannot be beaten, as described in the preceding paragraph.

Though a player may be under 21 in five cards, he loses if he draws another card and it carries him over 21.

Three Sevens. If a player's first three cards are sevens, giving him exactly 21, he immediately collects three times the amount of his bet and cannot be tied or beaten even if dealer also gets 21 later. This is played only occasionally.

8, 7, 6. If a player makes 21 with eight, seven and six, he immediately collects double the amount of his bet and cannot be tied or beaten. This is seldom played.

Dealer does not receive any bonus for making any of these combinations.

IRREGULARITIES. If a dealer fails to burn a card, he must, on demand, shuffle the remainder of the pack and burn a card before continuing the deal.

If dealer gives any player his first card face up, that player must still make his bet, but dealer must give him his next card face down. If dealer fails to give him his next card face down, the player may withdraw his bet and drop out for that deal.

* Many games do not limit this to a hand totaling 11.

Any player who stands must expose his face-down card as soon as dealer has stood or gone over. If that player has in fact a total of more than 21, he must pay dealer double the amount of his bet even if dealer has gone over.

If the dealer gives a player two cards on the first round of dealing, that player may choose which card to keep and which to discard; or may keep both cards, play two hands, and place a bet on each. He may not, however, play both cards as belonging to the same hand.

If dealer gives a player two cards on the second round of dealing, the player may choose which to keep and must discard the other.

If dealer gives a card to a player who did not ask for it, that player may keep the card if he chooses, or may refuse it, in which case it is a discard and is placed face up at the bottom of the pack. The next player in turn may not claim it.

If a card is faced in the pack, the player to whom it would fall may accept it or refuse it.

An irregularity must be corrected if discovered before the bet has been settled; after the bet has been settled, there can be no correction.

If dealer has a natural, but fails to announce it before dealing an additional card to any player, his hand constitutes a count of 21 but can be tied by the hand of any other player whose total is 21 in three or more cards.

STRATEGY: Formerly considered the second most favorable game to the player in the odds he bucked, computer studies have altered the recommended strategy so that the player has almost an even chance. In fact case-counters—players who memorize the cards that have already appeared—are unwelcome at the Black Jack tables, even though the house has altered its rules by adding decks, never dealing the last quarter of the stock and reserving the right to shuffle at any time. The important cards to remember are 5s (because dealer must draw to 16) and 10-cards, because a pack that is rich in high cards increases the chance that the house will go overboard.

The dealer's big advantage is that he plays last; before he plays he has collected from all hands that have already gone overboard. Casino rules require that the dealer draw to 16; stand on 17 or more. But this does not mean that the player should follow the same strategy; quite the contrary, the player should judge his action by the size of the dealer's up-card and the knowledge that the dealer will have to draw if his total is 16 or less. The effect upon the bettor's strategy is so profound that, for example, he should stand on 12 if the dealer's up-card is 4, 5 or 6.

The following chart summarizes the preferred action by the player. (*Soft* means a total arrived at by considering the ace as 1; *hard* refers to a hand that does not include an ace.)

Remembering whether the remainder of the pack is 10-rich or 5-rich will greatly improve your chances—but not your popularity. In a casino, the dealer will spot a case-counter pretty quickly. In a home game, especially if you do not spend a lot of time at it, it may not be noticed.

Insurance: When dealer's up-card is an ace and your hand has given you a natural, you may purchase insurance against his having a natural. Insurance pays you 2 to 1. If you invest half your bet in insurance, you have a sure win of 50% of that bet, whether he holds a natural or not. If he has a natural, you collect the insurance and get your stake back. If he doesn't, you collect your bet and lose the insurance. Correct odds against his having the natural are 5 to 2—but who can afford to turn down a sure thing?

Buy the bank? In home games, where dealer pays 2 to 1 for a natural, it will usually be worth buying the bank for three times the betting limit. Your maximum offer should not exceed four times, even though on such games the bank usually collects on ties. Also, the home banker is not bound to draw or stand, depending solely on his total. He can play as he deems necessary against all the opponents still remaining in the deal, or against the biggest bet.

CHART I. WHEN TO HIT AND WHEN TO STAND

YOUR TOTAL (in two or more cards)	STAND if dealer's showing card is	HIT if dealer's showing card is
8 to 11	Never stand	Always hit—but see below
12	4, 5, or 6	All other cases
13	2 or 3	All other cases
14, 15, or 16	2, 3, 4, 5, or 6	10, 9, 8, 7, or Ace
Hard 17 (such as 9 & 8)	Ace, 2, 3, 4, 5, 6 or 7	10, 9, or 8
Hard 18 (such as 10 & 8)	Always stand (but see Chart II below)	Never hit
Soft 18 (such as Ace & 7)	Ace, 2, 3, 4, 5, 6, 7, or 8 (but see Chart III below)	10 or 9
19, 20, or 21	Always stand	Never hit

CHART II. WHEN TO SPLIT A PAIR

YOU HAVE A PAIR OF	SPLIT if dealer's showing card is	DO NOT SPLIT if dealer's showing card is
Aces	Always split	
2's or 3's	2, 3, 4, 5, 6, or 7	10, 9, 8 or Ace
4's	5	All other cases
6's	2, 3, 4, 5, 6, or 7	10, 9, 8 or Ace
7's	2, 3, 4, 5,6, 7, or 8	10, 9, or Ace
8's	Always split	
9's	2, 3, 4, 5, 6, 7, 8 or 9*	10, 7, or Ace*
5's, 10's or face cards	Never split	Never split

CHART III. WHEN TO TAKE ONE DOWN FOR DOUBLE

YOUR FIRST TWO CARDS TOTAL (not including an Ace)	TAKE ONE DOWN FOR DOUBLE only if dealer's showing card is
11	Anything but an Ace
10	2 to 9, but not a 10, face card, or Ace
9	2 to 6, but not 7 or higher, or an Ace
Soft 17 (such as Ace & 6)	2 to 6

* The 7 has been included in both categories because the calculations appear extremely close. There seems to be some small edge in not splitting when dealer's card is a 7 on the grounds that your 18 will beat his 17 if his unseen card is a 10-card.

Faro

FARO, once the principal American gambling game, is not of American origin. Originally it was spelled Pharaoh, the name supposedly having been taken from the picture of a Pharaoh on French playing cards of the 17th century. It was known in England at least as early as 1700. In the 20th century it lost out to craps in American gambling houses, but is still played in a few places, notably in Nevada.

EQUIPMENT. On the Faro table there is a green cloth on which are enameled representations of the thirteen cards of the spade suit. At one end sits the dealer, with a dealing box in which a shuffled pack is placed face up. Other representatives of the bank are a *casekeeper,* who keeps track of the cards that have already shown up and therefore cannot reappear during the current deal; and one or more cashiers who pay and collect bets.

BETTING. All bets must be placed against the house. With the minor exceptions described later, all bets are even-money bets.

A player bets that a certain card will *win* by placing chips on the place in the layout reserved for that rank; this constitutes a bet that a card of that rank in any suit will win, though it is only the spade suit that is shown on the layout. Also, a player may bet on a card of any rank to *lose* by *coppering* his bet, which he does by placing a copper token on the chips.

By the manner in which he places his chips upon the layout, a player may also bet that any one of two, three or more cards will win, or, if the bet is coppered, that such card or combination of cards will lose.

THE PLAY. After any other player has had an opportunity to shuffle, the dealer shuffles the cards, has them cut, cuts them himself, and places them face up in the dealing box in which only the top card is exposed. Thus having them placed, he takes off the top card, which is called *soda* and "has no action"; this card does not affect bets, but is placed face up beside the box to found the pile of cards which win.

The next card is taken out of the box and placed a few inches away from soda; a bet on this rank loses, while a bet on the rank of the card left exposed in the box wins. This ends the first *turn;* bets settled by that turn are paid or collected, new bets may be placed, and the bets unsettled remain on the layout. The new bets having been placed, the dealer pulls off the exposed card and places it on the pile of winning cards; pulls off the next card, which loses, and places it on the pile of losing cards; and leaves exposed in the box another winning card.

This continues until three unknown cards remain in the box. Since the casekeeper has kept a record of the cards which have shown, the nature of the last three cards is known, and these may come up in any one of six different ways. No bets to win or lose are settled by the last turn, but the house pays 4-to-1 to anyone who guesses the order in which the last three cards appear. This is *calling the turn.* If the last three cards include a pair, it is a *cat-hop,* and the house pays even money to anyone who bets he can call the order in which they will come up.

Splits. A split occurs when two cards of the same rank come up in the same turn, so that the same rank both wins and loses. In such a case, the house takes one-half of everything that has been bet on that rank, the other half of each bet being returned to the player who made it.

STUSS

There is no difference between Faro and Stuss except that the latter is a far less elaborately established gambling game, the dealer merely holding one pack of cards in his hand and turning them up one by one, but with the same rules of play. In Stuss, when a split occurs, the banker takes all bets on that rank, instead of only half of them as in Faro.

Baccarat and Chemin-de-fer

THESE are among the games most often played for high stakes in the French casinos. Baccarat, the original game, has been almost replaced by its offspring, Chemin-de-fer.

BACCARAT

A banker is determined by auction, the high bidder putting up the amount of his bid as the bank. As many as ten other players may be "active" against him, seated in an established order of precedence usually depending upon the amount each of them bid. Other players in the room may also bet, but the banker is committed to pay bets against him only to the extent of his bank plus whatever winnings he has accumulated.

Each player in order of precedence may bet any amount up to the amount of the bank, less whatever has been bet by players preceding him. A player who calls *"Banco!"* bets the entire amount of the bank and all previous lower bets are cancelled. A player not seated at the table may bet only what is not covered by seated players, unless he bancos when no seated player has.

At least three, and often as many as six 52-card packs are shuffled together and placed in a dealing box called a *shoe*. Sliding the cards off the top of the pack, the banker deals three hands of two cards each, one at a time, one to his left, one to his right and one to himself. Players (*punters,* or opponents of the bank) may bet that the left will beat the banker, or that the right will beat the banker, or that both will beat the banker (a bet *à cheval*). A player who bancos may split his bet between the two sides as he pleases.

Face cards and tens count 0, aces 1 each, other cards their index value. When the total is 10 or more the 10 is deducted; *e.g.* a seven and a six, totalling 13, count as 3. Each player's purpose is to be as close as possible to 9 in two or three cards. First the hand on the right may stand or demand one more card, dealt face up; then the hand on the left has this privilege; then the dealer has this privilege.

214

The rules require that a player draw if his count is 4 or less, stand if his count is 6 or more, and use his own judgment if his count is 5. The dealer may use his own judgment whatever his count.

An original count of 8 or 9 is a *natural*. The holder shows this immediately and wins unless the opponent ties with the same number or wins with a natural nine against an eight. In the absence of a natural, dealer settles with each hand separately, winning if that hand is not so close to 9, losing if that hand is closer to 9, and tying if the two hands have the same figure.

If a player has bet à cheval, he wins if the banker loses to both hands; loses if the banker wins from both hands; and withdraws his bet unsettled if the banker wins from one side and loses to the other.

The banker may not reduce the amount of his bank (plus winnings) at any time, but may withdraw after any deal (*coup*) has been completed and the bets settled. If the banker loses his entire bank or if he withdraws, the bank is put up at auction again.

The cards are not reshuffled until the bank changes, or until there are only seven or fewer cards left undealt.

CHEMIN-DE-FER

The rules and objectives of Chemin-de-fer are the same as in Baccarat, but two instead of three hands are dealt and the right to bank moves from player to player in rotation to the right, as follows:

The first banker is selected at auction or by lot, and if the latter he states the amount of his bank. Other players in rotation to the right may take all or any portion of the bank until all has been covered. A person may banco as at Baccarat.

The banker then deals two hands of two cards each, one for his opponents collectively and one for himself. The player who made the largest bet against him plays the opposing hand. A natural is shown immediately and settled as in Baccarat; otherwise the punter, and then the banker, may stand or may draw one card. The hands are compared. If the banker wins or ties, he remains the banker; if he loses, the next player in turn to the right becomes the banker and states the amount of his bank; except that a person who bancos and wins may become the next banker.

Oh Hell, Oh Pshaw, or Blackout

THIS GAME, of mysterious origin, began to be popular in 1931. It has the rare merit of being extremely simple to learn, while affording extraordinary opportunity for skill.

PLAYERS: Three to seven. The best game is with four. Each plays for himself.

CARDS: The pack of 52. The cards in each suit rank: A (high), K, Q, J, 10, 9, 8, 7, 6, 5, 4, 3, 2.

DEALING. A game comprises a series of deals. For the first deal, each player receives one card; for the next, two; and so on to the point where the entire pack is dealt. The hands must be equal; therefore any extra cards left over in the last deal are put aside unseen. (Some play that the extra cards are exposed.) With four players, a game is thus 13 deals; with five, 10 deals; with six, 8 deals; with seven, 7 deals. With only three players, the game is better limited to 15 deals.

The deal rotates to the left. When more than one game is played without reseating the first dealer should be changed in each game, since the last dealer in a game has an advantage.

After every deal in a game but the last, the next card of the pack is turned up for trump. No card is turned for the last deal, which is played at no trump.

BIDDING. Each player in turn, commencing with eldest hand, must make a bid. This bid is the precise number of tricks that the player believes he can win. The minimum is "zero," often signified by "pass;" the maximum is the number of cards in the hand. Thus on the first deal the only alternatives are "zero" and "one." Each player contracts to win exactly the amount of his bid—neither less or more.

All the bids must be recorded by an agreed scorekeeper, and after the bidding is completed he should announce "over," "under," or "even," indicating that the total tricks bid exceed, fall short of, or equal the number of cards per hand.

THE PLAY. Eldest hand makes the opening lead. A lead calls upon each other hand to follow suit if able; if unable, the hand may play any card. A trick is won by the highest trump if any, otherwise by the highest card of the suit led. The winner of a trick leads to the next.

SCORING. A player who exactly makes his contract scores 10 plus the amount of his bid. A player who "busts" by winning more or less tricks than his bid scores nothing. The player with the highest total score at the end of a game wins.

Various methods of settlement are used. The winner may collect from every other player, according to the difference of respective totals. Or the winner may receive a game bonus of 10 points, and then each player may settle with every other upon the difference of scores.

(There is variation in the scoring of a "zero" contract. Some circles allow only 5 points; others allow 5 plus the number of cards per hand in the deal. The latter method takes account of the fact that zero contracts are easier to make when there are fewer cards in play.)

IRREGULARITIES. *Bid Out of Turn.* There is no penalty for a bid out of turn, but such a bid must stand. The turn to bid reverts to the rightful player. A player may change his bid without penalty before the player at his left bids.

A Lead or Play Out of Turn must be retracted on demand and the card played in error must be left face up on the table and played at the first legal opportunity. A card exposed in any way but legal play is dealt with in the same way.

Information. A player is entitled to be informed at any time how much any other player has bid, and how many tricks each player has won. Each player should keep his tricks arranged so that they may be counted by inspection.

Etiquette. By far the most important rule is one solely of etiquette. When a player sees that he is "busted"—unable to make his bid—he should refrain from communicating this fact to the table.

Spite and Malice

Primarily a two-hand card game of recent origin, Spite and Malice is especially popular as a husband-vs-wife game and in many areas has supplanted Russian Bank, which in some ways it resembles. The rules as originally played are given first, followed by variant rules worked out by Easley Blackwood (variants indicated in the original rules by an asterisk). Blackwood was first to publish a book on the game (*Spite & Malice*, Cornerstone Library) incorporating his variations and many suggestions for skillful play.

PLAYERS. Two.

CARDS. Two packs. Pack A is a standard 52-card pack. Pack B is a standard 52-card pack plus four jokers. The packs should be of different back designs or colors.

RANK OF CARDS. K (high), Q, J, 10, 9, 8, 7, 6, 5, 4, 3, 2, A (low).

PRELIMINARIES. Pack A is shuffled and divided into two 26-card packets, which become the *pay-off piles* of the two players. Each player turns up the top card of his pay-off pile; the higher card designates the first player, and if the cards are the same rank* the pay-off piles are shuffled and new cards turned up.

Pack B is shuffled by the first player's opponent, who deals a five-card hand to each player (one at a time, face down) and puts the remainder of Pack B in the center as the *stock*.

OBJECT OF THE GAME. To get rid of one's pay-off pile.

THE PLAY. Each available ace must be played immediately to form a *center stack*. There may be any number of center stacks. Each available two must be played, if possible, on an ace in a center stack.* Center stacks are built up in ascending order, regardless of suit—any deuce on any ace, any three on any two, etc. Both players play to center stacks.

Each player may have four *side stacks*. These are discard piles. A player may play only to his own side stacks and only from his hand. Any card may start a side stack. Side stacks are built downward, regardless of suit (any five on any six), or with like cards (any queen on any queen).

The top card of a pay-off pile may be played only to the center. When it is played, the next card is turned up. A card from the hand or from the top of a side stack may be played to the center. A card from the hand may be played to a side stack, but only one such card in a turn. A player may make as many legal plays to center stacks as he wishes but when he plays to a side stack his turn ends and his opponent's turn begins. Cards may not be moved from one side stack to another, or to fill a space.

A player may also end his turn by saying so, when he cannot, or does not wish to, play.

RULES OF PLAY. Each joker is wild and may be played in place of any card except an ace. If a joker becomes available at the top of a side stack, it may be played to the center.

At the beginning of each turn, a player draws enough cards from the stock to restore his hand to five cards.*

When any center stack is built up through the king, it is shuffled into the stock.

SCORING. The player who first gets rid of all the cards in his pay-off pile wins, his margin being the number of cards in his opponent's pay-off pile. If there are cards left in both pay-off piles and neither player can or will play, the winner is the player who has fewer cards in his pay-off pile and he wins the difference; but it is never legal to count the cards in a pay-off pile.*

BLACKWOOD VARIATIONS

PRELIMINARIES: A tie in the rank of the first turn-up card in the pay-off pile is broken by suit rank, spades (high), hearts, diamonds and clubs (low). Otherwise, suits ranks are of no consequence.

THE PLAY: An ace or a playable deuce on the pay-off pile or the discard pile *must* be played to the center. But a player is not required to play an ace or deuce from his concealed hand *except when both players claim to be frozen.* A player is not required to play a joker at any time, whether from concealed hand or from a discard pile. He may also declare himself *frozen* (unable to make a play or a discard) even though he has a playable card. If both players become frozen, voluntarily or otherwise, all of the center piles, discard piles and concealed hands are reshuffled into a new stockpile, five cards are dealt to each and the game continues. Only the pay-off piles remain intact.

If during one turn a player is able to play his entire concealed hand to the center (he may not use one for a discard) he draws five more cards and continues his turn.

A joker that becomes available at the top of a discard pile may be played to the center and called any rank. It does not necessarily retain the rank for which it was used in the discard pile.

Completed center stacks (ace to king) are added to the stock only when the stock is about to become depleted. If there is no completed center stack, the cards in the center stacks are shuffled to form a new stock.

Counting pay-off piles: A player may count his own pay-off pile and may require the opponent to count his and announce the total.

Scoring: In addition to one point for each card remaining in opponent's pay-off pile, winner gets 5 points for going out. Play may be for a series total (average win is 11 points in a game) i.e., winner is first to reach 25, 50, 100, etc. (But higher totals are unlikely to be reached in a single session.)

STRATEGY: The player must aim primarily at getting rid of his immediate pay-off card while at the same time endeavoring not to help opponent get rid of his. Discard piles should be maintained so as to give widest variety of discards; discard should be chosen so as to retain one or more discards for next turn. If possible, discard piles should not be blocked by doubling up with two or more cards of the same rank. If doubling up is necessary, try to confine such plays to cards at the head of the pile. Doubling kings or queens will rarely hurt. Starting all discard piles with cards of the same rank, or of high rank, is not desirable.

In some cases it may be wise to announce a freeze rather than foul a promising discard pile. In other cases you wish to avoid playing to the center a card that will permit opponent to get rid of his up-card on the pay-off pile, and will defer such a play by claiming a freeze. Even though a frozen player cannot draw until he has reduced his hand to less than five cards, strategy may demand such action.

Dominoes

DOMINOES are rectangular pieces of bone, ivory, wood, etc. Each *bone* is divided, by a line through the center, into two *ends,* and each end is marked by dots such as are used in marking dice. The commonest set of dominoes comprises 28 bones, as follows:

6-6, 6-5, 6-4, 6-3, 6-2, 6-1, 6-0
5-5, 5-4, 5-3, 5-2, 5-1, 5-0
4-4, 4-3, 4-2, 4-1, 4-0
3-3, 3-2, 3-1, 3-0
2-2, 2-1, 2-0
1-1, 1-0
0-0

Any domino set includes every possible combination of two numbers, from *blank* (0) up to its maximum. A set sometimes used extends to 12-12, and therefore comprises 91 bones.

The bones whose two ends are alike are called *doublets.* Each doublet belongs to one *suit* alone, while every other bone belongs to two suits. In the set up to 6-6, there are seven bones in each suit, but eight *ends* of any one number.

As between two bones, one is *heavier* than the other if it has more dots, the other being *lighter.*

THE DRAW GAME

PLAYERS. Best for two, but can be played by three or even four.

PRELIMINARIES. The bones are turned face down and shuffled. When there are two players, each draws seven bones and so places them that the faces cannot be seen by his opponent. The bones are usually made thick enough to stand on edge, so that they can be placed on the table before the player.

Three or four players draw five bones each.

THE SET. The first bone played is called the *set*. A common practice is to allow the player having the largest doublet to set it A better rule is to alternate in playing first, and allow any bone to be set.

MATCHING. After the set, the two players play alternately. (If there are more than two, the turn passes to the left.) A plays consists in placing a bone adjacent to one already on the table. The cardinal rule is that a bone so played must *match* that upon which it is played—the adjacent ends must show like numbers. *Example:* First player sets 6-6. Second can play only another bone of the 6-suit; suppose he plays 6-4. First player then may follow with a bone of the 6-suit or the 4-suit.

DOUBLETS. Each doublet must be placed *crosswise*. In the basic game, this placement of doublets does not alter the fact that there are always exactly two *open ends* in the layout. The sides of doublets are open; the ends closed; whereas the ends of non-doublets are open, the sides closed.

THE BONEYARD. The bones remaining of the original stock, after the original hands are drawn, constitute the *boneyard*. If unable to play in turn, a player must draw bones one by one from the boneyard until able to play. If he exhausts the boneyard and still cannot play, the turn passes.

Rules sometimes met are: Not all of the boneyard may be drawn; a player must play as soon as he is able; he may not dig deeper into the boneyard in hopes of getting a better bone. Neither of these rules is appropriate to the basic draw game.

SCORING. The first to get rid of his whole hand wins the deal. The winner customarily calls "Domino!" to signify the end of play. The winner scores as many points as there are dots on the bones left in the hands of his opponents. *Game* may be fixed at 50 or 100, or each deal may be treated as a separate game.

If the game ends in a block, with the boneyard exhausted and no player able to play, the one with the lightest total in his hand wins.

IRREGULARITIES. If a player draws less than the correct number of bones for his original hand, he must fill his hand from the boneyard whenever the error is discovered.

If a player draws more than the correct number for his original hand and looks at them, he is forced to keep them all.

If a player exposes a bone, in drawing for his original hand or later, he must take it into his hand.

If a bone is played that does not match, the error must be corrected on demand before the next hand has played, but if the error is not noticed until later it stands as regular.

MUGGINS (ALL FIVES, SNIFF)

Muggins, especially the variant Sniff, is considered by many the best of domino games. It is essentially the draw game, plus the rule that if a player makes the open ends of the layout total 5 or a multiple of 5 he scores that number. Sniff adds some special rules about the set.

To the rules of the draw game add the following:

PRELIMINARIES. To commence a game, shuffle the bones. Each player draws one, and the heavier bone will play first in the first deal. Thereafter the turn to play first rotates. The bones so drawn should be shuffled back so that they cannot be identified.

In two-hand, each player draws seven bones for his hand. With three or four players, each takes five bones.

THE SET. First player may play any bone. The first doublet played, whether set or played later, is *sniff*.

SNIFF. The sniff doublet is open *four ways*. There is free choice of which way to place it (when it is not set) or of how to play on it (when it is set). All other doublets must be placed crosswise.

MUGGINS. There may be two, three or four *open ends* in the layout, dependent on whether branches have been started on the side of sniff. A player scores the total of all open ends when his play makes the total a multiple of 5.

Care must be taken to count all the dots at the open ends, including the whole of a double (unless the doublet is sniff, placed endwise).

Points scored in play are called *muggins* points. Some follow the rule (as in Cribbage) that if a player overlooks a score his opponent may call "Muggins!" and takes the score himself. But this rule applies only by advance agreement. However, a player (including the scorekeeper) must announce a score on making his play in order to receive credit for it.

SCORING. Muggins points are scored when made. The play ends when one hand goes *domino*, or when the boneyard is exhausted and neither can play. The player with the lighter hand remaining wins the difference of total points in the two hands, taken to the nearest five. (That is, 2 becomes 0, 3 and 7 become 5, 8 becomes 10.)

The first to reach a total of 200 points wins the game, and if he reaches game during play, the deal is not finished out.

IRREGULARITIES. Same as for the draw game, except that if a player originally draws too many bones and looks at them, his opponent (before playing) may draw one of them, look at it, and then shuffle it into the boneyard. Once the opponent has played, the irregular hand stands.

ALL THREES

All Threes is in all other respects the same as Muggins, but scores are made by bringing the total of open ends to a multiple of 3.

BERGEN

Follow the rules of the draw game, with the following additions:

The highest doublet must be set. A player who makes both open ends of the layout alike scores 2 points for *double-header*; if there is a doublet on one end when both ends are alike, he scores 3 for *triple-header*. The player who wins the deal, either by going domino or having lightest hand in a block, scores 1 point. Game is 15 points.

MATADOR

Matador is the draw game with a different way of *matching*. Here ends match if they total 7.

Nothing can be played on a blank but a *matador*. There are four matadors: 0-0, 6-1, 5-2, and 4-3. These bones are "wild"; they may be played at any time, and with either end abutting the layout. The play of 0-0 leaves the end open only to another matador. Doublets are placed endwise, not crosswise, and are counted singly in matching: e.g., 2-2 matches with a 5, not with a 3.

THE BLOCK GAME

The Block Game is in all respects like the draw game except there is no drawing from the boneyard. A player unable to play in turn passes. If none goes domino, and none can play, the lightest hand remaining wins the total of all other hands. The two-hand block game is little played, since there is virtually no opportunity to overcome the luck of the draw, but with more players block is preferred to draw.

TIDDLY-WINK

Tiddly-Wink is one of the few games for a large number of players. It is best for six to nine. Each draws three bones. The highest doublet is set. Each hand in turn must play or pass; there is no drawing from the boneyard. There are two peculiarities in the play. There is only one open end—on the bone played last previously. Anyone playing a doublet, including the set, has the right to play again if able. The usual mode of settlement is for all players to ante before the draw; the player who goes domino wins the pool.

Backgammon

BACKGAMMON may be the oldest game still played. It was certainly played by the ancient Greeks and Romans. In England the rules of Backgammon were codified by Edmond Hoyle (about 1750) and the only significant change since has been the addition of doubling. The game we call Backgammon is often called Trictrac, as in France.

PLAYERS. Two. More than two may participate in betting, by Chouette (page 230).

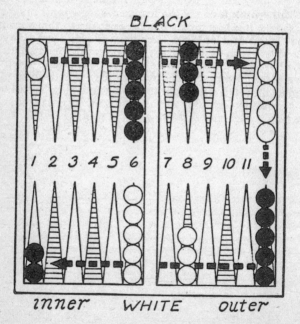

EQUIPMENT. The board (see illustration) is divided into two equal rectangles by *the bar*. One rectangle is the *inner* (or *home*) *table*; the other is the *outer table*. No marking on the board distinguishes the two tables; the players agree which is to be used as inner.

The players sit at opposite sides of the board, and may be designated as Black and White. Projecting from each side of the board toward the center are twelve *points*—elongated triangles. These points are of alternate colors.

Pieces. Each player is provided with fifteen *stones*, which are thick disks like checkers. The two sets of stones are of contrasting colors, which may be designated as black and white (although many different combinations are used).

The placement of the stones on the board for the commencement of a game is shown in the illustration.

Dice. Other equipment necessary comprises four dice and two dice cups.

Doubling Cube. This is a large cube bearing on its faces the numbers 2, 4, 8, 16, 32, 64. It is almost always used in the modern game.

NOTATION. Each point is designated by the initial B or W, according to the side of the board on which it impinges, followed by the numeral of its position counting away from the innermost edge. In this notation the initial array (see illustration) is:

> *Black:* W1 (2); W12 (5); B8 (3); B6 (5).
> *White:* B1 (2); B12 (5); W8 (3); W6 (5).

Each player's 7-point is called his *bar point*. (The 12-point is colloquially called the *comfort station*.) The two stones on the adverse 1-point are called *runners*.

COMMENCEMENT OF PLAY. Each player first rolls one die, and the higher number plays first. The two numbers cast are construed as his first roll. (*Variant.* First player makes a new cast of two dice for his first roll.) If equal numbers were cast first, both must roll again until different numbers turn up.

Object of Play is to move all 15 stones into the inner table and thence off the board. The first to *bear off* all his stones wins the game. The direction of movement of the White stones is from B1 to B12, then to W12 and thence to W1. The movement of the Black stones is in the opposite direction— W1 to W12, and B12 to B1.

MOVES. The player's cast of the two dice indicates over how many points he may move his stones. The following rules govern:

1. Two stones may be moved, one in accordance with each die, or the total may be applied to the move of one stone. Example: W's first roll is 6–3. Among the possible moves are (a) one runner B1–B10; or (b) one stone B12–W7 and one B12–W10.

2. Doublets *are taken twice over.* A doublet is the cast of two like numbers. Since a doublet is in effect four numbers, as many as four stones may be moved.

3. *A player must use both numbers of the roll if possible (or all four numbers of a doublet). If he can use either, but not both, he must use the higher (or as many as can be used of a doublet). If he can use neither, the turn passes to opponent.*

MAKING POINTS. A player *makes a point* when he places two or more stones upon it. A prime rule of the game is that stones of opposite colors may never occupy the same point at the same time. If one player *makes a point,* his opponent may not place a stone on it. Hence the rule:

4. *A stone may be moved to a point that is vacant, or contains a single adverse stone, or that has been made by the player, but may not be moved to a point made by opponent.*

A point made also acts as a blockade, preventing the opponent from touching on that point in passing. *Example:* W rolls 3–1 first, and moves W8–W5 and W6–W5, making his own 5-point. B then rolls 5–4. He cannot move a runner W1–W10. Although W10 is vacant, the runner cannot move 5 points (to W6) or 4 points (to W5) and therefore cannot move at all. This is the consequence of the rule:

5. *One stone may be moved for the total of the two dice only if it can first be advanced by one number under rule 4.*

BLOTS. A single stone on a point is called a *blot.* A blot does not *make* a point; on the contrary, if the opponent is able to move a stone to that point, or touch on it in moving one stone for the two dice, the blot is *hit* and is removed from the table. A blot that has been hit is said to be *on the bar,* for the reason that it literally is placed on the bar.

ENTERING. The first task of a player, when one or more of his stones are on the bar, is to *enter* them, for

6. *A stone on the bar must be entered before a player may move any other stone.*

A stone enters in the adverse inner table, on an open point of same number as appears on one of the dice.

Example: B hits a blot at a time when he has made his own 3-point, 5-point, and 6-point. To enter, W must roll 1, 2 or 4 on one of his dice. Each time he fails to do so, the turn passes to B, for W may move no other stone so long as one remains on the bar.

It is possible for a stone to be entered and moved out of the adverse inner table on the same roll. If a stone enters on a point where the opponent has a blot, it hits that blot.

When a player makes all six blots in his inner table, he has a *shut-out*. Any opposing man on the bar is then unable to enter and so has to move. First player alone continues to cast his dice, until the forced breaking of the shut-out opens possible entry to his opponent.

BEARING OFF. As soon as a player has moved all fifteen stones into his own inner table, he may commence *bearing off*. Note that:

7. *A player may not bear off so long as any of his stones are outside his inner table (in outer table, adverse inner table, or on the bar).*

Bearing off is the final act of taking stones from the inner table and putting them entirely away from the board. Once borne off, a stone never returns into play. The first player to bear off all fifteen stones wins.

A stone may be borne off a point of same number as appears on a die. *Example:* W has stones on all points of his inner table; on cast of 5–3 he may bear off one stone from his 5-point and one from his 3-point.

8. *In bearing off, the roll of a number higher than the highest occupied point may be applied to the latter.* Example: Player rolls 6–2, and bears off a stone from 2-point; there are no stones left on 6-point: then for the 6, a stone may be borne off the 5-point (or whichever is the highest occupied point).

If he can and so chooses, a player may use any or all of a roll to move stones within the inner table instead of for bearing off. *Example*: Player has three stones on his 6-point and two on his 4-point; he rolls 3–3; he may bear off two from his 6-point, or bear off one and move two from his 6-point to his 3-point, or move three from his 6-point to his 3-point and one from his 4-point to his 1-point.

DOUBLING. Backgammon is played for an agreed base stake. This stake may be increased by *doubling* during play, and also by *gammon* and *backgammon* (as below).

9. *A player may double only in his turn to play, before casting, and only when the last previous double (if any) was made by opponent or was automatic.*

If equal numbers are cast for the first turn, the base stake is doubled *automatically*. Some play that if equal numbers are cast repeatedly, the game continues to be doubled automatically without limit. But players should agree in advance as to automatic doubles, and the usual agreement is to allow only one.

Either player may make the first voluntary double. Thereafter doubles may be made only in turn, under rule 9.

When a double is made by the opponent, a player must either agree to play on at the increased stake or must forfeit the game at the previous stake.

GAMMON AND BACKGAMMON. If the loser has borne off at least one stone, he loses the *single* value of the game at that juncture, the base stake as increased by any doubles. But if the loser has not borne off a single stone, he is *gammoned* and loses *double*. If in addition to having borne off no stone, he has a stone on the bar or in the adverse inner table at the end, he is *backgammoned* and loses *triple*.

CHOUETTE. Chouette is a method of allowing the participation of additional players in a two-hand game. It is applicable to many games, but is most commonly met in Backgammon.

The participants draw cards or cast dice for precedence. Highest draw or roll becomes the *man in the box*; second-highest is *captain* for all the rest, who form a syndicate against the man in the box. Due notice is taken of who is third-highest, fourth-highest, and so on, for this order of precedence affects the future arrangements.

The actual play is between the man in the box and the captain. All other participants may freely advise the captain, who plays in their interest, but in case of disagreement on strategy the captain has final decision.

However, in any proposal to increase the stake, as by doubles in Backgammon, each participant is a free agent. He may drop out upon payment of the amount of the stake prior to the proposed increase. This right obtains whether the increase was proposed by his side or by the man in the box.

A player who drops, when another plays on, goes to the foot of the precedence list. If the captain drops, his place is taken by the highest-ranking member of the syndicate who is willing to continue.

If the man in the box wins the game, he stays in the box. The loser goes to the foot, and the next player in order of precedence becomes captain.

If the man in the box loses, he goes to the foot and becomes a member of the syndicate. The winner goes into the box, and the next player in order becomes captain.

The disposition of payments made by players who drop varies in different games. In some, the man in the box puts up a stake which is always met by the syndicate, regardless of how many of its members remain. When a member drops, he pays his forfeit to the syndicate. But in Backgammon, the man in the box has in effect a separate wager with every member of the original syndicate. If a member drops, he pays his forfeit to the man in the box. *Example*: Player "A" is in the box against "B," "C," and "D." Call the basic stake 1. After a few rolls "A" doubles. Only "D" drops; he pays 1 to "A." Later "B," the captain, decides to double back, against the advice of "C." The latter drops, and pays 2 to "A." The game continues and eventually is won by "B." "A" pays 4 to "B," and thus incurs a net loss of only 1. (In the other method of settlement, "A" would have lost 4, and "B" would have won all 7.)

IRREGULARITIES. *Cocked Dice.* The dice must be rolled together and come to rest flat (not "cocked") upon the table at the player's right, otherwise they must be thrown again.

Premature Plays. If a throw is made before an adversary's play is completed, or if either player touches a die before it has come to rest, the adversary of the offender may require a rethrow.

The player must leave his dice upon the board until his play is completed. Should he pick them up or turn them over before the completion of his play, the adversary may declare the play void and require the offender to replace the stone or stones moved and to throw again.

Errors in Set-up or Play. If an error has been made in the set-up, either player may correct it prior to the completion of his first play.

If an error in play has been made, either player may require its correction before a subsequent throw, but not thereafter. The stone played in error must be correctly played if possible.

STRATEGY. The first task of the beginner is to learn the board so that he can see moves at a glance instead of having to count them out.

The constant effort should be to make points, so as to impede the progress of adverse stones. At the beginning of a game, the points most valuable to make are one's own bar point and 5-point. Points in the inner table decrease in value away from the 6-point so long as no other points are made; the 4-point or 3-point is often made early, but the 2-point and 1-point rarely.

Do not wait for "naturals" (ideal numbers) to make points on your own side of the board. Bring down *builders* from the adverse 12-point into your own outer table, on casts of 4, 3, 2. The risk in leaving a blot is usually worth taking in the effort to build points around the bar.

The numbers 6 and below can be cast either as the total on both dice or the number on one of the two; both ways are included in calculation of the odds. If a given number must be thrown on a die, not as a total, the odds are:

To roll one given number, 25:11 against.
To roll either of two given numbers, 20:16 for.
To roll any of three given numbers, 27:9 for.
To roll any of four given numbers, 32:4 for.

OPENING MOVES. The best way to play one's first roll is in most cases time-honored and unquestioned. In the table below, the first choice given in each case is the 1750 recommendation of Edmond Hoyle. Hoyle suggested alternatives for some of the poor rolls, as 5-1, and the flexible rolls, as 4-4. All these alternatives are listed in the table, together with others preferred by modern Backgammon experts.

The moves indicated by asterisks (*) are deliberately risky. Their object is to make certain good points at once.

It is assumed that White is the first player.

ROLL		MOVE	ROLL		MOVE
6–5		B1 –B12	6–3		B1 –B10
6–4		B1 –B11		or	B12–W7
	or	B12–W7			B1 –B4
		B1 –B5		or	*B12–W7
	or	*B12–W7			W8 –W5
		B12–W9	4–3		B12–W9
6–2		B12–W5			B12–W10
	or	B12–W7		or	B1 –B5
		B12–W11			B12–W10
6–1		B12–W7	4–2		W8 –W4
		W8 –W7			W6 –W4
5–4		B1 –B10	4–1		B12–W9
	or	B12–W8			W6 –W5
		B1 –B5		or	B12–W9
	or	B12–W8			B1 –B2
		B12–W9		or	B1 –B5
5–3		W8 –W3			W6 –W5
		W6 –W3	3–2		B12–W10
	or	B12–W8			B12–W11
		B12–W10		or	B1 –B4
5–2		B12–W8			B12–W11
		B12–W11	3–1		W8 –W5
5–1		B12–W8			W6 –W5
		W6 –W5	2–1		B12–W11
	or	B12–W8			W6 –W5
		B1 –B2		or	B12–W10
	or	*B12–W7		or	*W6 –W4
					W6 –W5

Early Doublets. The recommended opening moves on doublets are given below. Each move is to be made with two stones together.

6–6. Move B1-B7 and B12-W7. Vacate B7 as quickly as possible. You will probably have to leave a blot there at some time; better to do so at once, before Black has built up his home table.

5–5. Move B12-W3. Not a very desirable roll, for repeated 5's in the early rolls are awkward. After the doublet, split your runners, so as to be able to play subsequent 5's with the advanced stone.

4–4. It is said "There is no wrong way to play double 4." Hoyle gives first choice to B12-W5, and second to B12-W9; B1-B5. Modern players reverse this order of precedence.

Other choices are W8-W4 and W6-W2, recommended by advocates of "Build the home table above all else," and B1-B9, recommended by advocates of "Run to the outer table or not at all."

3-3. Hoyle gives W8-W5 and W6-W3. His second choice is W8-W5 and B1-B4, but this is to be recommended only if Black has made his bar point. The modern second choice is B12-W7.

2-2. The classic move is W6-W4 and B12-W11. If Black has made his bar point, the preferable move is B1-B5.

1-1. Move W8-W7 and W6-W5. This is the best of early rolls, as it makes both key points at once.

The Forward and Back Games. Backgammon play is a race. The *forward game* is the natural course when the dice permit, but a succession of bad rolls often compels a player to try for a *back game.*

The back game is characterized by two or more points made in the adverse home table. If the enemy then blots (as he usually must, sooner or later) a runner will be hit, and the back player's whole army will then concentrate on preventing the safe return of this stone. A single stone trapped by a *walking prime* usually costs the game.

The Prime is a group of six adjacent points, all made by one player. An adverse stone manifestly cannot get past such a barrier.

The ideal way of walking a prime is to lay a blot (one of the three extra stones) on the point just ahead of it, then wait for a 6 and cover the blot from the rear end of the prime. If this process can be repeated without break, the prime becomes a shutout.

A prime wins more surely against a single adverse stone than against more. Two or more may be able to make a point in the path of the prime, which then becomes broken in crossing it.

Doubling. A player who doubles offers his opponent a 3-to-1 proposition. That is, the opponent should accept if he has as much as one chance in four to win. For, if in four cases of doubles, the acceptor wins once, he collects 2 and pays 6, a net loss of 4. This is exactly what he would have lost had he declined all four doubles.

ACEY DEUCEY

Acey Deucey is the favorite Backgammon game of the U. S. Navy, Marine Corps, and Merchant Marine. For the sake of uniformity, the rules are here given in the traditional terminology of Backgammon. But, of course, the Navy has its own lingo—to roll one die for first play is to *piddle* or *peewee*, the bar is the *fence*, the opponent's inner table is the *starting quarter* or *entering table* while one's own inner table is the *finishing quarter*, a blot or single man is *kicked* rather than hit.

1. Each player rolls one die, and the higher plays first. (Ace is high.) For his first play, winner picks up both dice and rolls them again.

2. All stones are originally off the board, as though on the bar. They must be entered in the adverse inner table in the usual way.

3. Having entered one or more stones, the player may use subsequent rolls to move these stones, or to enter additional stones, or for both purposes.

4. A blot may be hit and sent to the bar in the usual way and must be reëntered before the player may make any other move.

5. Doublets are used twice over, as usual.

6. On roll of 1–2 (*acey deucey*), the player (a) moves the 1–2; (b) names any doublet he wishes, and moves accordingly; (c) rolls again. If the player is unable to use any part of the roll, he forfeits the rest. *Example:* The player can move 2 but cannot use the 1. He may not name a doublet nor roll again.

It is permissible to name a doublet, only part of which can be used, although the player could name and use another doublet entire. *Example:* The player moves 1–2, and names 6–6, being able to move only three 6's. He loses the fourth 6 and does not roll again, even though he could have named 5–5, used all four 5's, and taken a second roll.

Some place a limit upon the number of successive rolls of 1–2 which a player can use, for example, that upon rolling a third 1–2 in succession a player must place his most advanced man on the bar and the 1–2, with all its privileges, belongs to his opponent.

7. Rules as to making points, hitting blots, and bearing off, are as in regular Backgammon.

8. *Settlement.* Here there is widest divergence of prac-

tice. Many play that the loser owes 1 point for every stone he has left on the board when opponent bears off his last stone. Others pay for each remaining stone its distance from the bearing-off edge. Some double the stake each time 1–2 is rolled. Some allow voluntary doubles, besides the automatics. Doubling for gammon and tripling for back-gammon are usually eliminated.

SNAKE

Black places his fifteen stones in the usual initial position; five on B6, three on B8, five on W12, two on W1. White places two stones on each of B1, B2, B3, and his other nine stones on the bar. First turn is decided in the usual way. White must enter all his stones before he can commence moving. All other rules are as in regular Backgammon.

Snake is primarily intended to give practice in how to play, and how to play against, a back game. It also gives an easy method of handicapping. The stronger player may take White, and may commence with three, two, one, or no points already made in the Black home board. At best (with three points made), the odds against White are about two to one.

Chess

MOST SCHOLARS believe Chess to have originated in India, at least as early as the 7th century A.D. Whether it is older depends largely on how you choose to define Chess. Certainly it was preceded by similar games of movement upon a board, the ancestors of Pachisi, Backgammon, etc. What might be called the modern era of Chess dates from about the 15th century, when the pieces reached their present form. The literature of Chess grew rapidly until it surpassed that of any other game and most other activities.

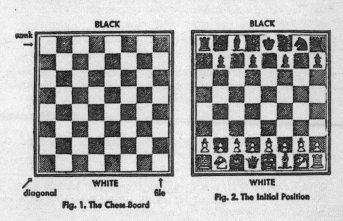

Fig. 1. The Chess-Board

Fig. 2. The Initial Position

PLAYERS. TWO.

EQUIPMENT. The Chess board is a large square composed of 8×8=64 smaller squares, colored alternately "white" (any light color) and "black" (any dark color). The two players are conveniently called "White" and "Black," after the color of the pieces used by each. The players sit on opposite sides of the board, which is so placed that each finds a white square at the corner near his right hand.

237

THE CHESS PIECES. Each player is provided with sixteen pieces, as follows:

	WHITE	BLACK
one king	♔	♚
one queen	♕	♛
two rooks	♖	♜
two bishops	♗	♝
two knights	♘	♞
eight pawns	♙	♟

The initial position of the pieces for the commencement of a game is shown in Fig. 2. The powers of the pieces are explained below.

The King (♔) may move one square at a time in any direction, on the rank, file, or diagonal. (See also *Object of Play.* The king may not move to a square attacked by an enemy piece.)

The Rook (♖) may move on the file or rank, any distance so far as the line is unobstructed by any other piece.

The Bishop (♗) may move diagonally any distance so far as the line is unobstructed. A bishop is thus tied to squares of one color throughout the game. As can be seen in Fig. 2, each player commences with one "white" and one "black" bishop.

The Queen (♕) combines the powers of rook and bishop, moving on any file, rank, or diagonal, any distance so far as the line is unobstructed.

The Knight (♘) has a peculiar move, best described as "from corner to diagonally-opposite corner of a rectangle three squares by two" (Dr. Lasker).

The knight move is a jump from point to point, not a line move, and cannot be obstructed by nearby pieces. In Fig. 3, if there were another piece on every square adjacent to the square occupied by the white knight, the white knight could still complete every move.

The Pawn (♙) in general moves forward on the file (away from the player) one square at a time. But from its original square on the second rank it has the option of advancing one or two squares. The pawn has some other peculiarities described in the next three sections.

WHITE

Fig. 3. The White Knight attacks all
the Black Knights

Fig. 4

(a) The Pawn attacks both Knights
(b) *En passant capture*
(c) Stopped pawns
(d) The Pawn promotes

PROMOTION. If a pawn reaches the eighth rank (farthest from the player) it *promotes*. See Fig. 4 (d). That is, it is replaced by a queen, rook, bishop or knight, at the option of the owner. Since the player usually chooses a queen, the strongest piece, promotion is often called *queening*. Promotion is permitted even though the player has not lost a single piece by capture; it is possible for three or more queens to be on the board at the same time.

CAPTURE. Pieces except pawns capture in the same way as they move. If any square that a piece can reach is occupied by an enemy unit, that unit can be captured. It is permanently removed from the board and the capturing piece occupies that square. (Capturing is optional; there is no compulsion to capture when able.)

The pawn cannot capture a piece ahead of it on the file, and therefore can be *stopped* by an adverse obstruction. The pawn captures on either square that is diagonally adjacent and forward of it. See Fig. 4 (a) and (c).

En passant capture. An advancing pawn is liable to capture by an adverse pawn on either adjacent file. A pawn is not permitted to escape this attack by use of the double move. In Fig. 4 (b) the White pawn has just moved up two squares from its original square. Had it moved only one square, it would have been attacked by both Black pawns. The attack is deemed to exist "in passing," so that either Black pawn can execute the capture, by moving diagonally to the square skipped over by the White pawn. The rules governing *en passant* capture are:

1. If a pawn makes a double-jump, it can be captured by an adverse pawn that could have captured it had it advanced only one square.

2. The *en passant* capture must be executed immediately or not at all; it may not be made at any later turn.

CASTLING. Once during a game a player may make a special move called *castling*. This is actually a simultaneous move of two pieces: the king and a rook. See Fig. 5. The circumstances in which castling is legal are:

1. Neither the king nor the rook has moved since the beginning of the game.

2. The squares on the rank between king and rook are vacant, and neither of the two adjacent to the king is attacked by an adverse unit. See Fig. 5(a).

3. The king is not in check.

The move *castling* is executed by first moving the king on the rank, two squares toward the rook, then placing the rook on the square passed over by the king. (Do not move the rook first, for if it is relinquished before the king is touched a legal move has been completed, and in strict play the transfer of the king can be barred. Moving the king first indicates the intention to castle, since at no other time may the king move two squares.) See Fig. 5 (b) & (c).

OBJECT OF PLAY. The object of play is to capture the adverse king. If a move directly attacks the king, the player announces "Check!" (The warning is customary but not obligatory.) His opponent must parry the attack or forfeit the game. The ways in which the attack may be met are: moving the king, capturing the attacker, interposing a piece on the line of attack.

When a check is announced and cannot be parried by any means, the king is said to be *checkmated* (or simply *mate*) and the game ends. The capture of the king is never actually carried out. A large proportion of games reach a decision without checkmate, one player resigning because he is satisfied that he cannot escape eventual checkmate.

DRAWN GAMES. A draw may result in any of the following ways:

Stalemate. If a player in turn to move cannot make any legal move, but is not in check, the position is a *stalemate* and is at once abandoned as a draw.

Insufficient force. If the pieces remaining on the board are too few and too weak to be able to administer checkmate by force, the game is abandoned. See *Minimum Forces*, below.

Perpetual check. If a player demonstrates that he can check the adverse king without surcease, he can claim a draw.

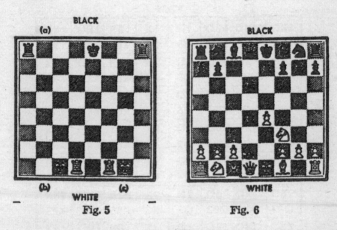

Fig. 5   Fig. 6

Recurrent position. If a position recurs three times in a game, identical as to the disposition of all pieces, and with the same player to move in each case, this player may claim a draw. (The draw is not automatic.)

Fifty-move rule. If during fifty consecutive moves no unretractable change has occurred (pawn move, capture, or castling), either player may call upon the other to demonstrate a forced win or to agree to a draw.

Agreement. A draw may occur by agreement between the players, neither being inclined to continue play. In tournament play, draw by agreement is permitted only after Black's thirtieth move.

NOTATION. *English Notation.* The notation largely used in England and the United States to record games is illustrated in Fig. 7. Each square has two alternative designations, according to the color of the moving piece. The abbreviation Kt for knight is sometimes replaced by N or S.

An example game record:

SICILIAN DEFENSE

	WHITE	BLACK
1	P - K4	P - QB4
2	Kt - KB3	P - Q3
3	P - Q4	P x P

The position after these three moves is shown in Fig 6.

BLACK

QR1 QR8	QKt1 QKt8	QB1 QB8	Q1 Q8	K1 K8	KB1 KB8	KKt1 KKt8	KR1 KR8
QR2 QR7	QKt2 QKt7	QB2 QB7	Q2 Q7	K2 K7	KB2 KB7	KKt2 KKt7	KR2 KR7
QR3 QR6	QKt3 QKt6	QB3 QB6	Q3 Q6	K3 K6	KB3 KB6	KKt3 KKt6	KR3 KR6
QR4 QR5	QKt4 QKt5	QB4 QB5	Q4 Q5	K4 K5	KB4 KB5	KKt4 KKt5	KR4 KR5
QR5 QR4	QKt5 QKt4	QB5 QB4	Q5 Q4	K5 K4	KB5 KB4	KKt5 KKt4	KR5 KR4
QR6 QR3	QKt6 QKt3	QB6 QB3	Q6 Q3	K6 K3	KB6 KB3	KKt6 KKt3	KR6 KR3
QR7 QR2	QKt7 QKt2	QB7 QB2	Q7 Q2	K7 K2	KB7 KB2	KKt7 KKt2	KR7 KR2
QR8 QR1	QKt8 QKt1	QB8 QB1	Q8 Q1	K8 K1	KB8 KB1	KKt8 KKt1	KR8 KR1

WHITE

Fig. 7

The initial of the piece moved is written before the hyphen, and the square moved to is written after. More data is added, if necessary to avoid ambiguity, as Kt (2) -Q4, "knight on the second rank to queen's fourth," in a position where the other knight also could move to Q4.

The symbol x, read "takes," indicates a capture. Black's third move above is "pawn takes pawn." Symbols commonly used are:

x   takes
ch   check
!   "Best" (of a move)
?   "not the best" or "bad"

Algebraic Notation. The notation preferred everywhere else, and used by problemists even in England and the United States, is also illustrated in Fig. 6. Each square has a single designation: the letter of its file and number of its rank, as f5. Besides avoiding ambiguity, this notation is more condensed, especially in the linear style. The moves leading to Fig. 6 are written (columnar form):

SICILIAN DEFENSE

	WHITE	BLACK
1	e2-e4	
2	Sg1-f3	
3	d2-d4	c5-d4:

The abbreviation of the piece is prefixed to each move except for pawn moves. Before the hyphen comes the square from which the piece is moved, and after, the square moved to. Linear writing is abbreviated by omission of the former square: *Sicilian.* 1 e4, c5; 2 Sf3, d6; 3 d4, c5:d4.

The symbols!, ?, are used in algebraic as in English notation; in addition the following are used:

:	takes
†	check
††	checkmate
O-O	castles on king side
O-O-O	castles on queen side

The abbreviation S for knight comes from the German *Springer.* The initials for the pieces of course vary from country to country.

MINIMUM FORCES REQUIRED TO WIN. If one side is reduced to king alone, the other can force checkmate if he has, besides his king, any of the following: one queen, one rook, two bishops, or a bishop and a knight. Insufficient to force checkmate are: one bishop, one knight, or two knights. (Queens and rooks are called *major pieces* because of their superior power; bishops and knights are *minor pieces.*)

A queen wins against a rook and usually against a rook and a pawn, but can only draw against a rook and a minor piece. Two bishops can usually draw against a queen, but bishop and knight or two knights usually lose.

A rook and a minor piece against a rook usually can only draw, and likewise a rook against one minor piece can usually only draw.

A single pawn cannot win unless it can be promoted. If the lone king can occupy the square in front of the pawn (before it has reached the seventh rank), the game is a draw, but it does not follow that the pawn can be queened in all other cases.

RELATIVE VALUES. The fighting power of the pieces is estimated to be in ratio; pawn 1, knight 3, bishop 3, rook 5, queen 9. More precisely, the following are shown by experience to be equivalent:

Queen=B+B+Kt+P=R+B+P
R+R=Q+P=B+B+Kt
Rook=B+P+P
B+B=R+P+P
Knight=P+P+P=Bishop

The knight and bishop are about equal, but the latter is more often favored by the position than the former. Two bishops together are usually stronger than an opposing bishop and knight, and stronger still against two knights.

KRIEGSPIEL

Kriegspiel is a way of playing Chess devised to add the element of the unknown.

It requires three boards, three sets of men, and the services of a third person. Each party has his own board, and the two players must be so placed that neither can see the other's board. (The players may be placed in different rooms, but usually agree to play in the same room so that each may hear what passes between the other and the referee.)

On his board, the player moves the pieces of his chosen color and must at all times keep them in the actual position to which they have been brought by his moves and captures by his opponent. The pieces of opposite color he may distribute on the board as he sees fit, in order to keep track of what he has discovered about the adverse position.

The referee announces alternately, "White has moved,"

"Black has moved," and so on, but does not state what the move is. But he says "No" whenever a player tries to make a move which, in view of the adverse position, is illegal. The referee therefore has to keep the actual position of both forces on his own board, to perceive and forbid illegalities.

Each player has the following sources of inference as to the adverse position:

(a) The referee says "No" to any illegal try; therefore by trying long-range moves of bishop, rook, queen, or pawn advances, etc. the player may detect the presence of obstructing adverse pieces. But if any such try proves to be legally playable, it stands as the player's move.

(b) When a move gives check, the referee states the fact and also the direction of the check, which must be one of: on the rank, on the file, by the knight, on the long diagonal, on the short diagonal. (In explanation of the last two: From every square of the board radiate two diagonals, one of which is longer than the other. From K1, the long diagonal extends to QR5, the short diagonal to KR4. From White's K3, the long is QR7-KKt1 and the short is QB1-KR6.)

(c) Whenever a move is a capture, the referee so announces, as by "White captures at his K5," but he does not state what was captured or by what.

(d) If the capture of a pawn by a pawn is *en passant*, the referee so states.

(e) At his turn to move, a player may ask the referee "Any?" meaning "Can any of my pawns make a capture?" The reply "Try" is affirmative, and the player must then make at least one try. Should his try be correct, it stands. Should it be incorrect, he may continue trying until he finds it, or he may at any time abandon the hunt and make another move.

(f) When the two players are in the same room, each may learn something from what the referee says to the other. *Example:* When the referee says "No" to a player on his third move, the likelihood is that he has moved a bishop to Kt2 or Kt5 and is trying to move it to the eighth rank to annex a rook or queen. In strict rules, the referee must nullify the effort of a player to deceive the other by trying moves he knows to be illegal, such as moving a knight like a bishop; in such case the referee says "Impossible" instead of "No."

Checkers or Draughts

THE STUDY of Oriental games indicates that Checkers had a common origin with Pachisi, The Mill and other board games, but not until relatively recent times has Checkers received the same serious consideration that has been bestowed from ancient times on Chess. In early times, it was fashionable to deprecate Checkers as "Chess for ladies." This evaluation has persisted in the name for the game, in many countries—in France, *jeu des dames;* in Germany, *Damenspiel;* in Italy, *il giuco delle dame.* But Checkers as a game of skill has been rated the equal of Chess by some who have mastered both games.

PLAYERS. Two.

EQUIPMENT. *The Checker Board* is identical with the Chess board—a large square composed of 8 x 8 smaller squares colored alternately dark and light. All play is conducted on the dark squares and each player must have a *double corner* near his right hand. The distinction between *double corner* and *single corner* may be seen in Fig. 1. Notice that in the diagram the pieces are represented on the light squares instead of the dark, but the "white" squares of the printed diagrams are actually the "black" squares of the board.

The Checker pieces, called *checkers,* are disks at least one inch in diameter and a little less than half as thick. Each player is provided with twelve pieces, of his own color. The initial position of the pieces is shown in Fig. 1.

PLAYERS. The players sit on opposite sides of the board. They are designated as Black and White, in accordance with the (approximate) color of the pieces used by each.

Black invariably makes the first move, and thereafter the players move alternately.

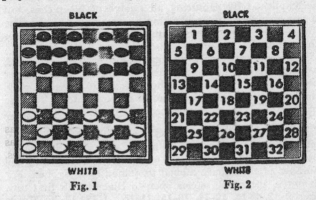

BLACK   BLACK

WHITE   WHITE

Fig. 1   Fig. 2

THE PLAY. The movement of the pieces is simple. A piece may move diagonally forward one square, if that square is vacant. Or it may *capture* an adverse piece which is adjacent, diagonally forward, if the square next beyond that piece is vacant. The capture is executed by jumping over the adverse piece to the vacant square and removing the enemy from the board. If the capturing piece lands on a square from which another adverse piece is attacked in the same manner, it continues jumping, in the same turn, to capture all adverse pieces it can. If able to do so, a player must capture rather than make a non-capturing move. Among several possible captures, a player may make a free choice.

Crowning. All pieces on the board at the onset are *single men.* A single man may move only forward. The row of squares at the Black or White edge of the board is called the *king row.* On reaching the adverse king row, a single man is *crowned* and becomes a *king.* Its promotion is indicated by placing upon it a second checker of the same color. A player is required by law to crown the adverse pieces that reach his king row.

A *king* has the same powers of move and capture as a single man, plus the right to move backward as well as forward. If a single man reaches the king row by capture, it has to stop to be crowned; it may not continue capturing (as a king) in the same turn.

OBJECT OF PLAY. The object of play is to deprive the opponent of the ability to move in his turn. This is usually accomplished by capturing all twelve of his pieces, but it can also result from blocking his remaining pieces. The first player to find himself unable to move in turn loses the game.

A *draw* results only by agreement, each player being satisfied that he has no prospect of winning. If one player proposes a draw and the other refuses to abandon play, the latter must within forty moves demonstrate an increase in his advantage, or else concede the draw.

NOTATION. The notation used in recording games is based on numbering the squares as in Fig. 2. A move is denoted by the number of the square moved from, followed by the number of the square moved to, joined by a hyphen. For example, the seven moves open to Black at his first turn are: 9-13, 9-14, 10-14, 10-15, 11-15, 11-16, 12-16. Moves may be written linearly, as in this example, or in a column. No mark is attached to show whether a move is made by Black or White. So long as there are no kings on the board, the numbers themselves show the color of the move, for Black moves up and White down. An example of opening moves:

                      11-15
                      23-19
                       8-11
                      22-17
                       9-13
                      17-14
                      10-17
                      21-14

The last two moves are captures. No mark is used to indicate a capture; the fact of capture is (except in long king tours) evident from the difference between the numbers. No noncapturing move can carry a piece to a square differing by more than 5.

A symbol much-used in annotation is the *star* (*). A *starred move* is the only one to win or to hold the draw.

RESTRICTION PLAY. Checker tournaments were formerly conducted in "go as you please" style—the contestants could play what openings they chose. The inordinately high proportion of draws resulting among experts led to the adoption of "restriction play."

Two-move restriction. Black and White each have seven possible first moves, so that there are 49 combinations for the first two moves. Two of these combinations are *barred* because they lead to loss of a piece without compensation: 9-14, 21-17 and 10-14, 21-17. In the two-move restriction, each of the 47 playable combinations is written on a card, and the opening to be played in each match is decided by drawing a card at random. Each match comprises two games, each player being required to play both the Black and White side of the selected opening.

Three-move restriction. Even the two-move restriction having been largely exhausted by top-flight players, the American championship tournaments now use a three-move plan. The number of combinations of the first three moves used at present for the field of chance selection is around 150.

OTHER CHECKERBOARD GAMES

THE LOSING GAME, OR GIVEAWAY CHECKERS. This is Checkers played with the object of getting rid of all one's pieces. A peculiarity of the game is that no draw is possible, unless a block be counted as such. But the game is consequently of relatively limited scope. Opening play is almost entirely concerned with luring or forcing an adverse piece to square 14 or 19, whence it can be forced to jump to 21 (by Black) or 12 (by White).

The Mill

THE MILL is believed to have had a common origin with Tit Tat Toe and Pachisi, in remote antiquity. The design of the Mill board has been found on Etruscan pottery, on Roman tiles, and carved on the steps of the Acropolis at Athens. In Elizabethan times it came to be called *Nine Men's Morris*, or simply *Morris*, from its fanciful resemblance to the morris (Moorish) dance. Another name, *Morelles*, derives from *merel* (old French, a counter or piece).

PLAYERS. Two.

EQUIPMENT. *The Board* is depicted at right. (The numbers, added here for reference, do not actually appear on the board.) There are twenty-four points, arranged in sixteen lines of three points each. The diagonal lines, such as 1-4-7, in the modern game are usually omitted.

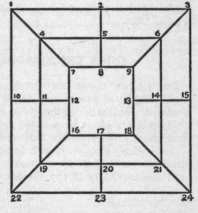

The Pieces are eighteen in number, in two contrasting colors, nine for each player. Ordinary checkers or poker chips will serve.

THE PLAY. Each player in turn places a piece on any vacant point, until all eighteen pieces are down. Then playing continues by alternate moves. A piece may be moved along a line to an adjacent vacant point.

The object, both in laying pieces on the board and in moving them, is to arrange three pieces of one's own color on a horizontal or vertical (not diagonal) line. Such an array

250

is called a *mill*. On making a mill, the player is entitled to remove one adverse piece from the board; pieces so removed are dead, and never return into play. The player who is first reduced to two pieces loses the game.

There are three rules governing the play:

1. A piece that is part of a mill may not be removed. *Example:* White, playing first, makes a mill in laying down, and removes a Black piece. Black, with the last piece he lays down, makes a mill; he may remove any other White piece, but not one of the three in the White mill.

2. If a mill is *opened* by moving one piece off the line, then *closed* by reversing the move, it counts as a new mill. *Example:* White has a mill on 1-2-3. If he is able to move 1-10, then 10-1, he is entitled to remove a Black piece.

3. A player who cannot move, in his turn to move, loses.

An optional rule, favored in children's games, is that when a player is reduced to three pieces he may move any piece to any vacant point, regardless of connections.

Another rule sometimes met is that a piece may be removed from a mill if only these three pieces are left on that side. The rule has application only where the "jumping" privilege is allowed the three pieces.

STRATEGY. There is little doubt that, with correct play on both sides, Mill is a draw. But no exhaustive analysis has been made.

The best points to seize in the opening are probably 5, 11, 14 and 20. Thus a game might begin: White 5, Black 14, White 20, Black 11.

After the opening, White 5, if Black fails to answer with 2, 4, 6, or 8, White can make a mill by force, but to do so at once loses the game.

Two mills are sure to win against one. One mill is left open, as a reserve against opening of the adverse mill, while the second is opened and closed. The most deadly form is the *double mill*. Suppose White to have pieces on 1, 2, 3, 4, 6. Then shuttling 2–5 and 5–2 closes a mill on *every* turn, and Black must resign.

Roulette

THE MOST celebrated seat of roulette is the gambling rooms at Monte Carlo, but it is a fixture in all gambling houses in North and South America, in Great Britain, and on the European Continent.

The Roulette Wheel

PLAYERS. Any number. All bets must be placed against the house.

EQUIPMENT. A "wheel" (see illustration), at either end of which there is a layout on which bets are placed. The wheel turns on a spindle and is divided into 37 (in Europe) or 38 (in America) sections in which a small ivory ball (which is spun in the wheel) may come to rest and designate a winning number.

These sections bear numbers from 1 to 36, of which half

are red and the other black; plus a green section marked 0, plus (on American wheels) a section marked 00.

THE PLAY. The players lay their bets on the layout in such a way as to indicate what number, color, or group of numbers they select to win. The house is represented by several *croupiers;* one of them, called the *tourneur,* then spins the wheel in one direction and tosses the ball into it in the opposite direction. When the wheel stops, the ball will be resting in one of the sections and the indicated number will win; bets on its color will win; bets on the dozen, the column, and the range of numbers (low, 1 to 18, or high, 19 to 36) of that number will win; bets on other numbers will be collected by the bank and bets may then be placed on the next coup, or turn of the wheel.

THE ODDS. For a winning bet on red, black, high, low, even or odd, the house pays even money.

For a winning bet on the dozen (1 to 12, 13 to 24, or 25 to 36) or on the column in which the winning number falls, the bank pays 2-to-1.

For a winning bet on the number itself, the bank pays 35-to-1; for a bet on either of two numbers, one of which wins, 17-to-1; for a bet on three numbers, one of which wins, 11-to-1; for a bet on four numbers, one of which wins, 8-to-1; for a bet on six numbers, one of which wins, 5-to-1.

The zeros. When a zero comes up, the house pays bets on the zero or on the zero and other adjacent numbers in combination with it, but collects all bets on other numbers, on even-money bets, and on the dozens and columns.

On the American wheel, one of the two zeros should come up twice in 38 times, so that the bank should win two out of every thirty-eight dollars bet against it, or 5.26%. On the European wheels, which have only one zero, the bank will win one out of every thirty-seven dollars, or 2.7%. At some casinos, the advantage of the bank is even less, because, when the zero shows, only half of the stakes on the even-money bets is taken.

SYSTEMS AT ROULETTE. There have been hundreds of betting systems devised, and books and pamphlets explaining them, but mathematically none of them is supportable. In the long run the bank will get its percentage of whatever money is bet against it, whether systematically or not.

Parlor Games

WORD SQUARES

ANY NUMBER may play. Each has pencil and paper, and draws a box of 25 squares, 5 x 5. Each in turn calls aloud one letter—any he pleases—until 25 have been called. As the letter is named, each player writes it into his own box—wherever he pleases. The object is to make as many good English words as possible, in the five rows and columns of the box. A word of five letters scores 10; of four letters, 5; of three letters, 2. The player with the highest total wins the game.

Some play that the first letter called must be placed in the upper left corner of the box.

It is usually advisable to aim for words with not more than one vowel, because experienced players called as few vowels as possible.

PASSWORD

Two partnerships of two players each play against each other. Partners sit facing each other. One player and his adjacent opponent (the "pitchers") agree secretly on a good English word. One of them now gives a clue to his respective partner. The clue may be only one word. It may be a proper noun. It may not contain any part of the secret word, or rhyme with the secret word. The first clue given must be a synonym or definition of the secret word; after that, there is no restriction.

The partner now attempts to guess the word. If he does not succeed in guessing the word, the other player now gives *his* partner a clue—the same one or a different one. Play continues until the word is guessed. Guessing the word on the first clue scores 10 points, on the second 9 points, and so on. If the word is not guessed after five clues by each side, the secret word is divulged and there is no score for the round. The team that guesses the word goes first in giving a clue for the next word.

No gesturing is allowed, no special intonations of the voice, no histrionics of any kind.

The partnership that first accumulates 21 points wins the game.

Password has been a popular television game, but with fewer restrictions on the permissible clues, gestures, etc.

CATEGORIES OR GUGGENHEIM

Any number may play. Each player is provided with a sheet of paper and a pencil. In a column at the left each writes a list of *categories,* selected by the players as a whole. The usual practice is to permit each player to name one category. A nomination may be vetoed, however, by majority vote.

To commence a round, the players agree on a key word, usually of five letters with no letter repeated, for example, COMET. Five columns are ruled off on the paper, and one letter of the key word is written at the head of each column.

A time limit for the round is fixed in advance (usually fifteen or twenty minutes). At the signal to commence, each player writes words on his paper, one in each row and column, each word fitting in the category of its row and having the initial letter at the top of the column. For example, a completed paper with four categories and five-letter key might look like this:

	C	O	M	E	T
1. Card games	Casino	Okla-homa	Michi-gan	Euchre	Twenty-one
2. Composers	Chopin	Offen-bach	Mahler	Elgar	Tschaikowsky
3. Capitals of U.S. States	Colum-bus	Olympia	Mont-gomery		Topeka
4. Words con-taining Q	Croquet	Opaque	Marquee	Equal	Toque

At the expiration of the allotted time, all players must stop writing. The lists are then compared and scored.

Each word scores one point for every other player who *did not* write it in his list. Thus, with seven players, if Euchre was named by only one player, it scores 6 points. If all players wrote the same word for the same category, as Chopin for "Composers" with initial C, none scores for it.

In certain limited categories, there may be no word with required initial (as there is no U.S. Capital with initial E). A player knowing this fact is *not* bound by rule or sportsmanship to announce it; he may benefit from the fact that others may search for a non-existent word.

The player with the highest total score wins the round. The key word should be changed every round, if not the list of categories, and effort should be made to vary the assortment of letters. Key words containing rare letters, as J, Q, X, Z, are usually barred.

Mah Jongg

MAH JONGG, of Chinese origin and probably more than 1,000 years old, is played with colorful tiles (recently also with printed cards) and other paraphernalia. Mah Jongg has enjoyed a tremendous resurgence under revised laws with Big Jokers added. In the following laws of the original game, an asterisk (*) denotes revisions to be found in "The Modern Game" (page 263).

PLAYERS. Four, each for himself.

EQUIPMENT. The original Mah Jongg set comprised 144 *tiles**—small rectangular blocks of wood with ivory or bone faces; 108 are *suit* tiles, 28 are *honors*, 8 are *flowers* (also called *seasons*).

Suits. Three: *bamboo (sticks), circles (dots),* and *characters (cracks, or actors).* Each suit comprises four duplicates each of tiles numbered from one to nine, inclusive.

Honors. Four duplicates each of *East, West, North,* and *South winds, red, green,* and *white dragons.*

Flowers. Individually marked, but assigned in pairs to the four winds.

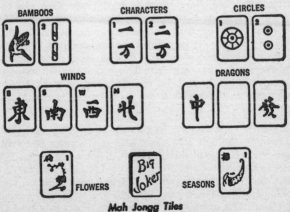

Mah Jongg Tiles

* Plus, in the Modern Game, 8 Big Jokers.

Accessory equipment includes two dice, a quantity of tokens used for scorekeeping, and four racks on which 14 tiles are placed.

PRELIMINARIES. One player selected by chance as *East*, has choice of seats. The others take seats as they please. They are called West, North, and South, in proper compass orientation. East collects or pays double, according to whether he or another player Mah Jonggs (goes out).* After each deal, each compass title passes to the player at the right.

WINDS. During the first deal, East wind *prevails*. A player who obtains a set of tiles of the prevailing wind scores more for them than for another wind. In the second deal, South wind prevails; in the third, West wind; in the fourth, North wind. This rotation is independent of the rotation of the East position at the table. After four deals players cast again for positions at the table.

THE WALL. Tiles are placed face down, and all players help in shuffling them. Then each player builds a wall parallel to his edge of the table, two tiles high and eighteen long (nineteen if Big Jokers are used). Each pile of two tiles is called a *stack*. The four walls are finally pushed together to form a hollow square in center of table.

BREAKING THE WALL. East casts the two dice and totals the two numbers. He counts off this number beginning at the right end of his wall; the selected stack is lifted out, and the two tiles are set face down on the wall just to the right of the break. The lower tile is placed adjacent to the break, and the upper tile at its right. The two are called *loose tiles;* whenever both have been drawn, another stack from the right side of the break is set on the wall to make a new supply.

DRAWING THE HANDS. Beginning with East, each player in turn to the left takes two adjacent stacks (four tiles) from the left side of the break, until each has twelve. Then each in turn takes one more tile, and finally East takes one extra tile. East thus draws 14 tiles, and each other player 13.

Flowers. The flowers are not counted as part of a hand of 13 tiles.* On drawing a flower, the player immediately

* See Modern Game.

places it face up before him and takes a loose tile to fill his hand. After the original hands are drawn, any flowers in the hands are *grounded*, and the players draw loose tiles in rotation beginning with East.

*Kong in Hand.** Any player who holds a *kong* (see below) in his original hand may at once ground it. The two end tiles should be turned face down to indicate that it counts as a concealed set (see below). The fourth tile of a *kong* is not combined in the total of 13 in each player's hand;* the player draws one loose tile, in turn, to fill his hand.

SETS. The object in play is to obtain *sets* of tiles as follows:
Chow: a numerical sequence of three tiles in same suit;
Pung: three like tiles, of same suit and rank, or three dragons of same color, or three winds of same direction;
Kong: a pung plus the fourth like tile.

A *Complete Hand* comprises four sets and a *pair* of like tiles—14 tiles. Since the hand during play contains 13 tiles, the 14th must be obtained by draw or taking a discard. The first player to show a complete hand wins the deal.

Whenever a kong is *grounded* (placed on the table), the owner draws a loose tile, thus maintaining 13 tiles in his hand exclusive of flowers and fourth tiles in kongs.*

A set is *concealed* if it was obtained by drawing from the wall. A kong must nevertheless be grounded to score as a concealed group; hence it is marked by turning end tiles face down. A set *from table* (completed by use of a discard) is necessarily grounded.

THE PLAY. East commences play by discarding one tile, reducing his hand to thirteen. Except as noted hereafter, each hand plays in turn, the rotation being to the right, counter-clockwise. In his turn, a player must either draw one tile from the wall (to the left of the break), or must use the last discard. He ends his turn by discarding one tile.

Discarded tiles are placed face up within the wall. Grounded sets are placed between wall and owner's rack.

Discard. A discard may be used if it can at once be grounded as part of a set. It must be claimed immediately, before the next hand plays. Any player can claim it, regardless of whether it is his turn to play. If there are several claims, they take precedence in order: for Mah Jongg (first

* See Modern Game.

claim), for pung or kong, for chow.* Among claims for the same purpose, the nearest hand has precedence. The player who obtains the discard grounds it with his set, then discards, and the turn passes to his right neighbor; intervening hands lose their turns.

Grounding sets. After commencement of play, a concealed kong may be grounded only after the player has drawn (from wall or table) and before he discards. A kong not grounded before another player Mah Jonggs, counts only as a concealed pung.

A player holding a concealed pung, and obtaining the fourth tile from the table, may ground only three of the tiles if he wishes, retaining the fourth. But if it is still in his hand when another deal ends, the set counts only as a pung. A player who holds or draws from the wall the fourth tile to match his grounded pung may, in turn, add it to the set to make a kong, and draw a loose tile. But a discard may not be claimed to be added to an already grounded pung.

MAH JONGG. On making his hand complete, four sets and a pair, a player may go out by showing his whole hand; he is the winner of the deal and play ends.

The tile needed to complete the hand, whether it fits with a chow, a pung, or the pair may be obtained by drawing from the wall or claiming a discard or *robbing a kong.* To rob a kong is to claim (for Mah Jongg only) a tile that another player has just added to his grounded pung.

The last fourteen tiles of the wall may not be drawn. If no player Mah Jonggs after the fifteenth tile from the end is drawn, there is no score, and East retains his position for the next deal. The player who draws the last available tile duly discards, and play continues so long as each successive discard is used.

SCORING.* Value of winner's hand is first computed, and each other player pays him this amount. If East wins, he collects double from each other player. The values of other three hands are computed, and players settle among themselves according to difference of scores. East pays or collects double the difference.

The value of a hand is the sum of points for sets, its *basic count,* doubled one or more times for special sets.

* But see Modern Game.

BASIC COUNT FOR ALL HANDS

CHOW	FROM TABLE	CONCEALED
Pung Suit ranks (1 to 9)	2	4
Pung of honors (winds or dragons)	4	8
Kong of *simples* (2 to 8)	8	16
Kong of terminals or of honors	16	32
Pair of dragons or of prevailing wind or own wind	2	2
Pair of player's own wind, when prevailing	4	4
Each flower	4	

DOUBLES FOR ALL HANDS

The number given is the actual factor by which the basic count is to be multiplied.

	FACTOR
Each pung or kong of dragons or prevailing wind	2
Pung or kong of player's own wind	2
Player's own flower	2
Bouquet of four flowers	16

(includes the double for player's own flower)

BONUSES FOR MAH JONGG HAND ONLY

	ADD TO BASIC COUNT
For going Mah Jongg	20
For drawing winning tile from wall	2
For filling the only place to complete hand	2

	FACTORS
Winning with last available tile or a subsequent discard	2
Winning with loose tile drawn after a kong	2
No chows	2
All chows and a worthless pair	2
All one suit, or all terminals with honors	2
All one suit, without honors	8
All terminals, without honors	Limit
All honors, without suits	Limit

LIMIT HANDS. In the American code, the limit that a hand may collect or be forced to pay is 500 (for East, 1,000). In the Chinese game, certain exceptional complete hands are recognized as *limit hands*—the owner collects the limit, whatever it may be. American players have gone far beyond the Chinese in inventing limit hands, including the *cleared hand* rule—the Mah Jongg hand may contain tiles of only one suit, besides honors; to reduce the number of draws, the flowers were made *wild*.

IRREGULARITIES. *Incomplete Set.* If the set of tiles is found to be incomplete, the deal is void unless a player has declared Mah Jongg, but scores made in all previous deals stand.

Exposed Tile. If tile is exposed in building wall, tiles must be reshuffled. A tile exposed in the act of drawing another must be shuffled with six adjacent stacks and that section of wall must be rebuilt.

Incorrect Hand. Player drawing less than correct number of tiles for original hand may draw balance before East's first discard; otherwise he must play with a short hand. If player draws too many for original hand, but does not look at any tile before error is noted, excess may be drawn by player sitting opposite and placed in open end of wall; but if player has looked at any tile, or error is not noted until East has made his first discard, the player must play with a long hand.

If a player fails to draw a loose tile to replace a flower or the fourth tile of a kong, or discards two tiles, or otherwise renders his hand incorrect, he may correct his error before the next hand is played (or before East's first discard); otherwise he must play on with an incorrect hand.*

Incorrect set. If a player grounds an incorrect set, he may retract it or otherwise correct his error before the next hand has played; otherwise he must play on with a foul hand. If he erroneously claimed a discard that he cannot use, and corrects his error in time, the discard is open to claim by the other hands.

*Short, long and foul hands.** A hand that is short or foul may not Mah Jongg; it is counted as usual for non-winners, except that double for flowers and for sets may not be applied. A long hand is scored as zero.

---

* But see Modern Game.

False Mah Jongg. If a call of Mah Jongg is incorrect, the hand being incomplete, short, long, or foul, false call ends the deal. Offender must pay limit to East and half the limit to each other player, or, if he is East, must pay limit to all. There is no settlement among other three players. East retains his position for the next deal, if he was not the offender.

THE MODERN GAME

Eight Big Jokers are added to the set. Laws, as well as new list of hands with which the player may Mah Jongg, are revised annually and published by the National Mah Jongg League.* For 1970–71, for example, number of flowers in play became six instead of eight; East no longer pays or receives double; if a player Mah Jonggs on a discarded tile, *discarder* pays winner double; others pay single, according to published value of hand, some of which count only if made *concealed.* Other laws differing from earlier game include:

Flowers are not immediately faced and replaced; they remain in play for use in certain prescribed Mah Jongg combinations; if discarded are called simply "Flower."

Matching dragons: Red-cracks; White-dots; Green-Bams.

CHARLESTON (*passing of tiles*): Before play begins, each player passes three tiles at a time, right, then across, then left. First Charleston is compulsory. A second, optional Charleston may be vetoed by any player. *Blind pass* of 1, 2 or 3 tiles is permitted on last pass of either Charleston. (Player selects 2, 1 or no tiles from hand; chooses, without looking at their faces, the same number of tiles from those passed to him from right; then completes pass of 3 tiles to left.) An extra "courtesy pass" to opposite player only, is optional. Flowers may be passed but not Big Jokers.

BIG JOKERS: May be used to represent any tile in any hand. If used in exposed set, any player may, during his regular turn, claim a Big Joker in exchange for tile it represents. (Exception: *see next page.*)

* National Mah Jongg League, 250 W. 57 St., New York, N. Y. 10019, from whom additional information may be obtained. A stamped self-addressed envelope must accompany the request for information.

Any hand completed without a Big Joker is paid double. If Big Joker was used, but was later claimed in exchange so that final winning hand includes no Big Joker, it is paid double.

A Big Joker may be discarded (usually as defensive strategy) and called the same as the previous discard. (When two tiles of same rank are discarded consecutively, the last must be taken, but Big Joker discard is an exception. First tile is taken and Big Joker becomes dead tile.

Quint: Five of a kind, made by using Big Joker(s).

CLAIMING DISCARDS: If more than one player claims priority goes to claim for Mah Jongg or to nearest player claiming for exposure. Priority is NOT affected by type of meld. Discard may not be claimed for exposure after next player in turn has discarded or declared Mah Jongg. Discard may not be claimed to complete a pair except to call Mah Jongg for either exposed or concealed hand.

ENDING PLAY: Play continues until last tile has been drawn from wall and thereafter as long as the next discard is claimed.

MAH JONGG HANDS: Since hands for calling Mah Jongg are changed each year, there is little point to listing them. An example of Mah Jongg hand according to 1970–71 rules:

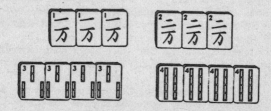

(Any four consecutive numbers; pung first two in one suit; kong next two in a second suit.)

BETTORS: Only four may play in any hand. If more than four are in game, out-player(s) may inspect all hands, choosing which player to back before first play is made. Bet is recorded secretly; cannot be changed. Bettor pays or collects same as player he has backed.

PAYMENT: Settlement is made only between Mah Jongg hand and other players. There is no settlement among other three.

PIE GAME: Many games limit a player's loss to amount of chips (discs) each player "buys" at beginning of game. A player who has lost all chips continues to play; chips he recoups are subject to pay-out on *future* hands.

IRREGULARITIES: Miscalled discard. Player must name his discard. If called incorrectly, there is no penalty if neither caller nor any other player has exposed any part of his hand. If claimant exposes any part of hand, game continues but offender's hand is dead. If one opponent exposes any part of his hand, the two intact hands continue to play. If only one player does not expose his hand, play ends and offender pays him double value of incorrect hand.

DEAD HAND: Too many or too few tiles, false claim of Mah Jongg, etc. Dead hand ceases play but pays winner full value of hand.

Dice Games

DICE are the oldest gaming implements known to man and innumerable games are played with them. Backgammon, Pachisi and other "track games" use dice as an adjunct to other equipment. Among games played only with dice Craps (or Crap-shooting) is most popular but there are many others. Some of them are described on the following pages.

CRAPS

PLAYERS. Any number may play.

EQUIPMENT. Two dice, of the same size, color, and markings. Each die should be a cube in the strictest sense, except that the corners may be uniformly rounded; each side should be approximately ⅝ inch, and no smaller than ½ inch. Each face of the die is marked with one to six dots, opposite faces representing reciprocal numbers adding to seven; if the vertical face toward you is 5, and the horizontal face on top of the die is 6, the 3 should be on the vertical face to your right.

THE PLAY. The players form a ring around the playing surface (floor, table, bed, etc.), which is known as the *center*. In a small game, each player may roll the dice once and the one rolling the highest total *shoots* first. In a larger game, the first shooter is usually the one who picks up the dice and offers a bet.

The shooter places some sum of money in front of him, and announces the amount. This is his *center* bet and other players are invited to *fade* it. The shooter is betting he will win; the players who fade him are betting he will lose.

The shooter takes the dice in his hand and rolls them out, preferably so that they hit a wall and bounce back, if the playing area affords the means to enforce this rule. The faces that are upmost when the two dice come to rest determine the number thrown.

Any one of five numbers thrown on the first roll settles the bets immediately:

Seven or *eleven* is a *natural* and the shooter wins.

Two, three or *twelve* is *craps* and the shooter loses.

When any one of these numbers is thrown, bets are settled, the shooter announces the amount he is next betting, and the game continues as previously described.

Points. If the shooter's number is four, five, six, eight, nine or ten, the bets are not settled. The number thrown becomes his *point.* He picks up the dice, shakes them and rolls them out again, and continues to do so until either (a) he shoots the same number again, in which case he *makes his point* (wins), collects his bets, and announces his next bet; (b) he rolls a seven, in which case he *sevens out* (or *craps out*) and loses the dice: he loses his bets in the center and the next player in turn to his left becomes the shooter.

So long as the shooter wins, he remains the shooter. But he may voluntarily pass the dice to the man at his left when the currents bets are settled.

When the shooter wins it is known as a *pass;* when he loses, it is known as a *miss.*

BETTING. Players place bets with one another. (In a gambling-house game, all bets must be placed with the house; that method of betting will be described later.) There are many bets in addition to the bets in the center between the shooter and the players who fade him. Some of these bets are as follows:

Come Bets. On any roll, one player may bet with any other player that the shooter "comes"—that is, that he will win in a series of rolls beginning with the next, as though the next roll were the first. The player who takes this bet is betting that the shooter "don't come." The former, who is betting that the shooter will win, is said to bet *right;* the other player is betting *wrong.*

Side Bets. Once the shooter has thrown a point, he and other players may bet that he will (or will not) make his point. If his point is six or eight, the odds are 6-to-5 that he will not make it; if his point is five or nine, the odds are 3-to-2 that he will not make it; if his point is four or ten, the odds are 2-to-1 that he will not make it. Bets on five, nine, four and ten are usually placed at the correct odds, but bets on six or eight are usually placed at even money, so that anyone betting that the shooter will not make his point has a considerable advantage.

Hard-way Bets. If the shooter's point is four or ten the odds are 8-to-1 that he will not make it by throwing 2-2 or 5-5 respectively. If his point is six or eight the odds are 10-to-1 that he will not make it with 3-3 or 4-4 respectively. If he sevens or makes his point any other way, he loses his *hard-way* (or gag) bet.

Proposition Bets. There are innumerable other methods of betting on what number or combination of numbers will or will not appear on the next roll or in the next two or three rolls; many if not most of these are "hustler's bets," offered by someone who knows he has the best of it mathematically if his bet is accepted.

IRREGULARITIES. If either die is resting against any object which causes any uncertainty as to which face is upward, it is "cocked dice" and the throw is void.

If either die rolls outside the playing surface in such a way that it cannot clearly be seen, the throw is void.

If a player picks up one of the dice while it is rolling and before either die has stopped rolling, the throw is void.

In case there is disagreement as to which player has faded all or any portion of the shooter's bet, precedence is given to (a) the player who has faded the last entire bet; (b) if it is the shooter's first roll, to the player who last lost the dice; (c) if it is not the shooter's first roll, to the player who faded the largest portion of the shooter's previous bet.

The shooter may withdraw any unfaded portion of his bet at any time, but may not withdraw any portion of his bet after it has been faded unless, before his first roll of the series, he withdraws his entire bet and passes the dice.

STRATEGY. Skillful play at Craps consists solely of knowing the proper odds and not making or accepting any bets which are mathematically unsound. A table of the proper odds in the most common cases is given later.

BANK CRAPS

In a gambling house, the players stand around a table on which a layout is marked to show the available bets and the odds offered by the house on each one. Bets are placed on this layout, and the dice are thrown on the same table.

A retaining wall surrounds the table, and the dice must be thrown so as to hit the wall and bounce back, or the dice must be thrown over a string stretched across the table.

The dealers pay and collect bets, and one of them handles the dice, recovering them when they have been thrown and returning them to the shooter.

All bets must be placed against the house. Many more such bets are invited than are found in a private Crap game; the layout illustrated is only one of dozens which are found in different parts of the United States.

The house derives its profit from the fact that it has a mathematical advantage in every bet; out of whatever money is wagered against it, it may expect to keep a certain proportion. The following table shows the most common bets, and how much the house should expect to keep out of every dollar bet against it; this is known as the "house percentage."

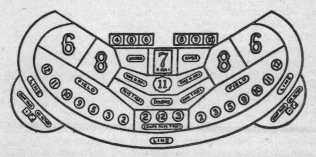

Layout of a Bank Craps table, using the word "for" and providing for a stand-off on 1-2 instead of 1-1 or 6-6 (see table of odds).

In some cases the odds offered by the house are even less than those listed above, in which case the advantage of the house is even greater. On many layouts the actual odds being offered are disguised by the use of the word "for." If the house, for example, pays 4-to-1 odds, the winner of a bet receives his $1 back together with $4 paid by the house, a total of $5. Some houses quote these odds by offering "five-for-one," meaning that for every $1 the bettor puts up, he receives, when he wins, $5—including his own $1. This is equivalent to odds of 4-to-1.

BET	CHANCES AGAINST		FOR	HOUSE PAYS	IN EVERY $1 BET HOUSE SHOULD WIN
Line (bet that shooter passes)	251	to	244	Even	1⅖¢
Don't pass (barring 1–1 or 6–6)*	976	to	949	Even	1⅖¢
Don't pass (barring 1–2)*	488	to	447	Even	4⅖¢
8 (or 6) before 7	6	to	5	Even	9 ¢
Hard way, 4 or 10	8	to	1	7–1	11 ¢
Hard way, 6 or 8	10	to	1	9–1	9 ¢
Craps (2, 3 or 12 on next roll)	32	to	4	7–1	11 ¢
7 on next roll	30	to	6	4–1	16⅔¢
Field (2-3-5-9-10-11-12)	19	to	17	Even	5½¢
Field (2-3-4-9-10-11-12)	20	to	16	Even	11 ¢
Field (2-3-4-9-10-11-12), paying double on 2 or 12	380	to	340	Even	5½¢
Any doubles on next roll	30	to	6	4–1	16⅔¢
11 (or 3) on next roll	34	to	2	15–1	11 ¢
2 (or 12) on next roll	35	to	1	30–1	14 ¢
Under 7 (or over 7)	21	to	15	Even	16⅔¢

CHUCK-A-LUCK (BIRD CAGE, HAZARD)

Popular in gambling houses, this is a game played with three dice. Usually the dice are placed in a cage shaped like an hourglass, bets being settled after the cage is turned over to make the three dice fall to another end and thus show new faces. Occasionally the fall of the dice is accomplished by putting them into a chute which covers their faces as they land on the table, until the bets have been placed and the chute is removed to reveal them.

Some houses use a very simple layout which provides only for bets on any one of the six numbers on each die; other layouts are far more complex, permitting bets on high numbers, low numbers, odd and even numbers, triplets ("raffles"), and even specific combinations of the three dice. When such a layout is used, specific odds are offered on each available bet.

When the more elaborate layout is used, the house collects all bets on high, low, odd, even, and on the combination

---

*If the shooter's first roll is the barred number, the bettor does not win his bet against the house; he may withdraw it, or may leave it to be settled by the next roll or series of rolls.

numbers (4 to 17) when any triplet appears; thus, a player who bets on nine does not win if the number is 3-3-3.

The following table shows the bets which are accepted and the advantage retained by the house in each case:

BET	CHANCES AGAINST		FOR	CORRECT ODDS	HOUSE PAYS	IN EVERY $1 BET HOUSE SHOULD WIN
High (11 to 17)	111	to	105	Same	Even	2¾¢
Low (4 to 10)	111	to	105	Same	Even	2¾¢
Odd	111	to	105	Same	Even	2¾¢
Even	111	to	105	Same	Even	2¾¢
A specified triplet	215	to	1	215–1	180–1	16 ¢
Any triplet	210	to	6	35–1	30–1	14 ¢
4	213	to	3	71–1	60–1	15⅓¢
5	210	to	6	35–1	30–1	14 ¢
6	207	to	9	23–1	18–1	21 ¢
7	201	to	15	67–5	12–1	9⅔¢
8	195	to	21	65–7	8–1	12½¢
9	192	to	24	8–1	6–1	22 ¢
10	189	to	27	7–1	6–1	12½¢
11	189	to	27	7–1	6–1	12½¢
12	192	to	24	8–1	6–1	22 ¢
13	195	to	21	65–7	8–1	12½¢
14	201	to	15	67–5	12–1	9⅔¢
15	207	to	9	23–1	18–1	21 ¢
16	210	to	6	35–1	30–1	14 ¢
17	213	to	3	71–1	60–1	15⅓¢

Superficially, it would appear that the house has no edge if it pays even money on a straight number bet; the bettor apparently has three chances in six to have his number show. But this overlooks the effect of doublets or triplets, for which the house still pays only even money. Bet a chip on each number and theoretically you should break even. But if the dice fall, for example, 1-1-2, you lose four chips and get back only two; if they fall 1-1-1, you lose five and get back only one.

FOUR-FIVE-SIX

Three dice are used. One player is chosen by lot to be the first banker, and he states the amount of his bank. Each other player, in order of precedence beginning at the banker's left, may take all or any part of the bank, or of whatever remains of it, until it is all faded; any unfaded portion is withdrawn by the banker. The banker then rolls the dice once.

If he rolls 4-5-6, or any triplet, he wins all bets.

If he rolls 1-2-3, he loses all bets.

If he rolls any pair plus six, he wins; any pair plus one, he loses.

If he rolls any pair plus two, three, four or five, the latter number is his *point*.

The banker continues to roll until one of these numbers appears. If it does not settle the bets, instead giving him a point, the dice pass to the player at his left.

This player then rolls to settle his bet with the banker; he wins if he rolls a winning number, loses if he rolls a losing number, and wins, loses or ties when he rolls a point number depending upon whether his point is respectively higher, lower, or the same as the banker's. His bet having been settled, the dice pass to the next player at his left, and so on until all bets are settled.

The banker has an advantage in Four-Five-Six, because he rolls first and there are more automatic winning numbers than losing numbers. His advantage amounts to about 2½% of all money bet against him.

When any player gets a Four-Five-Six or triplet against the banker, he becomes the next banker.

POKER DICE

Any number may play, each having one turn. Five dice are cast from a dice cup. In his turn, a player may cast the dice once, twice, or three times. His object is to get the best possible poker hand. The hands rank: Five of a kind (high), four of a kind, full house (three of a kind and a pair), three of a kind (straights do not count, and as there are no suits there can be no flush), two pair, one pair, high card. Aces (ones) are high, then sixes, fives, etc. Ties are broken as in Poker.

After his first cast, a player may pick up one or more dice and cast them again; after his second cast he may do the same; the third cast determines his hand. After any cast he may stand on what he already has and end his turn.

The highest hand wins. If two or more players tie for high, each of them gets three rolls to break the tie as among those who tied.